Aeropolis

Nerea
Calvillo

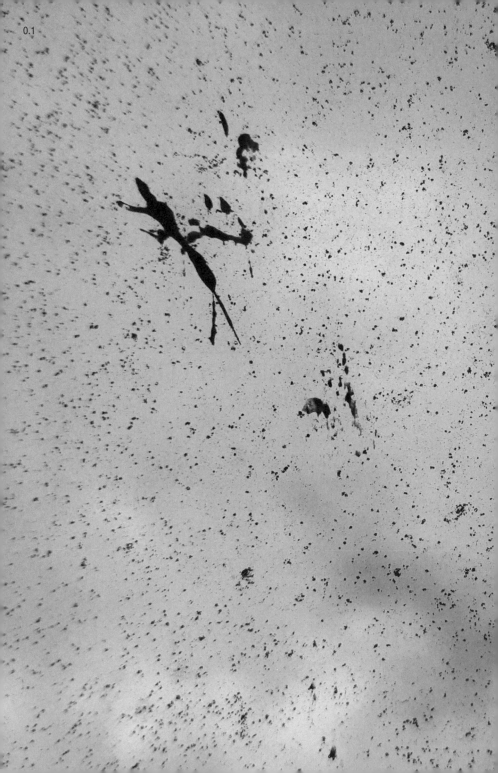
0.1

FOR THE LOVE OF AIR
BY MARÍA PUIG DE LA BELLACASA

Aeropolis moves, creates, multiplies airmaginations…

The small room I am in is made of air, filled with air that is many airs. This seemingly empty space surrounding me is inhabited. I'm in the company of, held by, more than human fullness, a medium invisible to my partial human eye. But it is not quite a medium either, because I am, this body is, also a medium for air. Embodying this inside outside of air is not just new knowledge for me, it is a learned sensation—one made possible by entering and experiencing Nerea Calvillo's *Aeropolis: Queering Air in Toxicpolluted Worlds*. This is a book that immerses us in air's materiality, and becomes a bodily experience. It feels like it contains more than what is in its pages, expanding registers of perceptibility.

Calvillo tells us her learning has been through "wondering, searching, exploring, trying, hunting." As a reader I can feel this, I can sense the intimacy that she has with words and their meanings, her love for writing and rewriting to carefully render a diversity of feelings—and, sometimes, the emotional rawness as it seeps through the pages of this book. Inseparably a thinker and a maker, Calvillo demands precision, she yearns for language (written and not) that exudes materiality and corporeality. Her curiosity is also generosity. She humbly recognizes the many collectives that make up *Aeropolis*'s diversities and mixtures—and that she does not know them all. To enter this book is to learn with Calvillo about a myriad of people and things that have taught, provoked, and recomposed her experience of air. *Aeropolis* does not read linearly. It does not impose a thinking, a form, a method. It does not even impose its own stories. It leaves impressions like cloud formations—collectively built up by strands of materiality and forces of wind, water, light… Sometimes gentle, other times stormy, always atmospheric.

Calvillo's pioneering work on air pollution, upon which this book is grounded and expands, reminds us that air has been and remains a dumpsite—filled with waste that we deem invisible because it so often literally is to the naked eye. And this waste is constantly in touch with us, through our bodies, our skin, the inner workings of our lungs, our bloodstreams, our cells. But while pollution and toxicity are mostly treated, and often rightly, as a matter of denunciation and opposition, this book works with and beyond that sense of outrage and repellence—and against the lucrative drive for solutionism and socio-technical fixes.

Air is/puts us in relation, in ways that un-locate our sensitivity to environmental troubles, circulating and binding the outside to the inside of bodies. Inhale... exhale... *Aeropolis* makes us wonder about what these stubborn movements of breath, movements that we are often unaware of, that keep so many earthlings alive, connect us to. At the same time, it obliges us toward those living within interlocking and unjust toxicity regimes. By eliciting the plurality of airs, Calvillo registers how pleasure and harm commingle in earth beings, as well as the elemental corporeality of matter. It is this troubling aesthetics that is at the heart, for instance, of Calvillo and her team's 2017 *Yellow Dust* installation: air pollution data is transformed into a yellow mist that is both gorgeous and unsettling, that may refresh your skin on a sweltering summer afternoon and at the same time allow you to sense the floating deadliness that touches you, and the interdependencies that make air both a commons infrastructure and a colonized dump. As part of this troubling aesthetics, the pleasures of *Aeropolis*'s queering ecologies are uneasy, uncanny, unsettling, compelling breathers into collective obligations.

Making-feeling, this book is also a learning experience in epistemic politics: about who holds knowledge about air; about how this knowing is counted or discounted; about what the consequences are when air inhabitants are quantified or counted as data, as evidence, as cause in very specific powerholding ways. *Aeropolis* argues against the inevitability of air designed to hurt, to kill. This is thinking that contests normativity. And so, while the openness to air's porous diversity extracts possibility out of the seemingly cemented futures of toxicpolluting regimes, these possibilities are inseparable from struggling to decolonize air, from questioning the chains of

8

causality, in and out of pores, lungs, soils, clouds... from making dominant data practices hesitate with alternative, interdependent, and specific toxicity practices and stories—from practicing queering.

This book is a love story for air, and a demanding invitation to design and make livable airs so that they matter otherwise. Engaging with *Aeropolis* is learning to care better for the air that holds us.

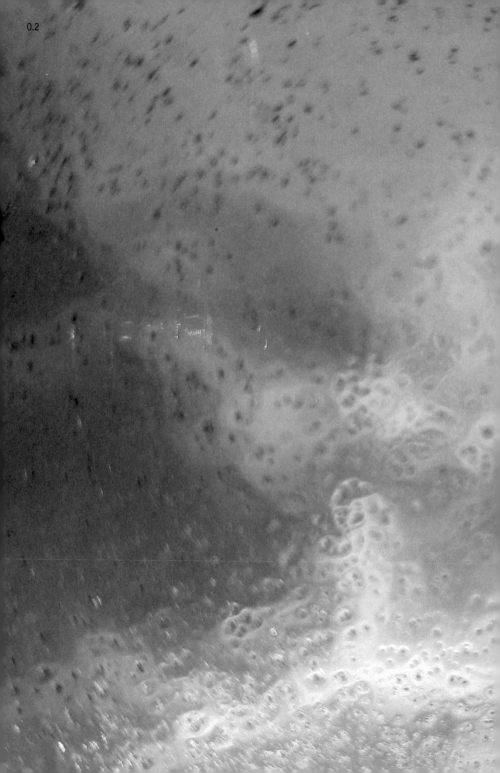

0.3

Intuitively, urban air is the negative of the city in three dimensions.

That which is above the sky-line.

But the air *is* city.

It is architecture, bodies, environment, soil, memory, affect, queer ecologies.

LIVING WITH AIRS

I tend to look outside my window, toward the sky, when prompted to think about air. As if there was an air "out there," an air that does not touch me or even concern me, although by now we know that it might be polluted. We tend to search for the line where the buildings end, for the contrails, for the clouds. But what exactly are we looking at?

Right now, from my window, I can see two layers of clouds hovering over the terrace houses across the street. The upper clouds, black and flat, are steady and threatening. The lower ones, white and fluffy, seem to move at the speed of a film on fast-forward. They move in the same direction, from right to left. The big puffs turn the sun on and off every few seconds. My neighbors, and the phantoms of the working class for whom these houses were built all over Victorian Britain, appear and disappear. My eyes try to quickly register the difference. I am in London, but I could be anywhere on this island. Seeing the same houses, the same sky, the same clouds running from the sea. In front of the window, a ray has illuminated yellow leaves holding stubbornly to their branches, keeping pulse with the wind. Through the narrow aperture I left open this morning to ventilate the room comes the smell of asphalt mixed with a dash of garlic from a tasty dish of an unknown neighbor. With the smell enters cold air and I feel goose bumps on my skin. I get up to close the window to keep in the warmth. With my hands on the frame and the cold breeze at my waist, I pause. I realize that my poor plants must dread the cold air—or maybe they crave water. Shall I close the window or leave it open? Who or what do I prioritize? My body's comfort, the plants' needs, or saving energy? The unbearable noise coming from the nearby construction site makes my hands push the frame down. Relieved, I notice how the high-speed film outside is now mute. But if I close my eyes, I can still feel the cold tickling the skin of my cheeks, dissolving in my throat. Two young sanitation workers rushing in zigzags down the street grab my attention. They sweat. While they frantically load the garbage truck with the remains of our consumerism, they breathe the fumes from the truck's exhaust pipes. Waste and smoke are part of their job. In the background, a radio announcer joyously informs listeners that the initial reaction to the results of the 2020 US presidential election has been one of hope from governments and environmental activists preparing for the United Nations Climate Summit that will take place next year in Glasgow...

THE IN-VISIBILITY OF AIR

Air is involved in (almost) everything. In fact, it makes (almost) everything possible: it creates and moves clouds, feeds plants, transports odors and voices, permits indoor inhabitation... it causes exposure inequality, technological developments, and political conflicts. And yet, air is still considered in popular discourse as a void, as emptiness, as a metaphor of lightness, as something external to us. How is this possible?

The feminist philosopher Luce Irigaray argues that this exteriority is the consequence of centuries of Western thought that has privileged the solid, the visible, the stable—while "forgetting" the materiality of everything else.[1] This forgetting can be, in part, explained because air itself escapes visibility, as the molecules that compose it are too small to be perceived by human eyes. But what Irigaray helps us see is how air has been *made* invisible, kept out of sight.

1 Luce Irigaray, *The Forgetting of Air in Martin Heidegger.*

Haven't we—(t)here—passed imperceptibility from one air to another? Fluid matter, voice, appearance. The possibility to breathe-live, the possibility to call-name, the possibility to appear-enter into presence. Heidegger does not recall this passage. He forgets the difference of air(s).

And in place of this forgetting? A certain void.[2]

For Irigaray, this designed invisibility, this void, is a philosophical problem, as it has configured a very narrow understanding of the world. But not only. This *in-visibility*—or tension between material and cultural forms of visibility and amnesia—has real, embodied consequences. It shapes what we think is natural, is urban, is human. And excludes all the things that are not: the in-betweens, the grays, the fluids, the forgotten.

For these reasons, air cannot be forgotten anymore.

And it can no longer be taken for granted.

Because "there is nothing more essential for life than air. And yet, because of air pollution, the simple act of breathing contributes to 7 million deaths a year."[3]

Because, as history has shown, air has been used as a free and limitless dumpsite for the waste of industrial production.

Because everything, and everyone, pollutes air—although at different scales and with different levels of responsibility.

Because this pervasive air pollution—and its inverse, access to clean air—is distributed unevenly and disproportionally—with the poor, the racialized, the displaced, the gendered bearing the brunt of its negative effects.

Because air is "fragile, it's technical, it's public, it's political, it could break down—it is breaking down—it's being fixed."[4]

19

2   Irigaray, *The Forgetting of Air in Martin Heidegger*, 28.
3   WHO Director-General Tedros Adhanom Ghebreyesus, "WHO Slashes Recommended Limits for Air Pollution, Which Kills 7 Million People per Year."
4   Bruno Latour, "Air," 2.

Because under the guise of good intentions, this fixing, entangled with ecosystem preservation, is often done "in exchange for the lives of Black people, the poor and other subalterns."[5]

Because the COVID-19 pandemic has made tangible how air interconnects bodies and transmits viruses or volatile compounds; how it can be the means of contagion or the delimiter of a safe space.

Because air has been specifically *designed* to kill. During World War I, in the trenches near Ypres, yellow clouds of chlorine gas annihilated whole battalions by "just" polluting their environment.[6] Decades later, atomic bombs became the epitome of mass destruction. Because this killing is state sanctioned not just in wartime but in everyday time. Because too many people have uttered "I can't breathe." Because this agony is also the rallying cry against anti-Black violence and the violence of modernity.

Because air *is* the possibility to breathe. And, well, in the words of artist, writer, teacher Ashon Crawley, because "it's all about breathing" and breathing points toward the collectivity of air:

> Air is an object held in common, an object that we come to know through a collective participation within it as it enters and exits flesh. The process by which we participate in this common object, with this common admixture, not only must be thought about but must be consumed and expelled through repetition in order to think. The always more than double gesture of inhalation and exhalation is a matter of grave concern given the overwhelming presence of air as shared object, the overwhelming presence of breathing as shared, common performance. In each movement of dilation is a displacement of one kind of matter into the space and plane of another. To fill lungs with air is to displace the carbonite matter that was previously within. To write narratives of flight

5   Malcom Ferdinand, *Decolonial Ecology: Thinking from the Caribbean World*, 85.
6   Peter Sloterdijk, *Terror from the Air*.

is to displace the common conceptions of the human, the subject, the object.[7]

For all these reasons air must be *de-in-visibilized*.

AIRS

And yet, what do we mean by air? From a scientific perspective, air is the combination of gases that compose the atmosphere, the gaseous layer that protects the Earth from excessive radiation and permits life. Put differently, air is the atmosphere's material composition. This material composition is often spoken about as a fixed amalgamation of gases, homogeneous in space and time. Within popular discourse this perspective belongs to the same conceptual framework that Irigaray criticized, the mistaken belief that something constant does not require attention. But air is not fixed. Air is an ecosystem of gases and solid particles. Gases that compose the atmosphere like nitrogen, oxygen, argon; particles such as dust and pollen suspended off the ground; molecules from human and animal skin, hair, and feces; microorganisms like virus, bacteria, fungus; anthropogenic gases like ozone, carbon dioxide, sulphides; anthropogenic particles like rubber, microplastics, heavy metals.[8] Air is a fluctuating and ever-reacting gaseous mass that cannot be fully captured in a single description. Air's composition is variable and diverse. "It is transformational, ecological and multiscalar."[9] To complicate things further, water vapor is another component of air. In Greek, the prefix "atmo" means water vapor. Therefore, is air "aero" and "atmo" at once? It is a slippery materiality that defies classification.

21

---

7   Ashon T. Crawley, *Blackpentecostal Breath*, 36.
8   Arborist William Bryant Logan collected air samples in different areas of New York City, where he found fungi, bacteria, pollen, dead skin cells, hair, cotton fibers, silica glass, and nail polish in various amounts. Logan's study shows not only that air is variable in different locations across a city, but also that it is a mirror of the activity that takes place in and around it. William Bryant Logan, *Air: The Restless Shaper of the World*.
9   Jussi Parikka, "New Materialism of Dust." Parikka observes how "materiality leaks in many directions."

Air is also referred to as a condition, or by what traverses it, or what it does, or how it is sensed. Air is sound, radiation, wind, pressure, temperature... it is smell, vision, erosion, movement, communication...

Air refers to different things across different forms of knowledge and is enacted in multiple ways.[10] It is a milieu, a gaseous chemical composition, a public health threat, a landscape, an invisible flow, an experience, an ontology, a weapon, a classical element.[11] For scholars in human geography or anthropology, air has become

22

10   Annemarie Mol's work on ontological multiplicity is useful to grasp how airs are enacted in different locations by different actors. See Annemarie Mol, *The Body Multiple: Ontology in Medical Practice*.
11   Fields of knowledge exploring urban air as an object of research have proliferated worldwide over the last century. There are chemistry research groups investigating the physical composition of the air; environmental researchers studying the weather and its impact on ecosystems; atmospheric scientists exploring air's dynamics; epidemiologists and toxicologists analyzing the impact of air quality on the human body and public health; engineers, chemists, and citizen scientists investigating instruments of measuring, modeling, and predicting air.

The humanities and social sciences have made important contributions as well: air has been used to describe eighteenth-century social conditions, and to illustrate the evolution of the concept of pollution (Rachel Carson, *Silent Spring*; Peter Thorsheim, *Inventing Pollution: Coal, Smoke, and Culture in Britain since 1800*).

Air has been a material for conceptual and formal research and investigation in the arts and, since the 1960s, has also sparked the imagination of popular culture: From artworks such as Marcel Duchamp's *Air de Paris* (1919) and Gordon Matta-Clark's *Fresh Air Cart* (1972); to novels like Albert Camus' *The Plague* (1947) and Geoff Ryman's science fiction work *Air* (2005); to films such as Fritz Lang's *Metropolis* (1927), Ridley Scott's *Blade Runner* (1982), Sofia Coppola's *The Virgin Suicides* (1999), Steven Soderbergh's *Contagion* (2011) and Béla Tarr's *Turin Horse* (2011); to Ferran Adrià's "gasification" of food, just to name a few.

Cultural geographers have explored the air as a territory with specific material, spatial, political, and experiential conditions. For instance, as the vertical space where other entities such as airplanes or balloons travel (Peter Adey, *Air: Nature and Culture*; Steven Connor, *The Matter of Air: Science and Art of the Ethereal*; Derek P. McCormack, *Atmospheric Things: On the Allure of Elemental Envelopment*; Sasha Engelmann and Derek P. McCormack, "Elemental Worlds: Specificities, Exposures, Alchemies"); as artistic practices (Sasha Engelmann, *Sensing Art in the Atmosphere: Elemental Lures and Aerosolar Practices*); or as spaces of territorial control or earth surveillance (Laura Kurgan, *Close Up at a Distance: Mapping, Technology, and Politics*; Mark Whitehead, *State, Science & the Skies*).

The social sciences have looked at how the knowledge of air is produced, the institutions that manage this knowledge, and what impacts these have in social and political configurations, including the reception of those materials in certain social groups and the political effects of their toxicity. And very importantly, how air pollution creates social inequality and environmental injustice (Michael Kennedy, "On Breath and Blackness: Living and Dying in the Wake of the Virus"; Stefanie Graeter, "Infrastructural Incorporations: Toxic Storage, Corporate Indemnity, and Ethical Deferral in Peru's Neoextractive Era"; Sara Wylie, Nicholas Shapiro, and Max Liboiron, "Making and Doing Politics Through Grassroots Scientific Research on the Energy and Petrochemical Industries"). Some scholars

a fertile conceptual space to capture atmospheric conditions that bring together the meteorological and affective,[12] a conceptual tool to help "deterrestrialize" anthropological thought,[13] or a thinking method in itself, like being in suspension.[14] These frameworks draw on the concept of "atmospheric attunements," which attempt to capture the complex entanglements between affective, physical, social, and climatic conditions whose properties cannot be defined in isolation.[15] To account for what cannot be grasped and yet is there; to recognize and value forms of sensing, describing, or perceiving aerial conditions that exceed scientific calculations:

> Atmospheric attunements are a process of what Heidegger (1962) called worlding—an intimate, compositional process of dwelling in spaces that bears, gestures, gestates, worlds. Here, things matter not because of how they are represented, but because they have qualities, rhythms, forces, relations, and movements. In the everyday work of attunement to worlding, spaces of all kinds become inhabited. Modes of existence accrue, circulate, sediment, unfold, and go flat.[16]

How then do atmospheric attunements change? Or, thinking with media theorist Desiree Foerster: "How long must such an effect

explore concepts of the air's location or position: urban air as a global zone of monitoring and research (Andrew Barry, *Political Machines: Governing a Technological Society*); *air milieu* (the space in which enemy bodies move) or surrounding air as opposed to air conditioning (Peter Sloterdijk, *Bubbles: Spheres Volume I: Microspherology*, translated by Wieland Hoban); or outdoor air, which relates to ideas of openness/enclosure. This links to technical strategies of air management: air control, environmental control, climate control, and even as a synonym of environment, climate, or weather. Other approaches explore its deadly potential: mist of death, death dust, radioactivity (Sloterdijk, *Terror from the Air*); or on the contrary, to questions related to the body or the essence of being, as the air or being in air (Derek P. McCormack, "Atmospheric Choreographies and Air-Conditioned Bodies") or unbreathed air (Beatriz Colomina, "Unbreathed Air 1956").

12   Derek P. McCormack, "Elemental Infrastructures for Atmospheric Media: On Stratospheric Variations, Value and the Commons."

13   Cymene Howe, "Life Above Earth: An Introduction," 207.

14   Timothy K. Choy and Jerry Zee, "Condition—Suspension."

15   Kathleen Stewart, "Atmospheric Attunements." Ben Anderson, "Affective Atmospheres."

16   Stewart, "Atmospheric Attunements," 445.

extend in time to become noticeable? Besides feelings, how else can I describe the effects of atmospheres on myself?"[17]

Air is multiple, diverse, a chemical composition and material state at once. It is (atmo)air. There are many airs.

Air is bodies, where "Every stir of the wind lifts particles of blue jean threads, plant hairs, skin cells, spores, yeast, algae, plankton, bacteria, pollen, soil, silica, soot, dead bugs, the scales of moth wings into it. Each cough or sigh or song releases more into the air."[18] It feeds all living entities. Animals, plants, fungi, cells. Through breath, air gets into human lungs, decomposes, and oxygen is distributed through blood to the rest of the body. Our brains need incoming air. Our nails need incoming air. The human body is a sophisticated air processor. It inhales oxygen and exhales carbon dioxide, volatile organic compounds, viruses and many other invisible particles back into the common air. Our physical and mental activities depend on the volume, composition, and speed of the air we breathe. Air is health and disease at once.

Air is affect. An embodied communication media. It relates bodies through sound and waves, permits language. It produces chemical sublimes.[19]

Air is architecture. The presence of air differentiates a building from a sculpture or a pile of materials. Because buildings are meant to be inhabitable, and to achieve this they need, before anything else, air. Inhabitation is having air to breathe. The air is moving architecture, exchanged with the exterior and managed through ventilation, heating, and breathing. Every room has its own aerial signature.[20]

24

17 Desiree Foerster, "Awareness for Atmospheres," 142.
18 Logan, *Air*, 90.
19 Nicholas Shapiro, "Attuning to the Chemosphere: Domestic Formaldehyde, Bodily Reasoning, and the Chemical Sublime." Thank you Nick for your key work and conversations.
20 Uriel Fogué has pointed out that, from this perspective, air can also be conceived as an architecture, in the sense that it is the result of a collective construction. Thank you, Uriel, for this insight.

Air is environment. As the background or stage par excellence, invisible, quiet, latent, and always there, noticing the air is bringing the environment to the fore while acknowledging its reciprocal relation with any entity that lives with air and in it. We live with/in air.

Air is soil, not only what is above the crust of the earth. It permits life underground, as well as death, decomposition, and regeneration.

Air is asthma; it is breathtaking.

Air is memory of industrial and biological inhabitation.

Air is contagion of ideas.

Air is contact zones and sacrifice areas.

Air is interspecies communication.

Air is power. The steam engine. Machine's fuel.

Air is the trace of past life in the present.

Air is the archive of the blood and bodies of those who worked in the past and in the present to change its composition.[21]

Air is warfare. Demonstrations. Revolts.

Air is rights. Citizenship

Air is a queer ecology. It gives and takes life. It is unstable, nonbinary, resists classification.

Air is all of this, and more importantly, it is what connects it all. Air is interdependencies and interrelation. We breathe because plants give us breath. We cannibalize each other through air, through multiple airs.[22] And, unfortunately, we also de-humanize each other through air, through multiple airs. As Black studies scholar Christina Sharpe reminds, "free air" was denied to those enslaved in the hold.[23]

What would it mean then to switch from air to airs?

---

21 Kathryn Yusoff, *A Billion Black Anthropocenes or None*.
22 As Emanuele Coccia claims in his suggestive and bold book *The Life of Plants*: "Breath is already a first form of cannibalism: every day we feed off the gaseous excretions of plants. We could not live but off the life of others." See Emanuele Coccia, *The Life of Plants: A Metaphysics of Mixture*, 47.
23 The entire chapter "The Weather" is worth reading. Christina Sharpe, *In the Wake: On Blackness and Being*, 104.

This reorientation toward the plural is an invitation to pay attention to the differences in and within air.[24] Airs recognizes how air is not the same in a remote forest, a rural area, a city, a neighborhood; along a busy road, at the top of a skyscraper, at the surface of a pond. Airs acknowledges that the effects of air depend on its composition and the entities that interact with it. Even at a microscopic scale one component can have multiple effects. Ozone is needed in the stratosphere, but at the ground level anthropogenic ozone is toxic. Carbon dioxide (CO_2) is fundamental for vegetable and human life, but in high concentrations it is part of climate change in the upper layers of the atmosphere. Airs demands specificity. The causes and consequences of certain aerial configurations, the actors involved, the who, where, and what that inhales, exhales, cohabits, and evades good or bad air. Airs points toward the multiplicity of aerial conditions, opening up the frame from gases and particles so that we can reconceive air itself.

De-in-visibilizing air requires us to re-materialize it, re-socialize it, re-politicize it, re-imagine it.

City Airs

This book is concerned with the airs just above the ground—the troposphere, the messy space where we breathe and live with others. They are not heroic spaces to be conquered or spaces of great disasters, but those of routine; airs that are different in every corner and circulate in unexpected ways, where the differences of

---

24 I cannot think of a better illustration than this paragraph by Toni Morrison: "So the ginger sugar blew unnoticed through the streets, around the trees, over the roofs, thinned out and weakened a little, it reached Southside. There, where some houses didn't even have screens, let alone air conditioners, the windows were thrown wide open to whatever the night had to offer. And there the ginger smell was sharp, sharp enough to distort dreams and make the sleeper believe the things he hungered for were right at hand. To the Southside residents who were awake on such nights, it gave all their thoughts and activity a quality of being both intimate and far away. The two men standing near the pines on Darling Street—right near the brown house where wine drinkers went—could smell the air, but they didn't think of ginger. Each thought it was the way freedom smelled, or justice, or luxury, or vengeance." Toni Morrison, *Song of Solomon*.

environmental injustice are most palpable. These airs we cannot escape, because they are the airs that come into our bodies through our lungs, the airs in which dogs bark, the airs where bees fly, the airs that spread pollen and carry kisses. The airs that are part of urban ecologies and territories, filling public spaces. But they are also the airs of capitalist, colonial, and neoliberal accumulation and the spaces of accumulation itself. They retain the heavy metals released by factory chimneys and toxic human-made chemical compounds. And at times the excess of some of their own components—carbon dioxide, carbon monoxide, nitrogen dioxide, and formaldehyde. The polluted airs. The ones that contribute to producing chemically altered lives and beings.[25]

In particular, I am interested in the airs of cities. The airs that 80 percent of the global population lives with. The airs of the nonevent, the everyday. The airs that cause slow violence and slow death.[26] The airs that are part and parcel of urban development, which distribute people, risk, and exposure. The urban transformations designed to improve the quality of its airs by displacing the source of pollution, by cleaning up or trying to pollute less.[27]

Architecture has joined these efforts primarily through sustainable technofixes, where air has been used for ventilation and climate control.[28] Sustainable technofixes aim to "solve" pollution problems through technology, leaving its social attachments and impacts

27

25 Or what Michelle Murphy has named "alterlives." Murphy's work has been crucial in shaping my critical understanding of air. My full appreciation. See Michelle Murphy, "Alterlife and Decolonial Chemical Relations."

26 Rob Nixon, *Slow Violence and the Environmentalism of the Poor.*

27 These urban interventions are immersed in a techno-scientific conceptual framework in which sustainability—to reduce environmental degradation while supporting economic growth and accumulation—is about protocols and efficiency. Where monitoring the environment is about taking the most accurate measurement, making the most perfect map, having the most suitable Air Quality Index, where massive geo-engineering projects are developed around the world to try to "clean" the air, as if pollution was a speck of dust to be swept off a table. But studies show that these interventions are not succeeding in removing pollution, let alone considering alternative forms of relating to air. They are based in the modern paradigm of zoning, inherited from hygienist thinking, where urban space is managed by delimiting areas and boundaries—producing social segregation and inequality.

unattended. While surely this kind of solutionism can temporarily alleviate local issues—crucial in contexts of lethal exposure—it often contributes to the problem. It perpetuates the idea that the environment is a resource for humans, an idea most starkly articulated in the concept of "ecosystem services," which evaluates ecosystems based on the economic and social benefits they provide to humans. These "solutions" are usually implemented quickly; they anticipate fast, recognizable results; they reinforce the belief—coursing through centuries of extraction and exploitation, settler colonialism and neoliberalism—that anything can be done to the environment.

Architecture has also mobilized air to "solve" some of its own challenges. It has turned it into a construction material, mostly through inflatable structures.[29] It has been used to challenge

28

28　In 1969, the historian Peter Reyner Banham recalled how the history of architecture had largely focused on material, historical, tectonic, formal, or functional aspects of built structures, leaving air and the environment as either void or emptiness (Peter Reyner Banham, *The Architecture of the Well-Tempered Environment*). Instead, he considered air movement and ventilation as fundamental to providing basic support for life. Banham traces the movement of air as a form of climate control back to 1840, when John Gorie, a doctor in Florida, tested a device to cool interiors and exteriors. Yet it was Willis Carrier's design of the first air-conditioner unit in 1903 that revolutionized and democratized indoor environmental control. While greenhouses and crystal palaces preceded this innovation, allowing for the inhabitation of new spaces (and a new collective spectacle for the masses), they remained large-scale technical feats on display. Air-conditioning units, from their early implementation in public buildings at the start of the twentieth century, as in Frank Lloyd Wright's 1906 Larkin Administration Building in Buffalo, and through to their use during the 1920s and 30s, led to a democratization of air manipulation and an idea of climate customization through user-friendly devices. In 1960, Buckminster Fuller scaled up the notion of climate control. He imagined a 4 kilometer transparent dome over New York City to regulate the weather and reduce air pollution. To produce, through the isolation of Midtown Manhattan, a reduction of energy consumption. Fuller brought together climate, energy, and land cost through air, anticipating that apartments inside the dome would be more expensive because they had better air quality. For a history of modern architecture and air control, see Daniel A. Barber, *Modern Architecture and Climate: Design before Air Conditioning* and Jiat-Hwee Chang and Tim Winter, "Thermal Modernity and Architecture." For the relationship between air condition, architecture, and institutional politics, see Paulo Tavares, "General Essay on Air: Probes into the Atmospheric Conditions of Liberal Democracy."

29　Air as a construction material was extensively researched during the 1960s and 70s in Europe and the US. One of its most common uses was as a vertical division, tested in 1930 by László Moholy-Nagy in Germany to challenge ideas of continuity, transparency, and enclosure. When plastics began to be mass-produced the air was also used structurally through pneumatic constructions, as in Warren Chalk's experiments in the 1960s and 70s, leading to entire imaginaries of mobile, ephemeral, and serializable architectures. I'd like to highlight the work of the Madrid architect J. Prada Pool, in particular his Instant City in Ibiza (1971), which became a technical achievement

disciplinary limits.[30] Or as an adaptor to the environment.[31] And yet, these operate in ways I am hoping to escape. Taking the air into account from a spatial design perspective can shift how architecture is conceptualized (from climate control machines to shelters), how the built environment is designed (beyond walls and borders, filters and sealed chambers), and how we define what air is (a chemical, a pollutant, an image, an element that can be controlled, designed, and taken care of). Although these relationships between the air and architecture have been in the background of the discipline, they become visible under dramatic events, as the artist and historian Susan Schuppli attests to in her *biography* of the dust of the World Trade Center on September 11, 2001, in New York City:

> As architecture collapsed into micro-spherical debris, it produced a billowy ash cloud that lingered for days obscuring

and a facilitator for new modes of constructing the collective through direct participation in defining spaces and pleasure.

30 Some projects have harnessed the materiality of air to demonstrate architecture's attachments and opportunities that are beyond the materials and realms that are considered architectural: Diller + Scofidio's Blur Building (2002), which uses water vapor to construct a cloud, or R&Sie(n)'s "Dusty Relief" building, which proposed capturing Bangkok's airborne dust to configure the skin of the building. For interior spaces, the artist-architect Olafur Eliasson and the architect Philippe Rahm have designed spaces through gradients of climatic conditions (see Philippe Rahm's "Digestible Gulf Stream," 2008).

31 The notion of architecture as shelter from a poisonous environment became prominent in the 1950s and 60s, when, post–World War II, the air was seen as a container of viruses or as a weapon of mass destruction. In this context, architecture became the space of hygiene and defense, as Alison and Peter Smithson illustrated in their House of the Future, built in 1956 as a prototype for an exhibition. For architecture historian Beatriz Colomina the house was an air control system, highly enclosed from the exterior to avoid contamination. It included multiple integrated devices to specifically manage air: air-conditioning units, an air wall to keep dust out, hot air as a drying device, and a window positioned in the ceiling to make visible a portion of the sky and the *unbreathed air*. Colomina's proposal that the material of the House of the Future is air is compelling; because of the multiple ways in which the air was used, it shifted ideas of hygiene and the relationship between the built structure and the body. Colomina, "Unbreathed Air 1956." Once aerial warfare stopped being a threat, the environment shifted from being poisonous to being fragile, and architecture needed to adapt to and work with it. I am reminded of the "bioclimatic architecture" of the 1980s and 90s, where the exterior was no longer considered a permanent threat to buildings but rather, a condition they needed to relate and adapt to. From a design point of view, it has been rapidly adopted by corporate architecture to draw from discourses of sustainability and efficiency, notably exemplified by Foster + Partners' Swiss Re building (2004), which is shaped by wind flows.

the boundaries between the terrestrial spaces of the built environment and the atmospheric realm into which its Twin Towers had previously reached. When viewed remotely from orbiting satellites this spatial fusion-confusion was confirmed, as neither a shift in scale, nor a pixel-by-pixel comparative analysis could disentangle pulverized architecture from airborne matter, or human remains from rubble.[32]

What is the role of the urban and the built environment in all this? If airs are designed by the city, can other airs be designed?

---

32 This text is fabulous, as it makes clear how architecture is dust, dust is architecture. See Susan Schuppli, "Impure Matter: A Forensics of WTC Dust," 120.

0.4

0.7

0.5

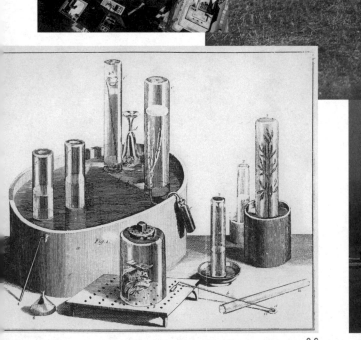

0.6

NOS ENTERAMOS DE QUE EL AIRE EXISTE
CUANDO NO PODEMOS RESPIRAR

0.9

0.8

0.10

0.11

0.15

0.12

0.13

THIS IS NOT A SOLUTION

0.14

0.18

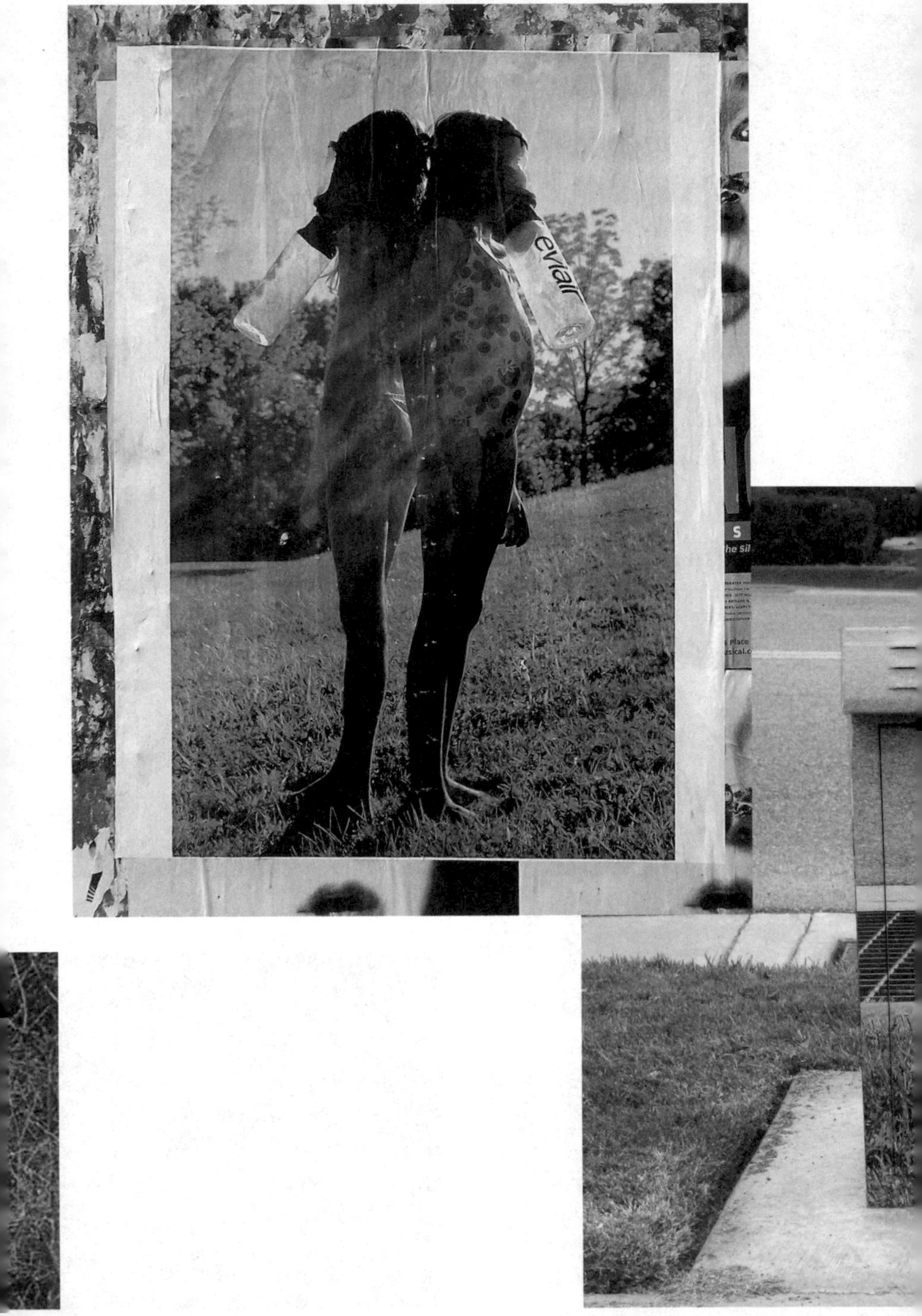

WORKS CITED

Adey, Peter. *Air: Nature and Culture*. London: Reaktion Books, 2014.

Anderson, Ben. "Affective Atmospheres." *Emotion, Space and Society* 2, no. 2 (2009): 77–81.

Banham, Peter Reyner. *The Architecture of the Well-Tempered Environment*. London: Architecture Press, 1969.

Barber, Daniel A. *Modern Architecture and Climate: Design before Air Conditioning*. Princeton, NJ: Princeton University Press, 2020.

Barry, Andrew. *Political Machines: Governing a Technological Society*. London: Athlone Press, 2001.

Carson, Rachel. *Silent Spring*. Boston: Mariner Books/Houghton Mifflin, 2012.

Chang, Jiat-Hwee, and Tim Winter, "Thermal Modernity and Architecture." *Journal of Architecture* 20, no. 1 (2015): 92–121.

Choy, Timothy K., and Jerry Zee. "Condition—Suspension." *Cultural Anthropology* 30, no. 2 (2015): 210–223.

Coccia, Emanuele. *The Life of Plants: A Metaphysics of Mixture*. Cambridge: Polity Press, 2018.

Colomina, Beatriz. "Unbreathed Air 1956." *Grey Room*, no. 15 (Spring 2004): 28–59.

Connor, Steven. *The Matter of Air: Science and Art of the Ethereal*. London: Reaktion Books, 2010.

Crawley, Ashon T. "Blackpentecostal Breath." *New Inquiry*, July 19, 2017.

Engelmann, Sasha. *Sensing Art in the Atmosphere: Elemental Lures and Aerosolar Practices*. London: Routledge, 2020.

Engelmann, Sasha, and Derek P. McCormack. "Elemental Worlds: Specificities, Exposures, Alchemies." *Progress in Human Geography* 45, no. 6 (2021): 1419–1439.

Ferdinand, Malcom. *Decolonial Ecology: Thinking from the Caribbean World*. Cambridge: Polity Press, 2022.

Foerster, Desiree. "Awareness for Atmospheres." *Excursions* 11, no. 1 (2021): 126–146.

Graeter, Stefanie. "Infrastructural Incorporations: Toxic Storage, Corporate Indemnity, and Ethical Deferral in Peru's Neoextractive Era." *American Anthropologist* 122, no. 1 (2020) 21–36.

Howe, Cymene. "Life Above Earth: An Introduction." *Cultural Anthropology* 30, no. 2 (May 25, 2015): 203–209.

Irigaray, Luce. *The Forgetting of Air in Martin Heidegger*. Translated by Mary Beth Mader. Austin: University of Texas Press, 1999 [1983].

Kennedy, Michael J. "On Breath and Blackness: Living and Dying in the Wake of the Virus." *Philosophy & Rhetoric* 53, no. 3 (2020): 286–292.

Kurgan, Laura. *Close Up at a Distance: Mapping, Technology, and Politics*. New York: Zone Books, 2013.

Latour, Bruno. "Air." In *Sensorium*. Cambridge, MA: MIT Press, 2006.

Logan, William Bryant. *Air: The Restless Shaper of the World*. New York: W. W. Norton, 2012.

McCormack, Derek P. "Elemental Infrastructures for Atmospheric Media: On Stratospheric Variations, Value and the Commons." *Environment and Planning D: Society and Space* 35, no. 3 (2016): 1–20.

———. "Atmospheric Choreographies and Air-Conditioned Bodies." In *Moving Sites: Investigating Site-Specific Dance Performance*, edited by Victoria Hunter, 79–94. London: Routledge, 2015.

Mol, Annemarie. *The Body Multiple: Ontology in Medical Practice*. Durham, NC: Duke University Press, 2002.

Morrison, Toni. *Song of Solomon*. New York: Picador, 1989 [1977].

Murphy, Michelle. "Alterlife and Decolonial Chemical Relations." *Cultural Anthropology* 32, no. 4 (2017): 494–503.

Nixon, Rob. *Slow Violence and the Environmentalism of the Poor*. Cambridge, MA: Harvard University Press, 2011.

Parikka, Jussi. "New Materialism of Dust." *Artnodes*, no. 12 (December 19, 2012).

Schuppli, Susan. "Impure Matter: A Forensics on WTC Dust." In *Savage Objects,* edited by Godofredo Pereira, 120–140. INCM, 2012.

Shapiro, Nicholas. "Attuning to the Chemosphere: Domestic Formaldehyde, Bodily Reasoning, and the Chemical Sublime." *Cultural Anthropology* 30, no. 3 (2015): 368–393.

Sharpe, Christina. *In the Wake: On Blackness and Being*. Durham, NC: Duke University Press, 2016.

Sloterdijk, Peter. *Terror from the Air*. Cambridge, MA: MIT Press, 2009.

    Bubbles: Spheres Volume I: Microspherology. Translated by Wieland Hoban. Los Angeles: semiotext(e), 2011.

Stewart, Kathleen. "Atmospheric Attunements." *Environment and Urban Planning D: Society and Space* 29 (2011): 445–453.

Tavares, Paulo. "General Essay on Air: Probes into the Atmospheric Conditions of Liberal Democracy." *Meusite* 1, 2008. https://www.essayonair.online/pagina-inicial.

Thorsheim, Peter. *Inventing Pollution: Coal, Smoke, and Culture in Britain since 1800*. Athens, OH: Ohio University Press, 2006.

Whitehead, Mark. *State, Science & the Skies*. Oxford: Wiley-Blackwell, 2009.

Wylie, Sara, Nicholas Shapiro, and Max Liboiron. "Making and Doing Politics through Grassroots Scientific Research on the Energy and Petrochemical Industries." *Engaging Science, Technology, and Society* 3 (2017): 393–425.

Yusoff, Kathryn. *A Billion Black Anthropocenes or None*. Minneapolis, MN: University of Minnesota Press, 2019.

IMAGES

0.1–0.3
Two years of particles in my window. London, 2018–2020. Courtesy of the author.

0.4
Wenceslaus Hollar, *The Greek Gods: Typhon*; print, 7×10 cm. Courtesy of the Thomas Fisher Rare Book Library, University of Toronto.

0.5
Ground Zero after the collapse of the World Trade Center, New York City, September 17, 2001. Photograph by Chief Photographer's Mate Eric J. Tilford. Courtesy of the US Navy.

0.6
Print showing equipment used by Joseph Priestley for studying gases. From Joseph Priestley, *Experiments and Observations on Different Kinds of Air* (London: J. Johnson, 1775–1777). Courtesy of the World History Archive.

0.7
Robert and Shana ParkeHarrison, *Suspension*, 2000. Courtesy of the artists.

0.8
Gas attack in Flanders on the Western Front during World War I, 1917. Courtesy of the US National Archives/Science Photo Library.

0.9
Tear gas action during the Gezi Park protests in Taksim Square, Istanbul, June 15, 2013. Courtesy of Mstyslav Chernov.

0.10
Andrés Rábago Garcia, "We realize the air exists when we cannot breathe." © 2023 Artists Rights Society (ARS), New York/VEGAP, Madrid.

0.11
Images of blue skies projected on an LED screen in Tiananmen Square to offset the dangerously high levels of pollution in Beijing, January 23, 2013. Photograph by Feng Li. Courtesy of Getty Images.

0.12
A cloud seeding rocket launched in Shijiazhuang, China, to stimulate rain, May 15, 2021. Photograph by Zhang Haiqiang. Courtesy of VCG via Getty Images.

0.13
Graffiti in protest of Boris Johnson's climate policies by the environmental organization Climate Rush. "This is not a solution," written in soot, 2013. Courtesy of Climate Rush.

0.14
A mother wearing a gas mask pushing a gasproof pram in Hextable, Kent, 1938. Courtesy of the Smith Archive.

0.15
US Navy sailors test the air quality at Camp Lemonnier, Djibouti, December 27, 2013. Photograph by Mass Communication Specialist 1st Class Eric Dietrich. Courtesy of the US Navy.

0.16
Schoolgirls' gas mask parade in Tokyo, 1936. Photograph by Masao Horino. Courtesy of Tokyo Metropolitan Museum of Photography/DNPart.com.

0.17
A road sign with an illustration of a cow releasing methane.

0.18
Image from the EVIAIR public art project in New York City by Raemann, 2019. Courtesy of the artists.

0.19
Josh Callaghan, vinyl mural on a utility box in Playa Vista, California, 2007. Courtesy of the artist.

Aeropolis, aeropolis, *Aeropolis*

falsification air

what can I pass on, you ask,
about methods of detecting the air?
it has become so habitual
I am not sure where to begin.
each morning I walk into the world
looking for signs. early, before light
is normalised by the shadow of buildings
and the gentle fraying of traffic. it seems the signs
are most attracted to states of dereliction.
to receive them, it helps to be empty
but imbued with residual function
like a disused water tower
or any number of withering technologies.
lie back. let the world grow over you
like weeds. consider the sheets of air
gridlocked in double glazing. now
are you beginning to understand?[1]

Aeropolis, THE CITY OF AIRS

I choose to use the heuristic of the city to qualify airs, to unpack
their "designed," built, terrestrial conditions, and to recognize the
urban environment's own form of air pollution. By this I do not
mean that air *is* or *performs* as a city; I do not compare it to other
models of urban or territorial organization.[2] I use the city as a

43

1   Daisy Lafarge, *Life Without Air*, 31.
2   The question I get most often when presenting this idea is: Why the city? Why not summon more
     specific concepts, like "megalopolis," "global village," or territorial concepts like "hydroterritories"?
     See, for instance, Lewis Mumford, *The Culture of Cities*; Marshall McLuhan, *The Gutenberg Galaxy*;
     and Erik Swyngedouw, Maria Kaïka, and Esteban Castro, "Urban Water: A Political-Ecology Perspective."
     I have stayed with the city because there is more information (scientific, cultural) about the air (quality)
     of cities and also, crucially, because the city is a more generic term. However, Aeropolis, as a
     framework, can be applied to any urban or territorial organization and at any scale.

conceptual image of a complex organization defined by visual, spatial, material, social, and political conditions, to help us be in air, to navigate it mentally and even physically, as an affective and embodied experience. And, inspired by anthropologist Hannah Knox, to consider air—as she does with climate—a form of thought.[3] I call this conceptual image Aeropolis.[4]

Aeropolis allows us to imagine the air's condition as a city in and of itself. Doing so encourages us to reimagine architecture and urbanism, to understand "this imagining and projectual process as an architectural exercise"—and as a form of design.[5] This city of airs moves away from solutionism, away from hygienist or risk assessment frameworks, allowing us to recognize that other stories about the environment and how it relates to more-than- and other-than-humans are needed.[6]

Identifying

The first premise of Aeropolis is that airs are not only gases and particles but natural-socio-technical "urban assemblages,"[7] which include, among many others, the agents that are integral parts of its production process, its management, and its suffering. From

3   Hannah Knox, *Thinking Like a Climate: Governing a City in Times of Environmental Change*.

4   In addition to referencing the Greek polis as the realm of the political, I appreciate the resonance this term has with popular culture. Aeropolis has been used to name various shopping malls, hotels, shops, and airport developments all over the world: a pavilion designed by Plastique Fantastique in 2013 and exhibited in Copenhagen; an aerospatial technological park in Andalusia, Spain; a car shop in Vilnius, Lithuania; a proposed 500-story building in Tokyo; hotels in Kuala Lumpur, Malaysia, and Moscow; "airport-driven" economic developments in Malaysia and India; and virtual cities in the videogames *MARDEK* and *Rayman*, among many others. Thank you, Uriel Fogué, for naming this city of the air.

5   In 1996, William Mitchell wrote *City of Bits* to describe the virtual environments produced by informational technologies. He, too, used the metaphor of the city to discuss the specific implications of this paradigmatic change in architecture and urbanism. See William Mitchell, *City of Bits*.

6   T. J. Demos, *Against the Anthropocene: Visual Culture and Environment Today*.

7   Drawing from Actor-Network Theory, Ignacio Farías and Thomas Benders articulate the concept of "urban assemblages" to highlight how cities are composed by overlapping socio-technical systems, which cannot be segregated by function or location, for instance. See Ignacio Farías and Thomas Benders, eds., *Urban Assemblages: How Actor-Network Theory Changes Urban Studies*.

this perspective, air stops being some generic, abstract entity and becomes something specific and situated. It permits us to open the epistemic frame to consider all the practices, people, and disciplines (beyond science and technology) related to and enacting airs, all the possibilities for acting and interacting with/in them. Thinking through these aerial assemblages facilitates the recognition of how airs have been materialized and composed and re-composed by different social, technical, and geopolitical processes, and how airs are harnessed to serve particular (often hegemonic) ways of ordering the world. To start testing Aeropolis, let's identify a few aerial assemblages: inhabitants, borders, and markets.

Inhabitants

Multiple creatures and objects conform to or move through the troposphere: birds, balloons, satellites, clouds... Surely all these things can be considered as inhabitants of Aeropolis. But I am interested in changing the scale of inhabitation, in zooming in to the life of gases and particles. What does it mean to radically decenter the human, to put the material composition of air at the center instead, to pay attention to their agencies, to recognize their diversity, and to focus on the microscopic and the invisible?[8] Most things on earth—and in the atmosphere—are composed of gases and particles and so, again, it could be argued that all of them are inhabitants of Aeropolis. However, gases and particles react with each other and transform other material states—oxidizing, eroding, corroding, diluting, exploding, and so on. Larger entities such as humans, animals, plants, factories, and aircrafts, for instance, transform the composition of airs in order to live and to function. In this framework, the inhabitants of Aeropolis are gases and particles, while the larger entities that create, transform, or exchange them are "metabolizers"—we will get to those later.

8   To consider gases and particles as the main inhabitants of this space is not a metaphor, nor an animist move. It is a rhetorical move to change scale and imagine Aeropolis from a different point of view.

The inhabitants of Aeropolis have different atomic configurations, they perform and react in different ways, they have different effects, they are produced by different sources, and the strategies needed to address them are different. And, as in any society, this recognition of difference is important for any kind of social justice to be possible. The components of the atmosphere, in variable proportions, form the largest share of Aeropolis's inhabitants. On average, they are nitrogen (N, 78 percent), oxygen (O_2, 21 percent), water vapor (0–7 percent), ozone (O_3), carbon dioxide (CO_2), hydrogen (H_2), and noble gases (like krypton and argon), which constitute the 1 percent of other substances. Within this 1 percent are most so-called pollutants—carbon monoxide, sulfur oxide, or ash, and only a few of these pollutants are monitored empirically in real time.[9] It can be argued that by measuring and monitoring these gases and particles, they have been given a collective voice by humans and thus can be understood as "representatives" of Aeropolis. Not only because they are taken as indicators of its quality, but also because being measured gives them political agency.

Without measurement, these gases and particles do not exist in legal terms, and therefore polluters cannot be held accountable. This is important, because the vast majority of Aeropolis's inhabitants, including some of the more toxic ones, are "unknown." Human communities are thus silenced when Aeropolis's inhabitants are not given the chance to speak—because corporations lobby against monitoring the chemicals they emit, because internationally approved air-quality sensors are expensive and not compatible with the airs of many cities,[10] because the management capacities of

9   I refer to them as so-called pollutants because most of these substances are released by both anthropogenic and natural sources, and yet this distinction is often not clear for non-experts. For instance, today more than half the CO_2 in the atmosphere comes from human activities, including motor traffic, other combustion of fossil fuels, and slash-and-burn agriculture. But atmospheric CO_2 is not poisonous per se; it is its effects that are toxic.

10 In Mexico City, for instance, they had to adapt the monitoring network to be able to measure and account for the specific qualities of its air. Natalia Verónica Soto Coloballes, *El Aire de Cada Día. Política y Medición de La Contaminación Atmosférica En La Ciudad de México (1960–2015)*.

councils and local governments are limited, and because the political will to know about the quality of airs is often diluted by more "pressing" issues. In addition, because gases and particles resist measurement. Therefore, to aim for social (human) justice, we either must give voice to more inhabitants or account for more forms of being "present" beyond the technical regime of representation. Which begs further questions: Who decides which inhabitants get accounted for? In what other ways are inhabitants made "present"?

Inhabitants have different natures too. Some are organic, like pollen and viruses. Others are traces of daily activities, like the cocaine molecules that have been found in the air in Madrid and Barcelona.[11] Some are traces of endangered species, ghosts of other presences. I remember reading a study conducted at the Hamerton Zoo Park in Cambridgeshire that identified the DNA of seventeen species of zoo animals, including tiger, dingo, and ruffed lemur, in the zoo's air. Can you imagine breathing a tiger?[12] It is hard for me to imagine, and yet…

You have 10-story buildings that leave more debris than these two 100-story towers. Where the fuck is everything? A serious weeklong search and we've found 200 in a pile of 5,000? What's going on? Where is everyone? Why aren't we finding more bodies? Cause it's all vaporized—turned to dust. We're breathing people in that dust.[13]

We breathe people, buildings, drugs, without even knowing it, which breaks down the very idea of boundaries and borders.

Borders

The anthropologist Timothy Choy beautifully describes how the limits and scales of air (and therefore of Aeropolis) are multiple and overlapping:

47

11 Cocaine has been found in two measuring stations in Madrid; see https://www.rtve.es/notlclas/20090513/cocaina-pulula-aire-madrid-barcelona/276523.shtml.
12 Robin McKie, "DNA from Thin Air: A New Way to Detect Rare Wildlife in Hostile Environments."
13 Susan Schuppli, "Impure Matter: A Forensics on WTC Dust," 128.

Air disrespects borders, yet at the same time is constituted through difference. Neighborhoods have different atmospheres; nations generate and apply different pollution standards; leaders worry about the state of their air compared to others. The winds themselves derive from differences in air pressure between regions, and similar relativities allow our lungs to inhale and exhale. Gradients, whose foundations are the contact and bleeding of difference, move air through the spaces we live and through our bodies.[14]

If it is already difficult to define the limits of global cities,[15] this difficulty is even more accentuated in the air because *everything* is fluid, mutable, and not easily apprehensible. Gases and particles are moved by the wind in multiple directions, traveling thousands of miles.

While Aeropolis's legal limits are, in principle, those of the city, the regulation of transboundary air pollution by the United Nations in the 1970s, for example, dissolved the geospatial limits of the air:

Some nation-states are net exporters of airborne pollutants, whereas others are net importers, and some will be more severely hurt by a changing regional or global atmosphere. The discovery of long-range air pollution did not result in the dissolution of spatial boundaries, though. Instead, it meant the transgression of earlier demarcations between local, national, and international environmental problems and the establishment of new ones. A new political geography of winners and losers was created, and new and different incentives for international cooperation were established.[16]

48

14 Thank you Tim for sharing your draft of air substantiations. It was transformative for my understanding of the ways in which air is material-socio-political. Thank you as well for your generous, inspiring, and unsettling work and attitude. See Timothy K. Choy, *Ecologies of Comparison,* 165.
15 Saskia Sassen, *The Global City: New York, London, Tokyo.*
16 On the effects of the definition of transboundary pollution as an issue of political concern, see Rolf Lidskog and Göran Sundqvist, *Governing the Air: The Dynamics of Science, Policy, and Citizen Interaction,* 5.

The dissolution of airs' geospatial borders has not diluted the xeno-phobic ideas that engender and maintain those borders. Particles understood to have originated elsewhere are described in the media as an "invasion" from the "other"—in Europe with dust from the Sahara and in Southeast Asia with the "yellow dust" from China and Mongolia.[17] And yet, sometimes countries are occupied *through* gases. As philosopher of science Bruno Latour points out, former US President Trump's withdrawal from the Paris Accord "was a declaration of war authorizing the occupation of all the other coun-tries, if not with troops, at least with CO_2, which America retains the right to emit."[18]

Aeropolis's physical limits may be impossible to determine because of the constant material fluctuation and movement of air. But the spatial configuration of the air at specific locations matters. It matters for environmental justice. It matters because different airs are unevenly distributed; because the overlapping geographies of polluting infrastructures and low-income communities mean that disadvantaged groups bear the burden of the highest concentrations of pollutants. Therefore, it is important to find ways to describe and manage those aerial differences, both in space and in height. On the ground, air-quality measurements have become just one point of reference, as the monitoring of the atmosphere has expanded to satellites orbiting the planet. And yet another vertical limit is rarely accounted for: The ground we walk on has been culturally thought of as a splitting surface between the Earth and the air. Soil, however, is 60 percent air. Because bacteria, roots, fungi, worms... they all need air.

Markets

Some of the inhabitants of Aeropolis have become, according to the United Nations, "a new commodity."[19] These are the greenhouse

17   For instance, see Financial District, "Yellow Dust Storm from China, Mongolia Invades South Korea"; Jon Herskovitz, "China's Killer 'Yellow Dust' Hits Korea and Japan."
18   Bruno Latour, *Down to Earth: Politics in the New Climatic Regime*, 84.
19   United Nations Climate Change, "Emissions Trading."

gases that engender climate change, of which CO_2 is used as the primary reference.[20] In an attempt to reduce CO_2 levels in the atmosphere, international institutions created a global carbon market in the late 1990s as an economic-environmental regulator of polluting activities. Through a "cap and trade" system, the most polluting countries and industries can buy the rights to emit CO_2 from those who do not reach their caps.[21] This shift from governmental policies to market regulation is critical.[22] It turns air pollution into a (peculiar) productive system, which removes the responsibility of governments to act.[23] What is bought and sold are the rights to emit, not the material itself—and, unlike scarce commodities such as oil and gold, there is a surplus of CO_2.[24] Other trading units are carbon offsets or carbon removal units, which are compensation projects to reduce or absorb CO_2. They can be clean energy

50

20 Greenhouse gases are water vapor, carbon dioxide (CO_2), methane (CH_4), nitrous oxide (N_2O), and fluorinated gases. United States Environmental Protection Agency, "Overview of Greenhouse Gases."

21 The carbon market was approved through the Kyoto Protocol in 1997 (and ratified in 2004), launching the first bonus to reduce emissions by more than 5 percent by 2012.

22 Sebastián Ureta, "'Because in Chile [Carbon] Markets Work!' Exploring an Experimental Implementation of an Emissions Trading Scheme to Deal with Industrial Air Pollution in Santiago."

23 Common resources are capitalized upon by linking some invisible components of the air with international markets through brokers, juridical bureaus, banks and financial entities, project developers, stock exchanges, the World Bank, and investment funds, among others. See United Nations Climate Change, "The Carbon Market."

24 These markets are huge. Carbon offsets are also purchased in voluntary carbon markets, tailored to allow individuals, companies, and governments to offset or compensate for their emissions. The United Nations Carbon Offset Platform announced in August 2020 that it had reached 2 million certified emission reductions (CERs) purchased and canceled since its launch in September 2015. As they define on their site, "CERs are emission reductions units emanating from projects located in developing countries under UN Climate Change's Clean Development Mechanism (CDM). These projects not only reduce greenhouse gas emissions but also support sustainable development in the project countries." See United Nations Climate Change, "The United Nations Carbon Offset Platform." CERs are a type of carbon offset measured in tons of CO_2, which turn forests, for instance, into trading elements. Many Spanish-led reforestation projects are located within Spain, like those managed by Bosquia o Reforesta. Others, like the Gandhi Project, managed by Selectra, have built wind turbines in India to promote efficient energy use, whereby the UK company can also claim to be aiding India in its development. These projects represent the paradox at the core of the carbon markets, where it is not clear who benefits from these projects. Take another recent example: The Repsol Foundation (the largest oil company in Spain) and KPMG have signed the "Green Engine–Carbon Turnaround" agreement to support the voluntary carbon market. See KPMG España, "Fundación Repsol y KPMG lanzan una iniciativa que ayudará a España a ser referente europeo en compensación de emisiones."

infrastructures, reforestation projects, cleanup initiatives in polluted areas, and others, which often take place in developing countries in the Global South due to cheaper and extractable land and labor.

From the beginning, there have been uncertainties about the transparency of the carbon market and carbon calculation, in terms of caps, emissions, sinks, and emission rights.[25] Carbon markets have become exclusively speculative, with the worst polluters reaping the biggest benefits.[26] Compensation projects, although "sustainable" on paper, often have unanticipated social and economic consequences that further impoverish local communities. These projects reproduce and intensify the colonial legacies of violence, exploitation, and suffering inflicted by the same countries in the Global North that now own or manage compensation projects. As public health researcher Sophie Pascoe recalls,

> Suau people's fears that their air and land might be stolen by climate change mitigation and conservation projects are tied to their experiences of colonization and missionization, as well as ongoing resource extraction through logging and land appropriation for export-oriented cultivation of oil palm.[27]

In addition to the detrimental social and economic effects of many compensation projects, their success in sequestering carbon—and therefore in balancing the overall quantity of CO_2 in the atmosphere—is questionable too.[28] Resource management and environmental justice researcher Hannah K. Wittman and international

25 See Kristin Asdal, "From Climate Issue to Oil Issue: Offices of Public Administration, Versions of Economics, and the Ordinary Technologies of Politics"; Anders Blok, "Configuring Homo Carbonomicus: Carbon Markets, Calculative Techniques, and the Green Neoliberal."

26 See, for instance, *Reuters*, "Carbon Markets Have a Goldilocks Problem."

27 Pascoe analyzed a REDD+ Pilot Project and a Save the Forest conservation program in central Suau, Papua New Guinea, twenty years later. Sophie Pascoe, "Stealing Air and Land—The Politics of Translating Global Environmental Governance in Suau, Papua New Guinea," 41.

28 A recent investigation into Verra, one of the world's leading providers of voluntary carbon offsets has found that "based on analysis of a significant percentage of the projects, more than 90 percent of their rainforest offset credits—among the most commonly used by companies—are likely to be

development scholar Cynthia Caron studied two first-generation carbon offset projects, a forestry project in Guatemala and a solar electrification project in Sri Lanka, to conclude:

> Local history and the current political-economic context help to explain the difficulty of meeting carbon sequestration objectives. In Guatemala, land use conflicts, struggles for control over scarce forest, and legal changes that criminalized subsistence activities such as fuel wood gathering undermined local farmer participation. In Sri Lanka, ethnic and social inequalities associated with the British estate system's oppressive living conditions for an ethnic minority group were deepened when tea-producing corporations striving to stay competitive in a global market saw that solar-home systems could be a means to increase worker productivity. Both projects also refocused attention from poverty alleviation and the improvement of rural life in their regions of implementation toward the pursuit of carbon offsets, in effect seeking to exchange mitigation objectives for development.[29]

The "host" countries of the Global South, whose CO_2 contribution is minimal, bear the burden and responsibility of creating these services for the polluting countries of the Global North. In return, these projects reproduce colonial forms of development, in tandem with the reproduction of paternalistic dynamics of colonialism and environmental injustice, what geographer Farhana Sultana has termed "climate coloniality."[30]

Despite all these failures, carbon markets are still in place.[31] They might not be working for emissions reduction, but they are

'phantom credits' and do not represent genuine carbon reductions." Patrick Greenfield, "Revealed: More than 90% of Rainforest Carbon Offsets by Biggest Provider Are Worthless, Analysis Shows."

29 Hannah K. Wittman and Cynthia Caron, "Carbon Offsets and Inequality."
30 Farhana Sultana, "The Unbearable Heaviness of Climate Coloniality."
31 Susanna Twidale, Valerie Volcovici, and Jake Spring, "Madrid Climate Negotiators See to Break Deadlock on Role of Carbon Markets."

working for those who profit from the speculative carbon market. Unpacking the inhabitants, borders, and markets of Aeropolis shows how air is forced to accommodate certain spatial or economic logics that, by its very nature, it cannot accommodate. It also shows us the fallacy of these systems, in all the ways that air refuses them (in having constantly mutating inhabitants, in not recognizing borders, in the difficulty of removing carbon from the atmosphere). This brings to the fore the intrinsic challenges of researching, working, and engaging with air: its imperceptibility, instability, mutability, fluidity, mobility. But it also reveals all the possibilities.

World-Making

Aeropolis is a world-making project. It aims to be propositional, to imagine, design, and construct space, theoretical and physical, anew—space that is intersectional, transfeminist, and queer. It is a framework that lets us experiment with how to live in this toxic polluted world and these troubled times. To identify the power relations, politics, and forms of management that configure, emerge from, and are affected by these materials, spaces, and bodies. And to create alternative ways of thinking, engaging, and transforming—through ecological relationships.

Aeropolis is indebted to the work of feminists of science, queer theory, and ecofeminist scholars and practitioners, as well as anticolonial environmentalists. From them I have learned to question what is taken for granted; to prioritize the relations between things; to take into consideration the power relations in knowledge production; to decentralize the human as the main actor or victim of environmental issues; to appreciate the relevance of transformative practices; and to dismantle the traditional dichotomies between nature and culture, body and mind, object and subject.[32]

32   This implies, in practice, challenging objectivity and taking responsibility for our own positions and the understanding that "humans" (and their bodies) are subject to ongoing co-fabrication—like any other socio-material assemblage; always considering interrelationships and acknowledging the

I have learned, for instance, that because pollen bonds to and travels with metal particles, growing in size and eventually creating "pollen storms" that can intensify asthma attacks, the dichotomy between the natural and the artificial does not even apply. I have learned to "see" how air is always relational and in constant and continuous transformation: always reacting, moving, and interacting with (other) beings, at all scales: spores, plants, animals, humans.

From feminists of technoscience I have also learned a particular attitude. I have learned, as Donna Haraway has suggested, to trouble—which in French means to make cloudy (cloudy!)—the past in order to tell a different story of the present and the future;[33] to be at ease with not having a solution for "the air-quality problem," as I am often asked to provide. Releasing ourselves from the solution means that we can speculate about a world different from our own, to spend time with what is possible and not just what is, and to think about how airs (and how we relate and live with them) could be otherwise.

Following feminist author María Puig de la Bellacasa, I consider Aeropolis a form of thinking with care, a way of "provoking political and ethical imagination in the present."[34] Aeropolis searches for what is missing in our understandings of the urban, for what is not visible in the ways in which technoscience sees the air, our bodies, and buildings. It searches for the practices of knowing the air that are not accounted for, practices that have often been made invisible, neglected, forgotten, left out through choices, histories, or policies.[35] Paying attention to airs and unpacking their material, social, and political assemblages provide us with an idea of what is

importance of how knowledge is produced. For more on feminist methods, see Christina Hughes and Celia Lury, "Re-Turning Feminist Methodologies: From a Social to an Ecological Epistemology"; Yasmin Gunaratnam and Carrie Hamilton, "The Wherewithal of Feminist Methods"; Sarah Whatmore, "Materialist Returns: Practising Cultural Geography in and for a More-than-Human World"; and Donna Haraway, "Situated Knowledges."

33 Haraway's work has been foundational for me and is behind my words and the words of many others whom I reference. See Donna Haraway, *Staying with the Trouble: Making Kin in the Chthulucene*, 1.

34 María Puig de la Bellacasa, *Matters of Care: Speculative Ethics in More Than Human Worlds*, 7.

35 Such as people's personal experiences of air quality or air-related local memories.

at stake, and how certain narratives are being articulated. All these caring practices are needed to gain a more complex understanding of airs' capacities and to expand techno-scientific practices. And they require that we *pay attention* to difference, to the uncanny, the dirty, and the unjust—which, as we know, are always made invisible.

Exploring difference, the uncanny, the dirty, and the unjust, is at the core of queer theories and activisms. It could be argued that air operates in a similar fashion to geographer Kathryn Yusoff's "queer coal":

> As an incorporeal materiality and as a *constitutive expression of subjectivity* that provokes an internal distortion—or queerness—in how we might "read" a genealogical account of fossil fuels—as fossil and fuel and mode of subjectification that disrupts asexual geologies...[36]

But in Aeropolis, queering is a practice, *the* mode of being with/in air. It is a practice that lets us understand the role of classification in the consolidation of power relations and inhabit the space of blurriness and contradiction. This is particularly useful in Aeropolis, as airs, too, break, demand, and blur cultural and social structures that are taken for granted. I think of Ashon Crawley's words on "*black pneuma*":

> The capacity for the plural movement and displacement of inhalation and exhalation to enunciate life, life that is exorbitant, capacious, and, fundamentally, social, though it is also life that is structured through and engulfed by brutal violence.[37]

Queering airs thus arouses the unresolved tensions between life and death, between abundance and deprivation, between inside

36 Kathryn Yusoff, "Queer Coal: Genealogies in/of the Blood"; emphasis in the original. See also Nigel Clark and Kathryn Yusoff, "Queer Fire."
37 Ashon T. Crawley, "Blackpentecostal Breath," 38. Thank you, Isabelle, for this reference.

and outside, between the incorporeal and the subjective where contact with toxic chemicals can produce "a series of pleasurable or unpleasurable bodily reactions, chill, pulse rush, adrenaline, heat, fear, tingling skin."[38] It recognizes, as feminist media theorist Magdalena Górska writes, that "breathing becomes an articulation of the suffocating operations of social norms and power relations."[39] It is this provocation, this distortion, this action, that interests Aeropolis.

aeropolis, THE AIRS OF A CITY

While Aeropolis is the conceptual and aspirational space of urban airs, it can also refer to the airs of a specific city, a *particular* socio-technical, urban-aerial assemblage of actors, regulations, qualities.[40] I call this version "aeropolis," with a lowercase "a." Exploring a city's aeropolis is a tool to gain resolution and get down (or up?) into the details. And, most importantly, it is a tool to understand what is at stake. If through Aeropolis we have identified inhabitants, borders, and markets—which are all very much dependent on the material qualities of airs—through aeropolis we will look for the metabolizers, urbanisms, and representations of a city to see who and what transforms its material and cultural reality and its imagination.[41] aeropolis can thus be put to work as a descriptor and as a method of intervention.

Describing

Take Madrid as a reference. It is one of the most polluted cities in Europe, as indicated by the Air Quality Comparative Analysis of

38 This book has been crucial to challenging the good/bad in human/nonhuman relations. Mel Y. Chen, *Animacies: Biopolitics, Racial Mattering, and Queer Affect*, 206.
39 Magdalena Górska, "Breathing Matters," 43. My thanks to one of the book reviewers for this reference.
40 Again, this heuristic can be used for any other spatial configuration.
41 We could also search for its governments, infrastructures, and sacred places, but I am going to leave that to the reader, who hopefully can imagine them in the aeropolis of their own city.

European Cities.[42] And yet, it is in a way a "conventional" city with regard to aerial matters; it does not have anything particular or dramatic (such as locale-specific pollutants or dangerous events). It is banal, aerially speaking, and therefore a perfect example of everyday city airs. And perhaps it is this mundaneness, this "non-urgentness" (compared to, say, Dubai or Beijing), that leaves space for speculation.[43] This generic condition makes Madrid a good case study to unpack. Madrid is also my hometown, and I realize I had for a long time been inhabiting Madrid's aeropolis without knowing it.

So, let's suspend ourselves. Floating in Madrid's airs. In Madrid's aeropolis.

Metabolizers

All living entities exchange various gases with others in their environments. They metabolize air, change its composition. They—and we—absorb and release, inhale and exhale. Constantly. Buildings, factories, any productive systems are metabolizers too, through combustion, exhaust, chemical release. What is at stake is the scale of and responsibility for this exchange, of who releases and absorbs what.

In Madrid's aeropolis, the best-known metabolizer is road traffic, which emits around 80 percent of the city's NO_2. What else is releasing gases or particles into the city's aeropolis? The only compilation of emitters we can draw upon is Madrid's Inventory of Emissions, which lists combustion in the production and transformation of energy, nonindustrial combustion plants, the extraction

57

42   Developed by the Department of Chemical Engineering at the Escuela Superior de Ingeniería de Madrid in 2008. Even though this document is not public, it has been cited in the "Estrategia Local de Calidad del Aire de la Ciudad de Madrid 2006–2010."

43   The empirical material on Madrid's aeropolis comes out of direct observations of the material and spatial instantiations of air-related matters, from archival work conducted in various city archives, interviews with some of the main stakeholders, analyses of the available online material on City Council web pages, and from resources published by the press and legal and civic associations. It also draws on my own experience through an ongoing collaborative visualization project called *In the Air* (2008–) and some of the projects developed through C+, the architecture office I founded in 2006.

and distribution of fossil fuels and geothermal energy, solvent use, road transport, other modes of transport and mobile machinery, treatment and disposal of residues, agriculture, and nature as "potentially polluting activities."[44] Other processes have larger temporal scales, such as urban development and infrastructural works.[45] And lately, methane emissions, largely produced by industrial farming, are considered even more toxic and responsible for climate change than is CO_2.

But there are also metabolizers that absorb or "capture" some of the above air pollutants. Plants inhale CO_2 and exhale oxygen to power photosynthesis, so that in the carbon economy, green areas are referred to as CO_2 "sinks." Humans do the reverse, as they inhale oxygen and exhale CO_2. Everything in the city participates in Madrid's aeropolis, with different temporalities and in relation to different components, so in a sense the building and functioning of the city itself builds its aeropolis.

Although metabolizers might seem to describe technical and automatic processes—as exchanges of gases—they are, obviously, legislated and controlled according to political interests and needs. A clear example is how road traffic is managed. After decades of neglect, the Madrid City Council, led by Manuela Carmena—the first left-wing mayor in more than twenty years—put air pollution at the center of its environmental agenda. It enforced traffic reduction warnings and established Madrid Central, a low-emissions zone that has become a core element of recent political battles, as

44 The Inventory of Emissions is the basis of the cost/benefit analysis of designed and implemented policies and interventions around air quality and climate change. The inventory of 2013 followed a methodology proposed by the EU and measured emissions in relation to greenhouse gases. Since 2019, there have been two inventories, one of greenhouse gas emissions and another one of pollutant emissions. See Madrid City Council, "The Inventory of Contaminant Emissions of Madrid 2019."

45 These are generally not taken into account in air-quality inventories or evaluation studies. However, the relationship between urban development and air quality became a matter of concern and a public controversy when Madrid presented its bid for the 2012 Olympic games, as it was one of the reasons why Madrid was eliminated. For a citizen response to this issue, see Karla von Ulme and Alan Fernández, "Siete Razones para Estar en Contra de Madrid 2012."

demonstrated by current right-wing mayor José Luis Martínez-Almeida's attempt to remove it on his first day in office.[46]

Urbanisms

Paying attention to aerial differences sheds light on airs' deep connection to the socio-geographical distribution of a city. How the inhabitants of Madrid's aeropolis are spatialized reveals the areas with the most prolonged and intensive exposure to pollution. These areas, when correlated with the city's population and geographical conditions, configure the urbanisms of Madrid's aeropolis, which show the spatial distribution of environmental inequality and injustice related to air pollution.

Madrid is a relatively flat city sitting in the center of the Castilian plain. The mountains in the northwest create winds that blow south, refreshing the warm summers and displacing air pollution. These winds, as in other cities, spatially organize the distribution of wealth. Wealthier neighborhoods are located in the northwest, closer to the mountains, which is to say, they have less pollution and more vegetation. Poorer neighborhoods are located in the southeast, thus they tend to be where air pollution settles. Some of Madrid's aeropolis urbanisms correlate with this spatial organization. The urbanism of particulate matter (PM_{10}), for instance, is mostly determined by Madrileños' average income per capita and age.[47] Madrid-aeropolis's urbanism of NO_2 is less clear, showing correlations only with the elderly and the Latin American populations who inhabit the city center.[48]

46 Euprepio Padula, "Almeida: 'Lo Primero Se Acabó Madrid Central'"; Marta R. Domingo, "Eliminar Madrid Central, Aprobar Chamartín, Bajar Impuestos y Desactivar los Semáforos de la A-5: Las Claves del Futuro Gobierno de Almeida."

47 Particulate matter (PM_{10}) is the designation for tiny (10µm diameter) particles such as fumes, fuels, or smoke, which can irritate the eyes and throat and exacerbate heart disease and some types of cancer. The main contributors of PM_{10} in Madrid are road transportation (roughly 65 percent), other modes of transport, and industrial and waste treatment processes. See Rosa Cañada Torrecilla, Maria Jesús Vidal Domínguez, and Moreno Jiménez, "Interpolación Espacial y Visualización Cartográfica para el Análisis de la Justicia Ambiental: Ensayo Metodológico sobre la Contaminación por Partículas Atmosféricas en Madrid"; María-Eugenia Prieto-Flores et al., "Contaminación del Aire,

Other urbanisms are configured more immediately around polluting infrastructures. In 1995, Madrid built its largest regional waste incineration plant on the southeastern edge of the capital by the city's largest informal settlement. This settlement, called La Cañada Real, has a long history of poverty, drugs, and national and international migration (from rural areas, people expelled from the city center, Spanish Roma, and Romanian and Moroccan people with links to the Roma communities), with very limited opportunities for social mobility. The construction of the incinerator sparked a controversy and strong resistance by environmentalists living in the neighboring areas, who set up associations like Rivas Aire Limpio and the platform Incineradoras No, and in 2016 sued the regional government for its lack of transparency, possible corruption, and failure to produce an environmental impact report.[49] These associations fought for air pollution data collection, and have recorded higher frequency of asthma and cancer among their neighbors than in the rest of the region. However, in 2019, the Madrid Council published an epidemiological study claiming lack of evidence of the impact of the incinerator on human health. The NGO Ecologistas en Acción challenged the validity of this study for insufficient data, and is engaged in an ongoing struggle against the government's obfuscation efforts.[50] Studies or measurements can be unreliable tools of manipulation. Urbanisms of aeropolis are deeply political.

Representations

Aeropolis's socio-technical assemblages are also cultural and semiotic. For centuries, Madrid's air has been one of its most representative elements. For instance, in the early seventeenth century,

Mortalidad Cardiovascular y Grupos Vulnerables en Madrid," 559.

48 People over 80 years old are more prone to cardiovascular diseases, which are exacerbated by NO_2 emissions. See Antonio Moreno Jiménez, "Población y Polución Atmosférica Intraurbana por Dióxido de Nitrógeno en Madrid."

49 Rivas Aire Limpio, "RIVAS AIRE LIMPIO."

50 Ecologistas en Acción, "El estudio epidemiológico sobre Valdemingómez no es válido," https://www.ecologistasenaccion.org/115128/el-estudio-epidemiologico-sobre-valdemingomez-no-es-valido.

when the renowned painter Diego Velázquez arrived in Madrid for the second time to paint a series of royal portraits of Kings Felipe III and Felipe IV, the queens and the prince, he took them out of the palace to the open air. Velázquez found the city's dramatic sky—its intense blue with spongy white and gray clouds, its vibrant yellow, orange, and pink sunsets—to be the best background to exalt the Spanish monarchy. Today, the sky is still the defining characteristic of the city, as can be seen in innumerable pictures taken by tourists, residents, and professional photographers alike.[51] However, all these pictures have been taken on days with low pollution. A picture of the city on a random day would reveal a brown-gray cloud covering the buildings and blurring the blue sky, what locals call *la boina*.[52] A question then emerges: Does Madrid need to change its icon, or should its true aerial conditions—as an index of the technological city[53]—be included in its representations? How/when has consciousness of the city's airborne pollution been registered and begun to compete with its iconic association with the sky?

Tall buildings are an intrinsic component of this tension. As icons that can render a city distinct and recognizable, like the "star-architect"-designed buildings of the 1990s and 2000s, these architectures have become air "measurers." In Madrid, the few towers that break an otherwise homogeneous skyline allow us to distinguish air quality according to how much of the tower is obscured by haze, as images used by the press to "evidence" pollution demonstrate.[54] Is architecture becoming the representational background for registering the urban environment and polluted air? It looks like neoliberal practices of urban development are, literally, erasing their own icons. But neoliberalism is quick to self-correct

61

---

51 This can be tested by looking at the picture-sharing platform Flickr, where under the tag "Madrid," what emerges are mostly pictures of its skies.

52 *Boina* is a beret.

53 Jussi Parikka, "The Sensed Smog: Smart Ubiquitous Cities and the Sensorial Body."

54 In a comparative analysis I conducted across digital newspapers from 2008 to 2011, I found that around 80 percent of them use the Real Madrid towers as a reference for air quality.

and capitalize upon its failures, and air pollution is now a key component of the real estate market: residential towers are built higher than the smog level, reserving fresh air and clear views for the uber-wealthy. Capitalism creates the conditions for its own acceleration.

If Aeropolis asks us to consider the microscopic and invisible "stuff" as inhabitants, aeropolis asks: How are inhabitants managed, produced, or sold? aeropolis aims to tell the story of a particular three-dimensional territory. A territory where every material entity, living or not, is part of metabolic micro—and macro—sequences of absorption or exhalation of gases and particulate matter; where some inhabitants have economic value and are traded like Apple or Google stocks; where certain urbanisms engender premature death or intensify social injustice; and where the "big" architecture becomes *the* scale of air pollution. Madrid's metabolizers, urbanisms, and representations have revealed how a specific aeropolis is designed—and all the biases that are expressed and enforced through design—and point to a way of thinking and designing otherwise.

Thinking-Designing-Making

Paying attention to the specificity of air permits us to understand where it reaches, how it interacts with humans and other-than-humans, and what it does in the world, materially, geographically, socially, symbolically. Paying attention to the specificity of air pushes design itself. In a city's aeropolis, design cannot be separated from how things are made. Paying attention to how things are made makes visible what it takes to make them, pushes *how* we design and build, how and when we get together to design. Paying attention to the specificity of air makes clear how design is not a linear sequence of "steps": thinking first, designing second, and making/building third. In a city's aeropolis, thinking-designing-making are entangled processes—interdisciplinary methods of knowing, engaging with, sensing, feeling, air.

You could describe this as a wondering process. Writing about the possibilities of anti-colonial thought, Black studies scholar Katherine McKittrick describes the Black Method as "a way of living, and an analytical frame, that is curious and sustained by wonder (the desire to know). This is a method that demands openness and is unsatisfied with questions that result in descriptive-data-induced answers."[55] Recognizing how different this project is from McKittrick's, I still hear her words and extend their legacies, through aeropolis, through my own thinking-designing-making, my own wondering. Because thinking-designing-making is, like wonder, a desire to know, doubt, question airs. And possibly, because Aeropolis would not exist if I had not wondered—feeling great surprise and admiration—every time I attuned to airs.

In sum, aeropolis is a tool for description and an interdisciplinary method for thinking-designing-making through materialized atmospheric experiments. And through air, for rethinking practices and understandings of nature, humans, bodies, disease, viruses, pollution, the city. This conceptual framework permits us to describe an ecosystem of particles and gases, bringing together toxic pollution, vegetable and soil reproduction, communication, and exchange. To understand the air-city, we cannot distinguish airs (as particles and gases) as separate from the physical, social, political entities that participate in their processes, because

> matter is becoming present to us in ways by which we, now, have no choice but to listen. But in doing so, it is asking to pay attention somewhat differently... If matter speaks, we need to tool our senses such that we learn to listen to its multiple and interrelated voices, and as such see and hear and feel how matter prefigures thought in important ways.[56]

63

55 Katherine McKittrick, *Dear Science and Other Stories*, 5.

This book has many aims. *Aeropolis* (the title of the book in italics) hopes to make airs sensible as multiple and diverse; to reflect on the conceptual, spatial, ecological, and social differences that constitute airs; to resist the tendency to flatten and homogenize the image of airs through philosophical matters, political interests, or just plain inertia; to explore how airs are complex physical, cultural, and political matter; to think with/in air from feminist and queer perspectives; to detect the specific airs of a city, and explore, materially, other forms of intervention in it; to imagine the city of (atmo) airs; and to reckon with what it means that "we are not inhabitants of the Earth, we are inhabitants of the atmosphere."[57] *Aeropolis* reorients how we get to know air, from seeing to feeling to sensing; it follows the past and present of air pollution, of pollen, of weeds; it looks down to think about what is up and vice versa; it attempts to trace the multiplicity of airs and airs as infrastructure. *Aeropolis* wonders. It asks questions to identify opportunities—possibly temporary, often ephemeral, but opportunities nevertheless—to think-design-make with uncertainty, openness, failure. It expands. Shares. Moves. Removes. Floats. Dissipates...

Sensing

Aeropolis wishes to be a tool to retool senses. A tool to sense differently.

A form of sensing that brings together all the etymological meanings of the word sense.

A form of sensing that makes air *sensible*: capable of being *perceived*, felt (sentir).

56 Mark Jackson and Maria Fannin, "Letting Geography Fall Where It May—Aerographies Address the Elemental," 436.
57 Emanuele Coccia, *The Life of Plants: A Metaphysics of Mixture*, 35.

A form of sensing that makes sense of how things (thoughts, theory, methods, sensors, designs, clouds, speculations) are done-made-assembled.

A form of sensing that makes us *sensitive* (susceptible to injury and pain) to airs. It aims to make us sensitive to the impact that airs have on other bodies, in other regions, in other ecosystems. To make us sensitive to the inequalities produced by and through airs.

A form of sensing that brings *sensuality* (carnal) to the air-city, and senses through attunement (technological, embodied, or otherwise). Attunement as sensorial but non-intuitive, precognitive but also cognitive, situated, technological, historical...

Aeropolis is a multisensor itself. Each chapter configures a different realm of perceptibility to sense the air in it. Living, breathing, seeing, touching, holding, queering. They can be read in any order. They do not configure a linear narrative or argument. They draw on similar and different references. They build their own bibliographies. They are repetitive (of authors, ideas, references). They establish both strong and loose connections. *Aeropolis* follows English and Gender studies scholar Jack Halberstam's approach to *Wild Things*, it does not provide a systematic review or genealogy of air, nor does this introduction. Rather, and I invite you to read "air" in place of *wildness*,

> it builds a lexicon within which wildness is the central principle. Appropriately, perhaps, there is not a central argument sweeping all the thoughts along toward a punch line; rather, I offer a vocabulary for wildness that might hold some of the pieces of this book in productive tension. Definitions of wildness will jostle with one another for classificatory dominance, and just as quickly as formulations of the wild emerge, they may just as easily recede into babble.[58]

58   Jack Halberstam, *Wild Things: The Disorder of Desire*, xii.

Sharing

Aeropolis was motivated by my architecture design teaching practice. First, because I am not convinced by the ways in which air is often mobilized in architecture (as technical thermodynamics, as formal airscapes, as polluted stuff to be technologically fixed). I am interested in other—feminist, queer, anti-colonial, anti-capitalist—forms of understanding airs and their pollution. And I am, with many others, convinced that this is the only way to live with toxicity and intervene in air pollution with social justice at the center. Second, because I have come to realize that the challenges we face in the classroom are related not only to air but also to understandings of "nature," "green," "the environment," buildings, plants, design, collaboration, disease... which are, at most, techno-solutionist. Thus, *Aeropolis* stands against understandings of air as a void, against size and strength, against huge cantilevers and facade compositions, against macho contractors and the tyranny of built square meters as the only criterion to evaluate the built environment. Against default white cubes and massive infrastructures justified through objectivity, efficiency, and cleanness—which, let us not forget, are colonial and extractive strategies.

I wrote *Aeropolis* to share what I have learned over the years. I wrote it for students, so that we could think-design-make with different references—and, hopefully, un-know the neoliberal understandings of "nature," "green," or "the environment" entrenched in mainstream architecture.[59] To share what I have learned from reading,

59 This book comes together after more than ten years of trying to get close to air through independent (and unstructured) research, through digital and spatial design, and through academic research. I guess you could say that my first "rational" incursion into urban air was through an attempt to visualize Madrid's air pollution data. In the process, I realized that air demanded more ways of being sensed, more ways of making sense of it. I conceptualized Aeropolis as part of my PhD thesis as a way to expand the notion of sensing. I continued enriching Aeropolis through reading, writing, talking, designing. *Aeropolis* as a book was unplanned, in the sense that it was never the goal or the end point of a very meandering path. In fact, I wrote it as a requirement of my academic job. Therefore, it is not a summary of these years of research, nor a conclusion.

making, conversing. To share how the things I have made are made—a process rarely discussed. Not necessarily so they can be made again (and therefore not as a method), nor as a reference of how things should be, but to grasp what it takes to think-design-make, from ourselves, colleagues, nonhumans, regulations, budgets, and so on.

I wrote *Aeropolis* to share how I have learned, because the references in architecture are too limited. I have learned by wondering, searching, exploring, trying, hunting. Without order or plan. Informally. Over time. Often unaware of it. Zooming in and out of disciplines, spaces, times, geographies, institutions, collectives... From the things, people, books, projects, images that have triggered, sparked, inspired, sustained this project. From the friends, artists, scholars, writers, curators, engineers, builders with whom I have shared experiences, conversations, projects, doubts, excitement, life. I have referenced as much as my (very poor) memory has allowed me to. To try to acknowledge the relations and obligations that come with reading and writing. As Métis/Michif anticolonial designer, researcher, and geographer Max Liboiron lucidly asks: "How do we recognize that our writing and reading come out from different places, connections, obligations, and even different worldviews, and still write and read together?"[60] To share for others to enjoy. To celebrate my aerial significant others, old and new. With the politics of citation in mind,[61] I have included the people and references I would like to share Aeropolis with or who are already there, together with ozone, metal particles, fungi, lead, and many other things—and not only the ones that "should" be.[62] Following Liboiron, I have used

---

60 Max Liboiron, *Pollution Is Colonialism*, 31.

61 For discussions on the politics of citation, I strongly recommend the reflections and genealogies of the concept in Liboiron, *Pollution Is Colonialism*; and McKittrick, *Dear Science and Other Stories*. I have borrowed from Liboiron their way of using footnotes and citations to acknowledge and celebrate their knowledge relations.

62 I have introduced the authors through their "professions" to give the reader an indication of the realm of knowledge their arguments derive from. I have tried to echo what each author uses in their institutional profiles. This is done with the understanding that to reduce these voices to one category

the footnotes to unpack concepts, translate ideas across disciplines, provide context, and show my relations with the authors or projects referenced, all academic and extra-academic, as part of my obligation to a diverse audience.

I'd like to also briefly share *how I have shared* in these pages.[63] A "how" shaped by airs' own requirements. The multiplicity, diversity, and situatedness of airs demands a way of writing that is active, filled with multiple voices, multiple breaths. So here are a few navigation tips: This is me.

These are my diffused thoughts—thoughts that might provide context, detail, history—and also my experiences and observations, auto-ethnographic glimpses, attempts at sense making.

These are other people's words. Diverse, like airs. Words that I bring in because they are inspiring, mind-blowing, productive, beautiful. Maybe too many? I hope not. They are such a pleasure to read—for ourselves, whispering, out loud.

I share floating in the air, suspended, in motion.[64] From a place of vulnerability, not "as an act of disclosure,"[65] which feels exciting, uncomfortable, challenging, difficult.

is always an impossible task as, first, most people cited here are multidisciplinary. Apologies if you do not feel accurately represented.

63 For an amazing articulation on how and why a book was written, I cannot stop reading McKittrick's spectacular first story *Dear Science and Other Stories*, which she calls "Curiosities (my heart makes my head swim)." It is an incredible introduction to the book, and a meta-introduction to the motivations, impulses, feelings, memories, instincts, questions, and pasts driving studies of and in the present.

64 When trying to think about my relations and obligations to Land, in response to Liboiron's call, I feel that throughout this project I have been suspended (in air?) in a transient flow of fluctuations—geographical, hormonal, affective, gendered. I have been queering, queer, queered. Such a state has inevitably permeated my days and my practices—and thus Aeropolis and *Aeropolis*. I share this—after a lot of thinking and numerous conversations (thank you, Uriel, María, Manu!)—as an obligation (Liboiron's term) to architecture students, to show not only that situatedness matters but that there are other—and more exciting!—ways of thinking-designing-making (and being) in a white, cis, male, heteronormative, and patriarchal field.

65 McKittrick, *Dear Science and Other Stories*, 7.

I wonder as a form of sharing or, more accurately, of having a conversation. I wonder frequently. I wonder to air—or ventilate—my thoughts. I wonder to air—or to share with you—my doubts, arguments, beliefs, or ideas (please write me if you have thoughts!). I wonder to leave assumptions about our beliefs hanging in the air—unresolved, unaddressed; or to leave them up—not decided, unsettled—in it. To try to prevent thoughts from disappearing into thin air—completely and without a trace. I wonder to build castles in the air—dreams, hopes, or projects about air that might be impossible, unrealistic, or have very little chance of succeeding.

This book is about airing air and cities. About environmental pollution and environmental justice. About ecology, inequality, architecture, urban space, smart cities... balloons, power plants, smoke, weeds. It gives relevance to air as a material and explores forms of transforming it. To think of air as an attitude, a method, and a political proposition, as an urgency and as a pleasure. Disclaimer: do not expect "solutions" or anything radically new. I have drawn on the work of many, so depending on where, what, and how you practice and with whom or what you have learned, you might be an expert, familiar, interested, or new to what you will find in these pages. Wherever you come from (intellectually, politically, affectively), I hope *Aeropolis* allows you to sense something unexpected, frustrating, inspiring, or different about airs. To find joy in sensing more aerial things. To walk away with a deeper sense of the implications of sensing air differently. And, why not, to walk—extremely happy—on air? To contribute to expanding the group of conspirers who, breathing together, work toward alternative futures, to imagine and test other worlds.[66]

I look again out the window. The spiderweb that grows larger every day has captured a tiny fly. Today the sky is

66 Timothy K. Choy, "A Commentary: Breathing Together Now."

gray, and the leaves still clinging to their branches are fluttering. I wonder if the wind that moves them contains sea droplets, algae, microplastics from the Thames River...

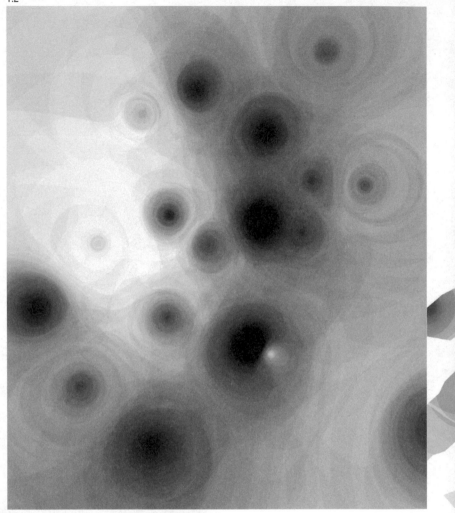

1.2

1.4

WORKS CITED

Asdal, Kristin. "From Climate Issue to Oil Issue: Offices of Public Administration, Versions of Economics, and the Ordinary Technologies of Politics." *Environment and Planning A: Economy and Space* 46, no. 9 (September 1, 2014): 2110–2124.

Blok, Anders. "Configuring Homo Carbonomicus: Carbon Markets, Calculative Techniques, and the Green Neoliberal." In *Neoliberalism and Technoscience: Critical Assessments,* edited by Luigi Pellizzoni and Marja Ylönen, 187–208. Oxford and New York: Routledge, 2016.

Chen, Mel Y. *Animacies: Biopolitics, Racial Mattering and Queer Affect.* Durham, NC: Duke University Press, 2012.

Choy, Timothy K. "A Commentary: Breathing Together Now." *Engaging Science, Technology, and Society* 6 (2020): 586–590.

⸻. *Ecologies of Comparison: An Ethnography of Endangerment in Hong Kong.* Durham, NC: Duke University Press, 2011.

Clark, Nigel, and Kathryn Yusoff. "Queer Fire: Ecology, Combustion and Pyrosexual Desire." *Feminist Review* 118, no. 1 (April 1, 2018): 7–24.

Coccia, Emanuele. *The Life of Plants: A Metaphysics of Mixture.* Cambridge: Polity Press, 2018.

Crawley, Ashon T. "Blackpentecostal Breath." *The New Inquiry,* July 19, 2017. https://thenewinquiry.com/blackpentecostal-breath.

Demos, T.J. *Against the Anthropocene: Visual Culture and Environment Today.* Berlin: Sternrberg Press, 2017.

Ecologistas en Acción. "El estudio epidemiológico sobre Valdemingómez no es válido," February 13, 2019. https://www.ecologistasenaccion. org/115128/el-estudio-epidemiologico-sobre-valdemingomez-no-es-valido.

Farías, Ignacio, and Thomas Benders, eds. *Urban Assemblages: How Actor-Network Theory Changes Urban Studies.* Questioning Cities Series. London and New York: Routledge, 2010.

Górska, Magdalena. "Breathing Matters: Feminist Intersectional Politics of Vulnerability." Linköping: Linköping University, 2016.

Gunaratnam, Yasmin, and Carrie Hamilton. "The Wherewithal of Feminist Methods." *Feminist Review* 115, no. 1 (2017): 1–12.

Halberstam, Jack. *Wild Things: The Disorder of Desire.* Durham, NC: Duke University Press, 2020.

Haraway, Donna. "Situated Knowledges: The Science Question in Feminism and the Privilege of Partial Perspective." *Feminist Studies* 14, no. 3 (October 1, 1988): 575–599.

⸻. *Staying with the Trouble: Making Kin in the Chthulucene.* Durham, NC: Duke University Press, 2016.

Hughes, Christina, and Celia Lury. "Re-Turning Feminist Methodologies: From a Social to an Ecological Epistemology." *Gender and Education* 25, no. 6 (2013): 786–799.

Jackson, Mark, and Maria Fannin. "Letting Geography Fall Where It May—Aerographies Address the Elemental." *Environment and Planning D: Society and Space* 29, no. 3 (June 1, 2011): 435–444.

Jiménez, Antonio Moreno. "Población y polución atmosférica intraurbana por dióxido de nitrógeno en Madrid: análisis desde la justicia ambiental basado en Sistemas de Información Geográfica." *Cuadernos Geográficos* 52, no. 1 (June 29, 2013): 84–107.

Knox, Hannah. *Thinking Like a Climate: Governing a City in Times of Environmental Change.* Durham, NC: Duke University Press, 2020.

Lafarge, Daisy. *Life Without Air.* London: Granta Poetry, 2020.

Latour, Bruno. *Down to Earth: Politics in the New Climatic Regime.* Cambridge: Polity Press, 2018.

Liboiron, Max. *Pollution Is Colonialism.* Durham, NC: Duke University Press, 2021.

Lidskog, Rolf, and Göran Sundqvist, eds. *Governing the Air: The Dynamics of Science, Policy, and Citizen Interaction.* Cambridge, MA: MIT Press, 2011.

Limpio, Rivas Aire. "RIVAS AIRE LIMPIO: La Incineradora de Valdemingómez. ¿Un Ingenio Invencible?" *RIVAS AIRE LIMPIO* (blog), March 17, 2016. http://rivasairelimpio.blogspot. com/2016/03/la-incineradora-de-valdemingomez-un.html.

McKie, Robin. "DNA from Thin Air: A New Way to Detect Rare Wildlife in Hostile Environments." *The Observer,* August 8, 2021, sec. Science. https:// www.theguardian.com/science/2021/aug/08/dna-from-thin-air-a-new-way-to-detect-rare-wildlife-in-hostile-environments.

McKittrick, Katherine. *Dear Science and Other Stories*. Durham, NC: Duke University Press, 2021.

McLuhan, Marshall. *The Gutenberg Galaxy: The Making of Typographic Man*. Toronto: University of Toronto Press, 1962.

Mitchell, William J. *City of Bits*. Cambridge, MA: The MIT Press, 1996.

Mumford, Lewis. *The Culture of Cities*. San Diego, CA: Harcourt Brace & Company, 1996.

Parikka, Jussi. "The Sensed Smog: Smart Ubiquitous Cities and the Sensorial Body." *The Fiberculture Journal* (2017): 1–24.

Pascoe, Sophie. "Stealing Air and Land—The Politics of Translating Global Environmental Governance in Suau, Papua New Guinea." *Conservation & Society* 19, no. 1 (2021): 34–43.

Prieto-Flores, María-Eugenia, Antonio Moreno Jiménez, Diana Gómez-Barroso, Rosa Cañada Torrecilla, and Pedro Martínez Suárez. "Contaminación del aire, mortalidad cardiovascular y grupos vulnerables en madrid: un estudio exploratorio desde la perspectiva de la justicia ambiental." *Scripta Nova. Revista Electrónica de Geografía y Ciencias Sociales* 21 (March 1, 2017).

Puig de la Bellacasa, María. *Matters of Care: Speculative Ethics in More Than Human Worlds*. Minneapolis, MN: University of Minnesota Press, 2017.

Sassen, Saskia. *The Global City: New York, London, Tokyo*. Princeton, NJ: Princeton University Press, 2001.

Schuppli, Susan. "Impure Matter: A Forensics on WTC Dust." In *Savage Objects*, edited by Godofredo Pereira, 120–140. Imprensa Nacional Casa da Moeda (INCM), 2012.

Soto Coloballes, Natalia Verónica. *El Aire de Cada Día. Política y Medición de La Contaminación Atmosférica En La Ciudad de México (1960–2015)*. México: Universidad Nacional Autónoma de México, 2021.

Sultana, Farhana. "The Unbearable Heaviness of Climate Coloniality." *Political Geography* 99 (November 1, 2022).

Swyngedouw, Erik, Maria Kaika, and Esteban Castro. "Urban Water: A Political-Ecology Perspective." *Built Environment* 28, no. 2 (2002): 124–137.

Torrecilla, Rosa Cañada, Maria Jesús Vidal Domínguez, and Moreno Jiménez. "Interpolación Espacial y Visualización Cartográfica para el Análisis de la justicia Ambiental: ensayo metodológico sobre la contaminación por partículas atmosféricas en Madrid." ISSN, 2011, 37.

Ureta, Sebastián. "'Because in Chile [Carbon] Markets Work!' Exploring an Experimental Implementation of an Emissions Trading Scheme to Deal with Industrial Air Pollution in Santiago." *Economy and Society* 43, no. 2 (April 3, 2014): 285–306.

Whatmore, Sarah. "Materialist Returns: Practising Cultural Geography in and for a More-than-Human World." *Cultural Geographies* 13 (2006): 600–609.

Wittman, Hannah K., and Cynthia Caron. "Carbon Offsets and Inequality: Social Costs and Co-Benefits in Guatemala and Sri Lanka." *Society & Natural Resources* 22, no. 8 (August 11, 2009): 710–726.

Yusoff, Kathryn. "Queer Coal: Genealogies in/of the Blood." *PhiloSOPHIA* 5, no. 2 (2015): 203–229.

IMAGES

1.1
Air pollution viewed from a cemetery in Madrid. Photograph by Santi Burgos. Courtesy of the artist.

1.2
Map of alerts and limits of particulate matter (PM_{10}) coinciding with areas with maximum and minimum population density in Madrid, January–October 2008, *LABO in the Air*, LABoral Centro de Arte y Creación Industrial Gijón, 2010. Courtesy of the author.

1.3
Accumulation of particulate matter (PM_{10}) alerts and limits in Madrid, January–October 2008, *LABO in the Air*, LABoral Centro de Arte y Creación Industrial Gijón, 2010. Courtesy of the author.

1.4
A car passes the entrance mark of Madrid's first environmental zone, "Madrid Central," at Puerta de Toledo square, June 27, 2019. Courtesy of Thomas Holbach.

1.5
Thousands protest for the preservation of the inner-city environmental zone in Madrid, June 29, 2019. Courtesy of Thomas Holbach.

BREATHING POLLUTION (AND TOXICITY)

I remember the first time I saw an image of Beijing blanketed in smog. I remember it because I had been trying to make air pollution visible through data visualizations, to "see" the composition of air, to know more about it. Then, suddenly, through this small printed image, I felt that I had "seen" air for the first time. There it was. "The air." The pollution in the city transforming conditions of visibility and movement.

Some months later, similar images from other cities started popping up in the news: Lagos, Delhi, Santiago de Chile... in each case, there was a grayish or yellowish smog solidifying what would otherwise be considered not there, empty. Grayish or yellowish smog reminding us, through the masks worn by workers and passersby— pre-COVID 19—of all that we took for granted.

But this was not the first time the air had become visible, and definitely not the last. Humans have been compelled to look up to the sky for all sorts of things: gods, weather, birds, planes. But it was the industrial revolution that really made the air itself visible—and smellable—on an urban scale.

"Pollution is a social construct, but the stuff that this concept signifies is very real indeed," writes historian Peter Thorsheim.[1] Tracing the history of dirty air in the UK, Thorsheim shows us how what counts as pollution or what counts as "pure" air has developed in a nonlinear way; he shows us how these designations shift; how they intertwine scientific, social, cultural, and political preoccupations. For instance, he describes how in Europe in the early nineteenth century, it was widely accepted that miasma—an invisible form of "bad air" thought to carry diseases—was the most lethal environmental hazard in urban areas, occasionally rendered visible in

[1]   For a detailed and fascinating account of the evolution of pollution as a social and cultural construct, see Peter Thorsheim, *Inventing Pollution: Coal, Smoke, and Culture in Britain since 1800*, 201.

fog.[2] By the mid-nineteenth century, the use of coal to heat homes and power steam engines for transport and industry filled the air of cities with a thick black smoke, blurring the contours of buildings, machines, and humans. Surprisingly, this man-made smoke was, at first, not considered pollution. On the contrary, it was seen as a kind of disinfectant—something that would get rid of miasmas—and otherwise experienced as a nonthreatening nuisance—something that stained clothes and buildings, occasionally darkened streets, and reduced visibility. However, over time, smoke was re-signified. It shifted from being a disinfectant to a poison. As the smoke became darker and thicker, respiratory difficulties increased. The germ theory of disease gained traction, and social dissatisfaction with the unbearable living and working conditions grew. A moral correlation between dirt and social degeneration emerged. The smoky acidic gases inflicted material and aesthetic damage as well, darkening and eroding stone facades throughout the city. And yet despite these negative associations, as urban dwellers cohabitated with this black cloud—accepted as a sort of fact of life—they referred to it simply as fog. For Thorsheim, the use of this term had the effect of naturalizing smoke until the turn of the twentieth century, when H. A. Des Voeux, treasurer of the Coal Smoke Abatement Society, suggested the use of the combined term "smog" to keep present the anthropogenic component of the air that enveloped urban dwellers.[3] By the early 1900s, Britain's urban

2   Miasma was considered invisible but was recognizable through its pestilent smell. It was thought to originate from the decomposition of organic matter caused by urban multispecies cohabitating with their own exhalations, waste, and excrement; it was understood to carry cholera, malaria, and other biological infectious diseases considered airborne at the time. Fog, the white and blurry condensation of water droplets, was also considered a natural (though visible) hazard. Sharing its smell and poisonous associations with miasmas, fog was thought to emerge from marshlands and other dump areas away from cities. The two were seen to occasionally overlap in urban areas, instances where in the public imagination fog made miasmas visible. This was one of many attempts to make sense of the damage caused by invisible and smelly gases, so poignantly represented in the anthropomorphized drawings of the "miasma" published in newspapers. See Thorsheim, *Inventing Pollution*.

3   Thorsheim, *Inventing Pollution*.

air had become visible and was understood to have the capacity to damage human health. But it was London's Great Smog that became a turning point.

On a cold, bright December morning in 1952, a very thick cloud of smog covered the whole city of London and stayed put for four days. This black, sticky presence disrupted and upended city life: production halted, crime escalated, deaths quadrupled. The smog made visible the lethality of smoke air pollution and its broad economic consequences. For geographer Mark Whitehead, this event marked a change in atmospheric governance. As the air became a social, political, and cultural concern that needed to be managed, its lethality—or its toxicity—and its socioeconomic effects had to be measured, registered, and, in many cases, prevented.[4] Whitehead details how after the chaos of the Great Smog the government organized the Beaver Committee to study the impact of smog on physical, social, and economic health. The committee corroborated what scientists had known for a long time: that smog had ongoing—even if not visible—effects on the health and well-being of the population and pushed for smoke abatement regulations. Their work led to the Clean Air Act of 1956, the first piece of air quality legislation passed by any state in the world to outlaw smoke production, to legislate appliances and technology, to explore alternative energy sources, and to transform cities through smoke-free zones. It was thought that improving the quality of air would improve social and economic issues—such as reducing crime and increasing productivity, turning the atmosphere into a tool *of* governance. The awareness of airs' slipperiness as both life-giving and death-dealing led to more

4   Through the 1850s, Whitehead explains, air quality was monitored by the government through human smoke surveillance programs—the first smoke inspectors, who reported on smoke through observation and smell, were deployed in Birmingham. But the eventual development of demography and meteorology, along with a new military interest in air pollution after World War I and the availability of aerial surveillance systems after World War II, permitted the geocoding of the atmosphere, and therefore systematic management. For a detailed account of atmosphere governmentality shifts in this period, see Mark Whitehead, *State, Science & the Skies*.

scientific, legal, technological, and social transformations. The Clean Air Act of 1956 catalyzed subsequent clean air acts, which aimed to control the burning of coal and promoted the switch to gas energy. As new technologies were developed and new routine dependencies on them formed, urban airs became transparent again. Smog became a harm of the past and air pollution a risk under control.

But the atmosphere continued to be the dumpsite for industrial and capitalist practices, where the eventual (invisible) pollution of the air was considered their unintended—and inevitable—effect. What remained "forgotten" until the 2000s was the understanding that what had killed thousands of people across industrializing cities was not a one-off event but an indicator of the cyclical damages produced by limitless capitalist accumulation, overproduction, and ongoing colonial relations.

POLLUTION OR TOXICITY?

Scientific and institutional contexts use "air pollution" or "air quality" to "describe the importance of clean air for human health, a livable society, and a sustainable environment. But, what is clean air, or rather, what makes air polluted?"[5]

Dirt, disease, bacteria, virus, contaminant, pollutant. Allergen (foreign substance causing allergic symptoms), toxin (nonliving biological substance that creates harm), toxicant (anthropogenic substance that creates harm), pathogen (microorganisms and parasites), poison (common word for a toxic substance). These and other terms describe the harming capacities of microscopic entities suspended in air. Some refer to an entity that harms (toxin or pathogen); others to a type of harm (poison or allergen). Despite all their differences, air is often referred to as polluted or toxic. In the dictionary, and even colloquially, the differences between toxicity

82

5   Rolf Lidskog and Göran Sundqvist, *Governing the Air: The Dynamics of Science, Policy, and Citizen Interaction*, 1. See also Andrew Barry, *Political Machines: Governing a Technological Society*.

and pollution are clear: Pollution is defined as "damage caused to water, air, etc. by harmful substances or waste," whereas toxicity is defined as "the level of poison contained in a drug, or the ability of a drug to poison the body."[6] Despite their differences, both terms are often used synonymously. Both imply a threat to (human) existence, but scientists cannot agree on what pollution or toxicity is in specific instances. Sometimes there are even discrepancies in what counts as evidence of the existence of a potentially harming substance—a particle of NO_2, for instance.[7] Some scientists struggle to define what causes harm. Is it a particular molecule? Is it the compound that this molecule creates with other substances? Or is it the object made of these substances that harms?[8] There are different meanings of toxicity and its relation to causality.[9] And what is considered "acceptable" harm or damage changes over time with social and political norms and their relationship to care, and depends on what and who is being impacted.

In Aeropolis, understanding this complex—and uncertain—distinction between pollution and toxicity matters. Why? Because

---

6   *Cambridge Dictionary.*

7   Medical anthropologist Emma Garnett accounts for these definitional conflicts among scientists working in different capacities on the same project about the human impacts of air pollution. A molecule of NO_2 meant one thing for scientists *modeling* air pollution and another for scientists *monitoring* air pollution. As a consequence, they could not integrate their data into a single NO_2 data set. See Emma Garnett, "Developing a Feeling for Error: Practices of Monitoring and Modelling Air Pollution Data," and the rest of her wonderful work.

8   Métis/Michif anticolonial designer, researcher, and geographer Max Liboiron explains how scientists cannot agree on what is toxic in plastic marine pollution: the chemicals that comprise plastic, the specific combination of molecules that configure each type of plastic, or the disintegrated microplastic particles themselves. See Max Liboiron, "Redefining Pollution and Action: The Matter of Plastics."

9   Feminist sociologist and philosopher Astrid Schrader, when looking at how different research groups tried to locate the causality of the massive death of fish off the coast of Maine in 1991, realized that: "The scientists' incoherent and sometimes interchangeable usage of the terms 'toxicity,' sometimes referring to 'toxi(co)genicity' (producing toxins), and other times to 'ichthyotoxicity' (fish killing) may have contributed a great deal to the controversy over Pfiesteria's 'toxicity.' Various articulations of toxicity imply different notions of causality... The more important distinction for my purposes is that the former [ichthyotoxicity] suggests toxicity as a harmful or deadly relationship, whereas the latter [toxi(co)genicity] associates toxicity with an inherent property." For more details on the difference between these three terms, see Astrid Schrader, "Responding to *Pfiesteria piscicida* (the Fish Killer): Phantomatic Ontologies, Indeterminacy, and Responsibility in Toxic Microbiology," 290.

each term is connected to a different set of cultural assumptions, infrastructures, and ways of understanding the body and its relation to the built and natural environment—and therefore to politics. Because toxicity and pollution each have a different focus, they point in different directions, and often lead to different—and at times divergent—forms of action and intervention. Because, in the everyday, toxicity and pollution are measured, regulated, or acted upon by different practices that involve different types of experts, communities, tools, or spaces to detect harm, define acceptable limits, or design solutions. To unpack these differences, I am reminded of historian and feminist STS scholar Michelle Murphy's concept of "regimes of perceptibility." Murphy writes:

> Produced by assemblages that are anchored in material culture, regimes of perceptibility establish *what phenomena become perceptible*, and thus what phenomena come into being for us, giving objects boundaries and imbuing them with qualities. Regimes of perceptibility populate our world *with some objects and not others*, and they allow certain actions to be performed on those objects.[10]

What would it mean to consider toxicity and pollution as two distinct (yet interrelated) regimes of perceptibility? What assemblages (everyday activities, technologies, groups of people, and laws) are they produced by? What becomes perceptible—and imperceptible—through these two regimes? Which forms of harm and accountability are implied, and how are their physical consequences managed and rendered knowable? Furthermore, what solutions are implicit and practiced in each? Breathless in Beijing, anthropologist Victoria Nguyen observed that daily practices make the air—and its pollution—more real, and therefore more prone to

84

10   Italics are mine. See Michelle Murphy, *Sick Building Syndrome and the Politics of Uncertainty: Environmental Politics, Technoscience, and Women Workers*, 24.

transformation and action.[11] So, I also ask: what are the everyday practices that render pollution and toxicity perceptible?

Now as I write this, the SARS-CoV-2 pandemic has spread throughout the world and, with it, air has become culturally present in a, possibly, unprecedented way. It could be said that we are witnessing these two regimes of perceptibility that sense differently the cause of the pandemic (molecular or environmental), where we place blame (on a virus or on the structuralconditions that have engendered the contagion among humans), and where or what is held accountable (local or national governments, international health institutions, labs, individuals). Although it is easy to see how toxicity and pollution are connected at different scales, the impacts of who and what is harmed, and the implications of "what to do" are divergent.

Inhaling and exhaling have become health risks with social and political consequences. When paying attention to inhaling we are more focused on the toxicity of the virus that might enter our bodies with the air we breathe, and consequently we are more focused on ourselves: our protection, antibodies, vaccines, isolation. When focusing on exhaling we pay attention to where we might be polluting the air (that others breathe) with our virus, and therefore pay attention to other bodies, physical distance, ventilation, and air circulation.

Although COVID-19 has made explicit that "we live and breathe in shared air space, we share a substrate that is a surround that is a medium, whereby our interiors are interior to each other,"[12] let's follow our breath to recognize the differences in focus, forms of harm, and accountability between the realms of perceptibility of toxicity and pollution. Let's follow our breath as a way to follow

85

11   Victoria Nguyen, "Breathless in Beijing: Aerial Attunements and China's New Respiratory Publics."
12   Mel Y. Chen and Timothy K. Choy, "Corresponding in Time," 797.

airs. With each breath, gases and particles are exchanged between our bodies and the airs we are immersed in and part of. Correlated yet divergent, breathing in and breathing out point toward different directions, as lenses or sensors that reveal different things.

Breathing in is a movement inward, where the body absorbs, processes, or lets go of each air molecule. In this process we can identify what air does to bodies—nurture or harm.

Breathing out is a movement outward, where we can trace the impact that our exhalations produce on any entity in front of us.

Both are forms of exchange, and yet the possible type of harm and the responsibilities between particles and the body are opposed. Let us follow breath to unpack the differences across toxicity and pollution practices and their environmental and political potential.

Breathe in.

Breathe out.

TOXICITY PRACTICES

Breathing in gets us close to the toxicity regime of perceptibility. Along with all the microscopic molecules from the world around us, breathing carries us inside the living body to flesh, fluids, organs, bacteria, bones. And yet, despite air being the stuff of life, the toxicity regime of perceptibility exposes us to a realm of harm and risk, not pleasure. The goal of what I refer to as *toxicity practices* is to identify the harm made by substances that enter the body through the mouth, nose, and/or skin. As in toxicology or detective stories, toxicity practices, mostly conducted between laboratories and policy makers, search for chemical interactions at a molecular level. The causality of harm in these cases always needs to be proven, either by finding traces of a toxic substance or by locating the deteriorating effects of a poison in specific organs: lungs, heart, nervous system, brain, bones... the list grows by the day.

86

But where is toxicity located? Rather than things being toxic, toxicity—and the harm it inflicts—depends on the dose, on duration, on exposure, on the specific constitution of the body. That is why we speak about the *level* of toxicity. The definition of this level, especially since chemical interactions are invisible, requires a quantitative framework that correlates the quantity of a substance and the intensity of its effects in and across similar bodies.[13] Thus, finding evidence of causality requires a lot of effort: laboratory tests, regulations, epidemiological and toxicological studies to test the thresholds, among others. In *Sick Building Syndrome and the Politics of Uncertainty*, Michelle Murphy accounts for all the emotional labor, technologies, social organizations, and scientific research that it took for women working in office buildings built in the 1950s and 60s to prove that their workplaces were making them sick. That is, what it took to make their health problems, symptoms, and reactions to the gases released by the plastics that composed most of the interior finishes "count" as evidence of toxicity.[14] One of the main challenges they faced was that the toxicological experiments conducted by scientists to prove causality

were only concerned with materializing physiological reactions to chemicals that were both regular—that is, replicable—and specific—that is, a signature physiological reaction for that chemical. Bodies, likewise, were investigated as objects that reacted specifically, predictably, and consistently to chemicals... [and] while toxicology was undoubtedly effective at rendering

13 The standardization of harm configures a generic (healthy) body as the reference, disregarding the complex interactions that take place across human and nonhuman molecules. The generic bodies defined by toxicological studies at times are not even human, as "laboratory based toxicological research depoliticizes and depersonalizes chemical exposure by using genetically standardized model organisms such as rats or zebra fish and by modelling single chemical exposures in controlled conditions rather than investigating the complexity and heterogeneity of lived human exposures." See Sara Wylie, Nicholas Shapiro, and Max Liboiron, "Making and Doing Politics through Grassroots Scientific Research on the Energy and Petrochemical Industries," 404.

14 Murphy, *Sick Building Syndrome*.

perceptible certain kinds of occupational disease, it simultaneously lent a narrow shape to what counted as a significant chemical exposure, creating a domain of imperceptibility where other reactions fell. Reactions to combinations of chemicals or to chronically low-level exposures, as well as rare or variable reactions all fell outside the practices of toxicology and industrial hygiene. The dominant assemblage in toxicology not only rendered perceptible the specific bodily effects of chemicals, it also set up criteria by which one could exclude a bodily condition from the category of occupational disease.[15]

These exclusions—all that is excluded from the "regular" and "specific" demands of toxicology—mean that many symptoms, social groups, and practices are left out of regulations, rights, and accountability. Therefore, today, communities and NGOs working to address environmental injustice—the recognition that environmental harm disproportionally affects disenfranchised communities—are demanding the legality or acceptance of alternative forms of evidence, such as citizen science-produced data, public epidemiology, or people's experiences.

In sum, for toxicity practices, understanding "how much"—substance or time—and causality are the main goals. In a fragile and always complicated balance between economy and health, safety limits are established to guarantee "safe" cohabitation with possibly harmful substances.[16] But in Aeropolis, causality is even more

15 Murphy, *Sick Building Syndrome*, 96.
16 In Aeropolis, safety limits are established by Air Quality Indexes (AQI) that, as well as communicating the level of toxicity of the air, make recommendations for the type of activities that should be done in the open air. Although considered a device to regulate "air pollution," AQIs only regulate the limit concentrations of gases or particles in relation to human health, so they only regulate the toxicity of the air. Max Liboiron calls this a "threshold theory of pollution," but I am considering here the threshold theory as part of the toxic world, as it is committed to finding causality (even if it is by epidemiology than toxicology) and therefore the "healthy human levels." We can say that AQIs measure the toxicity of the air, not its pollution, as they only measure the five components in relation to human health. This form of biomonitoring has the potential to induce social and political change, as governments can be held accountable for air quality. But it also has the potential to further privatize risk, where

difficult to prove. Whether or not urban airs support life depends on the specific relationship between concentrations of certain gases or particles, the built environment, and the bodies with which they interact. These relations are ever changing, and "ecosystems differ in their sensitivity to pollutant uptake, and societies differ in how they are affected and have different capacities for resilience."[17] The invisibility of air is, in the literal sense, up against the inscrutability of causal relations in massively complex statistical and political machinations. The only molecules that are monitored and regulated are those found to harm humans consistently across cities—CO, PM, NO_2, O_3, in the case of urban air. This framework therefore misses other toxicities and does not take into account their chain of consequences for animals and plants, and leaves other gases or particles that might be less commonly found but highly toxic unexamined— like hydrogen chloride, asbestos, mercury, and all the unlisted chemicals leaked or spilled by factories into bodies of water.

Even in moments of industrial disaster, which make the danger of certain chemicals, components, or production processes known, many chemicals are considered proprietary information—trade secrets that do not need disclosure.[18] This means that when studies cannot be conducted, toxicity cannot be proven; as a consequence,

89

only the privileged can make choices on when or how to be outdoors. See Michelle Murphy,"Chemical Regimes of Living"; Liboiron, *Pollution Is Colonialism*, 56.

17 Lidskog and Sundqvist, *Governing the Air*, 5.

18 Take, for instance, the disaster in Bhopal in 1984, which caused 2,000 deaths and affected more than a million people. Methylisocyanate (MIC), a synthetic component of pesticide, leaked from a Union Carbide Corporation (UCC) pesticide plant in Bhopal, India. "The toxicological properties of MIC were also known before the Bhopal accident, although in less detail than the compound's physical and chemical characteristics. The UCC manual warned that MIC was irritating to the eyes and chest and that overexposure could kill people. Understandably, the UCC manual focused mainly on the short-term hazards of contact with MIC. The chemical's long-range health effects were largely uninvestigated before the Bhopal tragedy. Independent scientists were deterred from experimenting with the compound because its chemical, physical, and biological properties made it difficult to work with. As a result, the best available evidence on MIC's toxicity was that produced by UCC's own staff toxicologists. The company, however, treated this information as a trade secret. Even after the disaster it was shared only with federal agencies such as the National Toxicology Program and the Environmental Protection Agency (EPA)." See Sheila Jasanoff, "The Bhopal Disaster and the Right to Know," 1115.

toxicity does not exist in legal terms. In other words: because the cause of the damage is difficult to establish or has not been established yet (intentionally or not), there is no accountability. In Murphy's words, again: "The absence of specificity could be used to claim nonexistence."[19] This nonexistence can be gendered, as in the case of women workers in office buildings, but it can also be racialized, marginalized, naturalized... This is a strategy very commonly used by oil and gas companies and other big polluters, state officials, doctors, and insurance companies involved in a labor of confusion that sustains extractive capitalism.[20]

Toxicity Practices beyond Levels

Scholars have proposed conceptual openings to this narrow human-centric framing of techno-scientific toxicity practices. Paying attention to toxicity's relationality, feminist sociologist and philosopher Astrid Schrader has suggested that toxicity is an emergent condition that takes place through the interaction between bodies under specific environmental conditions—as opposed to a "bad substance" held in some bodies.[21] Queer interdisciplinary scholar Mel Y. Chen extends the relationality of toxicity even further, as a specific form of affect and being affected by nonhumans, as "an 'assemblage' of biology, affect, nationality, race, and chemistry," where amounts are inconsequential and affectivity is what matters.[22] For Chen, "unlike viruses, toxins are not so very containable or quarantinable; they are better thought of as conditions with effects, bringing their own affects and animacies to bear on lives *and* nonlives."[23] Thus toxic encounters depend on the

---

19   Note that "specificity" here is a technical term, "a signature physiological reaction for that chemical." Murphy, *Sick Building Syndrome*, 92.
20   For an interesting ethnography of the ways in which different actors consciously work to confuse residents and other parties, see Javier Auyero and Debora Swistun, "The Social Production of Toxic Uncertainty."
21   Schrader, "Responding to *Pfiesteria piscicida* (the Fish Killer)."
22   Mel Y. Chen, *Animacies: Biopolitics, Racial Mattering, and Queer Affect*, 206.
23   Chen, *Animacies*, 196, 209, 211.

specificity of the substance, the materiality and histories of bodies, and their accumulated experiences. Exploring how they cohabitate with high levels of mercury in their bodies, Chen continues:

> A few pedestrians cross my path, and before they near, I quickly assess whether they are likely (or might be the "kind of people") to wear perfumes or colognes or to be wearing sunscreen. I scan their heads for smoke puffs or pursed lips pre-release; I scan their hands for a long white object, even a stub. In an instant, quicker than I thought anything could reach my organs, my liver refuses to process these inhalations and screams hate, a hate whose intensity each time shocks me.[24]

Both Schrader and Chen extend toxicity practices across levels and individual bodies in space and time. Therefore, toxicity is necessarily situated in considerations of how harm is socially, culturally, and racially inscribed, and in the effect and the lived-ness of exposure.[25] How, for whom, when, under which circumstances, and where do toxic interactions occur? And where are power and inequality present in those interactions?

Historian of science Gabrielle Hecht follows these uneven relations of global power to other sites and territories, exposing, in the context of radiation waste projects in France and South Africa, how toxicity practices are uneven in geographical and historical substance-body relations, and how this unevenness reinforces inequality and poverty. For instance, Hecht details how toxicity is defined and regulated differently (by design) in the Global North and the Global South, where materials and practices considered toxic (and therefore banned) in the Global North are permitted and even imposed onto the Global South, sustaining an ongoing toxic

24 For Chen, this accounting for toxicity and intoxication alongside sense memory—what they call the "toxic sensorium"—is a method to grasp a queer "worlding" of and with chemicals. See Chen, *Animacies*, 198.
25 Linda Nash, *Inescapable Ecologies: A History of Environment, Disease, and Knowledge.*

colonialism.[26] Anthropologist Vanessa Agard-Jones offers an eye-opening account of the multiscalar—spatial and temporal—condition of environmental toxicity, and of the intimacies and embodiments attendant to producing "alternative evidences" of toxicity. It is with and through the experiences of queer bodies that certain histories become visible. Inquiring with her queer friend Marc about the presence of organochlorine pesticide, used on banana plantations, in Martinique and Guadeloupe's air—and consequently in soils, bodies, waters, and in every millimeter of the islands—Agard-Jones sharply shows us what it might mean to recalibrate the very frame we use to locate forms of injury:

> any analysis of Marc's health (as well as that of his fellow Martinican residents) would be incomplete without an analysis of how their bodies are produced through and via engagements with the local, regional, and global forms of power that have made the island's chlordécone contamination possible. What chlordécone has done and continues to do is to call attention to the intimate ways Martinican bodies are connected to commodity chains, to uneven relations of colonial/postcolonial power, and thus to world systems. Taking a chlordécone molecule as a unit of analysis recalibrates the scale of ethnographic practice, bringing us not only to the body, but also to the chemicals circulating within and beyond it.[27]

These accounts rearticulate toxicity beyond levels, where toxic interactions are situated and differential in relation to geopolitical structures and economic interests enacted through extraction and exploitation.

26 Gabrielle Hecht, *Being Nuclear: Africans and the Global Uranium Trade.*
27 Vanessa Agard-Jones, "Bodies in the System," 191.

Toxicity Practices' Interventions

My interest in these openings does not dismiss the strong damaging capacity of certain substances or the need to prove the existence of toxic interactions. Toxicity practices—the damage-based research that searches for quantification, causality, and at times responsibility in toxic interactions—are often fundamental for fence-line communities as a way to prevent further molecular injuries and toxic exposure and to obtain reparation, medical services or compensation for harm.[28] However, the main repertoire of material and spatial interventions to prevent or repair toxic interactions, namely containment (i.e., isolation, quarantine, physical protection), counteraction (i.e., adding a substance that kills or neutralizes the "toxic" one), and eradication are not as simple as they are often presented. They might work temporarily for some, but they work against the liveliness and dynamism of matter and bodies. Containment, counteraction, and eradication often have their own negative effects—physical, psychological, economic—that often become even more damaging and enduring than toxic interactions.

Looking at the specific forms of relationality in toxic encounters sheds light on other forms of intervention. For instance, in order to move away from the re-victimization of some communities and "inspired by practices that render life possible in criminalized and chemically assaulted worlds," anthropologist Kristina Lyons instead pays attention to what she calls "the tenacity of life."[29] While Lyons writes this in the context of Putumayo in the Colombian Amazon—

28 The reliance on quantitative evidence as the path to justice has proven to be less straightforward than expected, because it requires institutions (with the capacity and political will) to act. Also, Murphy cautions against the idealization of toxicity practices, as they might have undesired negative effects: "despite often antiracist intentions, this damage-based research has pernicious effects, placing the focus on chemical violence by virtue of rendering lives and landscapes as pathological. Such work tends to resuscitate racist, misogynist, and homophobic portraits of poor, Black, Indigenous, female, and queer lives and communities as damaged and doomed, as inhabiting irreparable states that are not just unwanted but less than fully human." Michelle Murphy, "Alterlife and Decolonial Chemical Relations," 496.

29 Lyons, *Vital Decomposition: Soil Practitioners and Life Politics*, 3; Kristina Lyons, "Chemical Warfare in Colombia, Evidentiary Ecologies and Senti-Actuando Practices of Justice."

an area devastated by war and ecocide for decades—she provides a different (and more positive) entry point to worlds embedded within toxic relations. Lyons proposes a methodology that shifts away from searching for harm to locating life embedded not only in place but in history and accumulated experiences.[30] These life-affirming methods show alternative paths for environmental harm reduction by moving away from—unsuccessful—solutionist approaches oriented toward removing the toxic and repairing "the" past. Observing what emerges, what lives and creates life, makes visible practices that are already there—albeit disregarded.

Throughout the pandemic, toxicity practices have been deployed by most governments to protect humans from the "incoming" virus. The enormous international machinery of biomedical research has been put into high gear to understand the effects of the virus on human health, and its concentrations, distances, and contagion routes. The interventions that tend to constitute toxicity practices have been put to the test: containment of airborne particles and humans through protection (masks), isolation (at the scale of the body, house, and the city), lockdown (travel restrictions, curfews), and boundaries (walls, borders). These measures have been turned on and off, opened and closed, shuttered and unshuttered for public health, diplomatic, and economic reasons. The built environment has become the context and an instrument to manage and organize life, from domestic quarantines to "safe" capsules, bunkers, sealed buildings, and autonomous systems—available only to a few.[31] That the built environment does this work, that it

---

30 This method resonates with anthropologist Anna Tsing's renowned work on mushrooms as traces of vitality within the ruins of capitalism. See Anna Lowenhaupt Tsing, *The Mushroom at the End of the World: On the Possibility of Life in Capitalist Ruins*.

31 See Lydia Kallipoliti, *The Architecture of Closed Worlds* for fascinating research on historical projects that attempted to create sealed and artificial interior environments.

encloses or closes off certain communities and ways of living, was experienced for the first time by many in the context of the pandemic. And yet, we cannot forget that for many others this containment is not crisis-specific but an ongoing part of daily life.

We are also experiencing, or witnessing in real time, what we already knew: that toxicity practices' interventions do not work because the virus mutates, because total isolation is impossible, because the most vulnerable groups cannot isolate (the unhoused, frontline and health workers, and others) and because for many, isolation can be far more dangerous (they may be experiencing hunger, domestic violence, and abuse).[32] The rapid spread of the virus has made visible the abandonment of public health infrastructures—and the welfare state, where it existed—holding government accountable for decades long austerity measures, international health organizations for their lack of power, funding, and coordination, and the shameful global inequality in terms of medical access, job security, and general social and economic precarity, among others. So, what has created more harm, the virus or inequality?

Breathing in takes us to the microscopic world of situated chemical interactions. But, expanding the idea of toxicity, it also takes us to the accumulated social, spatial, personal, and shared histories of suffering.

Breathing out orients us back outside the body.

95

32 Toxicity practices' interventions might reduce the level of contagion among certain communities and therefore human deaths, but COVID-19 is still contagious.

POLLUTION PRACTICES

With each exhale our attention moves away from the human body, from our nose and mouth outward. If we go where the air goes, we might encounter what it encounters, touches, and impacts. But how far does air go through each exhalation? What is the reach of its effects?

What I call *pollution practices*—the ones that permit us to know, sense, and act on polluted landscapes, not the ones that create pollution—are spatial and temporal, and affect bodies, spaces, and territories. Pollution practices, which are mostly enacted through fieldwork and laboratories, are attuned to the effects of "harmful" substances or waste (or any other material that, when displaced, might be detrimental) on air, water, and soil (or mountain, beach, and city). Native algae can pollute rivers. Soil nutrients can pollute lagoons. Cow manure can pollute soil.

Breathing out makes legible that there are more entities besides microscopic elements that can create damage, more forms of harm, more entities damaged, and, most importantly, that the damage produced is *through* the damage to an environment.[33] Therefore, pollution practices are driven by the "who," "where," and "how" more than by the need to prove causality through "how much" substance or time, at the core of toxicity practices.

In fact, in anthropologist Mary Douglas's canonical work on pollution, *Purity and Danger: An Analysis of Concepts of Pollution and Taboo*, she claims that "dirt is essentially disorder. There is no such thing as absolute dirt: it exists in the eye of the beholder."[34] Her widely cited definition of dirt as matter out of place suggests that pollution does not require an evidentiary regime but a cultural

---

33 Liboiron provides a great example: fish die because they become trapped in fishing nets, not because they ingest a harmful substance. For more on marine pollution, see Liboiron, "Redefining Pollution and Action."

34 Mary Douglas, *Purity and Danger: An Analysis of Concepts of Pollution and Taboo*, 2.

framework with a system of classification to contend with this disorder. One that relies on ideas of purity and the rejection of unwanted elements. One that cannot always be quantifiable. For Douglas, pollution breaks the conceptual system that sustains what is clean or pure and what is not. Her approach, criticized for being only cultural,[35] is still relevant here. In part because the difference between physical and cultural forms of pollution is blurry,[36] in part because systems of classification are culturally bound.[37] And because culture defines what and how we intervene.

In Aeropolis—the city of airs—the very idea of air purity is a paradox: one percent of the composition of air is, by definition, "matter out of place," which includes—among other elements— almost any material that makes up our built environment and is released by our daily activities: dust, sand, pollen, heavy metals, drugs, human hair, feces, spores, and bacteria. So, when is all this matter "out of place" considered pollution? Also, the incessant movement and transformation of airs might turn air into two something seen as "unwanted" elsewhere. For instance, the Sahara's dust is often presented in the European Union (EU) media as air pollution that interrupts everyday lives: transportation, leisure, and forms of production, a nuisance that seems to become more disruptive because of its origin. As the *BBC* put it a few years ago in an article titled "Saharan Dust: Why Your Car Is Covered in Red Dirt": "many drivers are asking why their cars are covered in red-colored dirt— and the answer lies in Africa."[38] The EU turns African dust into dirt. But if we follow the Sahara's dust particles thousands of kilometers

97

35 Liboiron, "Redefining Pollution and Action."
36 As with the dichotomy between "physical" and "cultural," "scientific" and "cultural" and "quantitative" and "qualitative" are always flawed and limited.
37 See, for instance, anthropologist Kelly D. Alley's account of the divergent approaches to the polluted waters of the Ganges River: Hindu communities surrounding the Ganges have different understandings of how the religious purity of the river interweaves with the physical pollution of the water. Kelly D. Alley, "On the Banks of the Ganga."
38 *BBC News*, "Saharan Dust: Why Your Car Is Covered in Dirt," https://www.bbc.co.uk/news/uk-scotland-48037362.

over the Atlantic Ocean, we can see how they condense water and produce rain, sedimenting the phosphorus that traveled attached to them and providing essential nutrients to depleted soils—making possible the Amazonian rain forest, livelihoods in the Caribbean, and agriculture in the southeast of the United States. So "the residue of the desert creates the rain to keep the rain forest."[39] Letting ourselves go with the wind reveals how even the tiniest particle has far-reaching and interdependent ecological consequences.

Pollution Practices beyond Substances

Max Liboiron's work *Pollution Is Colonialism* made me travel much farther than I could have imagined.[40] Through historical references, the book unpacks how pollution has always been used to name a deviation. Displaced matter. The unwanted. The invader. The other. The foreign entity that reveals the boundary between what existed and what is "new." What belongs and what does not. But, in practice, what counts as "otherness" depends on how the relationships between the body, nature, and the built and natural environment are conceptualized, and how the boundaries or the skins between them are constituted.[41] The focus on the "otherness" of pollution has been shared historically with other marginalized humans— queer, poor, displaced, women, Black, Indigenous, and others— leading very often to racist and eugenic projects that have transferred attributes—like "invasive" or "undesirable"—across bodies, spaces, and environments and affected their lives and livelihoods.[42] Furthermore, "otherness" travels across bodies. Sociologist Javier Auyero and social anthropologist Debora Swistun explain how

39 William Bryant Logan, *Air: The Restless Shaper of the World*, 94.

40 This book is mind-blowing, funny, and a good companion to have nearby. It is full of jewels like "Land is a verb" and the ones that follow. My gratitude to Max for being a reference on how to do and be in academia, for their generosity and commitment. Max Liboiron, *Pollution Is Colonialism*.

41 See the wonderful book by Linda Nash, *Inescapable Ecologies: A History of Environment, Disease, and Knowledge*.

42 Nerea Calvillo, "Toxic Nature: Toward a Queer Theory of Pollution."

ignorance about what is actually polluting means that social bias misnames the polluting entity. It is poverty, not the environment, that pollutes, they argue.[43]

And yet, Liboiron reframes the question of what pollutes beyond particular substances and their interactions to consider the structural violence produced by the systems where polluting is part and parcel of their functioning. Reframing proposals where pollution has been articulated as the inevitable, and necessary, consequence of capitalism and colonialism,[44] Liboiron argues that,

> pollution is not a manifestation or side effect of colonialism but is rather an enactment of ongoing colonial relations to Land. That is, pollution is best understood as the violence of colonial land relations rather than environmental damage, which is a symptom of violence.[45]

For Liboiron, pollution is also property, it produces whiteness, its goal is structural unevenness.[46] And the "solutions" and forms of studying pollution are colonial too:

> In the case of pollution, a focus on capitalism misses relations that make Land available for pollution in the first place. It can miss the necessary place of stolen Land in colonizer's and settler's ability to create sinks for pollution as well as stolen Land's place in alternative economies (via a communal commons) and environmental conservation (via methylmercury-producing hydroelectric dams). Pollution, scientific ways of producing pollution, and actions to mitigate pollution are not examples of, symptoms or metaphors for, or unintentional by-products of colonialism, but rather are essential parts of the interlocking

43 Auyero and Swistun, "The Social Production of Toxic Uncertainty."
44 See Jason W. Moore, *Capitalism in the Web of Life: Ecology and the Accumulation of Capital.*
45 Liboiron, *Pollution Is Colonialism*, 6.
46 Liboiron, *Pollution Is Colonialism.*

logics (brain), mechanisms (hands and teeth), and structures (heart and bones) of colonialism that allow colonialism to produce and reproduce its effects in Canada, the United States and beyond.[47]

Thus the damage in the pollution realm is environmental. It is often systemic. It encompasses chemical, physical, and affective harm, as well as emotional, aesthetic, and economic harm.[48] All living entities—from animals to microorganisms—are eventually damaged by colonialism and neoliberalism, sometimes by direct contact with a pollutant, sometimes through more far-flung acts of limitation, experiencing diminished livelihoods, reduced food sources, and circumscribed mobility.

Pollution Practices' Interventions

In pollution practices, cleaning is the core intervention, which has been practiced from the scale of the home to the scale of cities and beyond. For instance, cleaning was at the core of the hygienist project of modernity, which since the early twentieth century has triggered many of the urban transformations that we live within and uphold today.[49]

Cleaning implies that pollution can be undone to reach a previous (read: clean, pure) state by removing the unwanted "other"—that is, by depolluting.[50] But actually, cleaning is moving dirt, waste, or unwanted substances from one place to another, carrying with it

47 Liboiron, *Pollution Is Colonialism*, 15.
48 As the reader may have noticed, many of these experiences of suffering were also part of toxicity practices. Indeed, as I mentioned before, pollution and toxicity practices overlap and have many things in common. And yet, what distinguishes them is their focus. In pollution practices the chemical interactions among elements are important, and so are their threshold levels. And yet, other questions are often more pressing, such as where the pollution comes from and where its economic harm is experienced. While toxicity thresholds aim to prove evidence of harm, pollution thresholds aim to prove how much harm is acceptable.
49 Fernando Dominguez Rubio and Uriel Fogué, "Technifying Public Space and Publicizing Infrastructures"; Uriel Fogué, "Ecología Política y Economía de la Visibilidad de los Dispositivos Tecnológicos de Escala Urbana Durante el Siglo XX: Abriendo la Caja Negra."

environmental and social effects. In many ways this colonial impulse to clean, this corrective to move "matter out of place," is to put matter in places that are considered already dirty or expendable— and this is obviously racially, socially, and economically determined. It also externalizes waste and the polluting—like the extraction of natural resources or the labor of waste management—structural to global racial capitalism.[51] Other forms of cleaning are camouflage strategies. As pollution can often be seen, smelled, or touched, polluted sites are often rendered invisible, through difficult access, being literally hidden (think of the trees planted around oil and gas extraction infrastructures) or because the communities that inhabit toxic sites are considered disposable.[52] This project of purity and hygiene, activated through medicine and technology, no matter its intention (like a "solution" to urban density), has fueled colonial, genocidal, and ecological destructive projects.[53]

Cleaning is an old strategy often materialized through buildings in the form of ventilation, air "purification," air extraction, and so on. However, the notion of cleaning is dependent on a spatial and geographic distinction between inside air (what needs to be protected, kept clean) and outside air (a no-man's-land that can be polluted). This distinction, I argue, is one of the causes of the current climate crisis and ecocide. Thus this book—*Aeropolis*—explores the airs that inhabit streets and open spaces in urban environments, what I will call from now on "open airs."[54] Opposed to the "architectures of air" built through air conditioning and accessible only for the well-off,[55]

50 Carmella Gray-Cosgrove, Max Liboiron, and Josh Lepawsky, "The Challenges of Temporality to Depollution & Remediation."
51 See, among others, Moore, *Capitalism in the Web of Life*; Kate O'Neill, *Waste*.
52 Thom Davies, "Slow Violence and Toxic Geographies: 'Out of Sight' to Whom?"
53 Alexis Shotwell, *Against Purity: Living Ethically in Compromised Times*.
54 Open airs attend to air conditions and geographies that are made peripheral, exterior, edged out of spaces of support, access, civilian life, and so on, like prisons and poor housing conditions. So with open airs we are also working through a way of expanding and reframing the "outdoor" to spaces of confinement or exclusion without reproducing the siloing of these sites.
55 Jerry Zee, "Breathing in the City: Beijing and the Architecture of Air."

open airs are conditional and inevitably shared. They are a political condition that connects us as breathers through "respiratory distress and systemic breathing disorders, as well as agitations for some-things-else."[56] It is also the airs where environmental injustice is most extreme, and therefore the ones that are most urgent to tackle.

Since the onset of COVID-19, botanists, environmentalists, and economists have argued (from what I have called a pollution practices perspective) that the cause of so much suffering and death is not the virus "out of place" but the rampant urbanization, the destruction of the environment, and the decline in biodiversity. Neoliberal accumulation has enabled this pathogen spillover. Blame cannot be placed on the virus, they argue, for the virus is just an indicator of structural forms of violence— poverty, forced migration, and political control—and the consequences of agroforestry, industrial farming, and other capitalist practices of resource exploitation.[57]

And yet, ventilation has become the strategy to "stay safe" from the virus indoors. Stronger filters, faster air renovation conditioning systems, open windows. The pandemic has flipped the entrenched equivalent between safety and indoors. Poorly ventilated spaces have become more lethal, as seen in the high number of deaths attributed to COVID-19 in prisons. Outdoors, or better, open airs, have become the new "safe" space.[58]

56   Timothy K. Choy, "A Commentary: Breathing Together Now," 586.
57   Chuang Collective, "Social Contagion: Microbiological Class War in China," https://chuangcn.org/2020/02/social-contagion.
58   Indoor air has been thought to be unsafe before. For instance: in New York City during the 1918 influenza pandemic, radiators were run very hot to keep apartments warm in the winter so folks could keep their windows open. However, there have not been events of that scale until the COVID-19 pandemic, so it was felt as something of the past.

TOXICPOLLUTION: THE PERSISTENT WORLD OF INDUSTRIAL CHEMICALS

At times, the rhythms of breathing in and breathing out are disrupted. Similarly, industrial chemicals complicate the distinction between the toxicity and pollution realms of perceptibility.

In the form of substances, compounds, and gases, industrial chemicals resist organic decomposition, accumulate over time, and eventually become toxic for all species. These persistent chemicals induce slow violence to humans and other beings, make traceability and causality even more difficult or impossible to detect, and bring together instantaneous and geological time scales. This slow violence is not simply an accumulation of harm over time. It is also the violence of being considered disposable and without agency or hope. As anthropologist Thom Davies argues, citing philosopher and political scientist Achille Mbembe,

> Mbembe introduced necropower to encompass the "subjugation of life to the power of death." This is more than the Foucauldian idea of the right to kill but rather the right to expose people to the possibility of death; in other words, not to make someone die but to let them. This subtle distinction between "make die" and "let die" violence goes some way to explain the experience of slow violence at the hands of an unlocatable, dispersed, and contested polluter. No one is being actively killed through pollution as a means of biopolitical control. Rather, communities who have been "designated expendable" are allowed to suffer the attritional violence of environmental pollution, often through the "violent inaction" of regulating authorities.[59]

As industrial chemical pollution *is* toxic, from now on I will refer to it as *toxicpollution*. Air is one of toxicpollution's main vehicles

---

59 Thom Davies, "Toxic Space and Time: Slow Violence, Necropolitics, and Petrochemical Pollution," 1540.

and environments. Air contains and carries with the wind all sorts of industrial residues to the most remote corners of the globe. Microplastics have been found deposited on Mount Everest, in the Arctic, in the deep seas. CO_2 released by fossil fuel combustion and deforestation has increased the concentrations of CO_2 in the atmosphere, raising the temperature of the planet. Incoming substances dilute or spread in the air, becoming part of it. They recombine according to radiation and humidity. Synthetic chemicals might change or mutate, but they never disappear.[60] The small amounts of industrial chemicals ingested through breathing make causality difficult to prove. On top of this, air cannot be contained, hence human isolation or moving far away from the source of pollution are temporary solutions, fundamental for the livelihood of fenceline communities but not for altering the basic composition of the air. The carrying capacity of the winds and the activity of the earth's crust ensure that, no matter how far away or how deep in the ground certain chemicals are displaced or captured, they end up affecting the whole planet: ashes released by the eruption of a volcano in Iceland in 2013 were found in Australia, and the radiation storms emitted in the Fukushima nuclear plant disaster in 2011 circled the globe twice. Industrial chemicals in the form of plastics, gases, and particles are characterized by mobility, extreme latency, collaboration, additive effects, and ubiquity—qualities that make any form of control challenging. Besides, even if the chemical composition between, let's say, two particles of dust is similar, matter is not universal. Each particle of dust has its own signature, which connects it to social and environmental histories that also need to be accounted for, reckoned with, situated in time and in place.[61]

Moving away from matter but acknowledging its material effects, Michelle Murphy proposes studying the "chemical infrastructure" that supports and perpetuates chemical pollution, searching

60   Gray-Cosgrove, Liboiron, and Lepawsky, "The Challenges of Temporality to Depollution & Remediation."
61   Agard-Jones, "What the Sands Remember."

for the places and practices distributed in space and time that relate to and are affected by toxicpollution.[62] Murphy attends to chemical exposures, a practice that is "as much about figuring life and responsibilities beyond the individualized body as it is about acknowledging extensive chemical relations."[63] Exposing chemical infrastructures also shows that toxicpollution reproduces power and injustice due to its permanent relation with settler colonialism, white supremacy, and gender inequality, among other forms of oppression. In the same spirit, Liboiron insists that we

> move beyond the usual articulation of plastics and their chemicals as autonomous, wayward particles that cause harm to instead talk about scales of colonial violence. This is not an academic exercise. It is the groundwork we need to do anticolonial science, research, and activism in ways that decrease the reproduction of colonial land relations by positing other types of relations with plastics.[64]

Because, as they continue, "both pollution and its industrial chemicals are best understood not as wayward molecules, but rather as regimes of living, ways of living with and within colonial political economies."[65]

I am interested in the notion of "harm ecologies" to account for the dynamic, multilayered, interrelated, cross-temporal, cross-spatial, and intersectional human and nonhuman forms of harm created by toxicpollution and persistent chemicals, which are active across "chemical ecologies" of molecules, compounds, objects, lands, infrastructures, oceans, bodies, airs, waters, politics, cultures, and affects involved in ways of living within colonial political economies. This concept is useful to visualize the impossibility

62 Michelle Murphy, "Chemical Infrastructures of the St. Clair River."
63 Murphy, "Alterlife and Decolonial Chemical Relations," 497.
64 Liboiron, *Pollution Is Colonialism*, 83.
65 Liboiron, *Pollution Is Colonialism*, 82.

of cleaning as there is no way back to a pure state (it never existed before) because chemical ecologies are entangled. Therefore, if a harming substance is removed, other forms of harm persist or are activated, like the black lungs of miners in the Ostrava region in northeast Czech Republic[66] or the toxic chlordecone used in pesticides now found in the soil and groundwater in Martinique and Guadeloupe.[67] In addition, the lack of linearity in chemical ecologies distributes causality and responsibility widely, making interventions even more difficult.

Toxicpollution requires a new form of politics aware of the materiality of chemical pollution, a politics of slow and intimate activism, whose "achievements" might be difficult (or impossible) to measure, but which has the power to cope and test other futures.[68] Living in a toxicpolluted world also requires learning to inhabit polluted environments. This does not mean accepting the status quo. Rather, as anthropologist Kim Fortun remarks, it means rejecting ideas of purity, rejecting the dichotomy between good and bad.[69] Because reality is more complex; because those dichotomies do not provide the specificity we all need to intervene; and because good and bad are easily co-opted by politicians and large corporations who promote their "good" contributions to humans and the environment as they hide their damaging effects. This line of reasoning does not imply that toxic chemicals need to be produced or that they are not harmful. On the contrary. It aims to widen the spectrum of what counts as harm, including the power relations embedded in notions of purity, cleanliness, and pollution.

What remains an open question is how to intervene in the toxicpolluted world. What would it mean to forbid waste externalization—to the atmosphere, poor neighborhoods, natural

66 Magdalena Górska, "Breathing Matters: Feminist Intersectional Politics of Vulnerability."
67 Malcom Ferdinand, "De l'usage du chlordécone en Martinique et en Guadeloupe: L'égalité en question."
68 Max Liboiron, Manuel Tironi, and Nerea Calvillo, "Toxic Politics: Acting in a Permanently Polluted World"; Manuel Tironi, "Hypo-Interventions: Intimate Activism in Toxic Environments."
69 Kim Fortun, "From Latour to Late Industrialism."

environments, overseas territories, other countries—and make every country, city, and neighborhood cohabit with the waste they produce? Would it eradicate the production of industrial chemicals? Would it require structural changes like degrowth or an alternative to neoliberal racial capitalism? How can these interventions have social justice as their primary goal, understanding the complexity of achieving it?[70]

Designing in Toxicpolluted Aeropolis

Material "otherness" produces different modes of harm. What is at stake is not *if* a material "pollutes" or is "toxic" but rather *how* each term carries with it a model of what society is and what it can be. Each designation constructs different worlds. Prioritizes different things. Therefore, embracing one or another is always a political (institutional or not) decision that immediately directs *how* to intervene in and design within a toxicpolluted world.

Throughout the pandemic anthrologists, urban planners, architects, and many others have been asked to speculate on how cities could be different; how they should be redesigned to prevent or protect from future pandemics. The proposals aligned with toxicity practices is sprawl; they distance one family unit from another. Isolation, walls, enclaves, low-density urbanization, growth. These are the conceptual and physical tools and spatial models of toxicity practices. And yet, these "solutions" seem to exacerbate the harmful conditions that gave rise to the pandemic in the first place—like deforestation and its consequent loss of biodiversity. The proposals aligned with pollution practices reconsider the possibilities of the hyper-dense city; they minimize land occupation.

---

70 For a discussion on the challenges of environmental justice, see Kim Fortun, "Afterword: Working 'Faultlines.'"

The tension between these two models is difficult.
Yet it is inevitable that the very terms of the city—
density, community, hybridity, public spaces—will be
reconsidered and negotiated in urban futures.[71]

New urban models are needed in a toxicpolluted world. Urban models that think about the fabric of a city, social justice, and the environment all at once. Urban models that juggle the management scales of multispecies toxic interactions—architectures of dense isolations? Hyper-dense scattered neighborhoods? Permanent social distancing? Urban models that negotiate the complicated tension between "protecting" human bodies and "protecting" the environment, keeping always present the reality that "protection" can only be for some—humans, environments—and *require* the destruction of others, as settler colonialism and conservationist projects have shown.[72] Urban models that account for harm ecologies; that are framed through the pollution lens... and all its inherent contradictions and paradoxes; that radically stop destroying ecosystems; that cohabit with future viruses; that understand that barriers, envelopes, or walls can only be porous; that insist that "otherness" is always material, social, cultural, and political; that consider, engage with, and take care of Aeropolis.

One of my favorite COVID-19 memes argued that virtual/
online meetings are like séance sessions, as often the only
spoken words are: Can you hear me? Are you there?

In the first year of the pandemic, whenever I entered
a room, I found myself asking the microscopic virus
possibly floating in the air the same questions: Can you
hear me? Are you there?

71   Richard Sennett, "Cities in the Pandemic."
72   As political ecologist and environmental humanities scholar Malcom Ferdinand argues, this destruction is *the* condition for capitalism, colonialism and imperialism to function. Malcom Ferdinand, *Decolonial Ecology*.

I maybe once asked these questions out of fear—out of feeling like I needed to know and register whatever possible infection was in the air—but we've had to learn to live without actually seeing the virus. Public health mandates required other untrained sensoria. At first, it was touch; and the world around a collection of threatening surfaces—that could be cleaned. Then, it was breath; and the world around an invisible threatening cloud—that could enter my lungs just by my privilege of being allowed to breathe. These questions now seem like a way to summon and proceed from the uncertainty of not knowing.

Breathe in.

Can you hear me?

Breathe out.

Are you there?

2.3

2.4

2.6

2.5

2.7

2.8

WORKS CITED

Agard-Jones, Vanessa. "Bodies in the System." *Small Axe: A Caribbean Journal of Criticism* 17, no. 3 (November 1, 2013): 182–192.

———. "What the Sands Remember." *GLQ: A Journal of Lesbian and Gay Studies* 18, no. 2–3 (June 1, 2012): 325–346.

Alley, Kelly D. "On the Banks of the Ganga." *Annals of Tourism Research* 19, no. 1 (January 1, 1992): 125–127.

Auyero, Javier, and Debora Swistun. "The Social Production of Toxic Uncertainty." *American Sociological Review* 73, no. 3 (June 2008): 357–379.

Barry, Andrew. *Political Machines: Governing a Technological Society.* London: Athlone Press, 2001.

Calvillo, Nerea. "Toxic Nature: Toward a Queer Theory of Pollution." In *Environmental Histories of Architecture,* edited by Kim Förster. Montreal: Canadian Centre for Architecture, 2022.

Chen, Mel Y. *Animacies: Biopolitics, Racial Mattering, and Queer Affect.* Durham, NC: Duke University Press, 2012.

Chen, Mel Y., and Timothy K. Choy. "Corresponding in Time." *ISLE: Interdisciplinary Studies in Literature and Environment* 27, no. 4 (November 1, 2020): 795–808.

Choy, Timothy K. "A Commentary: Breathing Together Now." *Engaging Science, Technology, and Society* 6 (2020): 586–590.

Chuang Collective. "Social Contagion: Microbiological Class War in China." https://chuangcn.org/2020/02/social-contagion.

Davies, Thom. "Slow Violence and Toxic Geographies: 'Out of Sight' to Whom?" *Environment and Planning C: Politics and Space* 40, no. 2 (April 10, 2019): 409–427.

———. "Toxic Space and Time: Slow Violence, Necropolitics, and Petrochemical Pollution." *Annals of the American Association of Geographers* 108, no. 6 (November 2, 2018): 1537–1553.

Domínguez Rubio, Fernando, and Uriel Fogué. "Technifying Public Space and Publicizing Infrastructures: Exploring New Urban Political Ecologies through the Square of General Vara Del Rey." *International Journal of Urban and Regional Research* 37, no. 3 (2013): 1035–1052.

Douglas, Mary. *Purity and Danger: An Analysis of Concepts of Pollution and Taboo.* Classics Series. London: Routledge, 1966.

Ferdinand, Malcom. "De l'usage du chlordécone en Martinique et en Guadeloupe: L'égalité en question." *Revue française des affaires sociales,* no. 1–2 (2015): 163–183.

———. *Decolonial Ecology: Thinking from the Caribbean World.* Cambridge: Polity Press, 2022.

Fogué, Uriel. "Ecología Política y Economía de la Visibilidad de los Dispositivos Tecnológicos de Escala Urbana Durante el Siglo XX: Abriendo la Caja Negra." *E.T.S. Arquitectura,* Universidad Politécnica de Madrid, 2015.

Fortun, Kim. "From Latour to Late Industrialism." *HAU: Journal of Ethnographic Theory* 4, no. 1 (June 1, 2014): 309–29.

———. "Afterword: Working 'Faultlines.'" In *Technoscience and Environmental Justice,* edited by Gwen Ottinger and Benjamin R. Cohen. Cambridge, MA: MIT Press, 2011.

Garnett, Emma. "Developing a Feeling for Error: Practices of Monitoring and Modelling Air Pollution Data." *Big Data & Society* 3, no. 2 (2016).

Górska, Magdalena. "Breathing Matters: Feminist Intersectional Politics of Vulnerability." Linköping: Linköping University, 2016.

Gray-Cosgrove, Carmella, Max Liboiron, and Josh Lepawsky. "The Challenges of Temporality to Depollution & Remediation." *Surveys and Perspectives Integrating Environment and Society,* no. 8.1 (November 26, 2015).

Hecht, Gabrielle. *Being Nuclear: Africans and the Global Uranium Trade.* Cambridge, MA: MIT Press, 2012.

Jasanoff, Sheila. "The Bhopal Disaster and the Right to Know." *Social Science & Medicine* 27, no. 10 (January 1988): 1113–1123.

Kallipoliti, Lydia. *The Architecture of Closed Worlds.* Baden, Switzerland: Lars Müller Publishers, 2018.

Liboiron, Max. *Pollution Is Colonialism.* Durham, NC: Duke University Press, 2021.

———. "Redefining Pollution and Action: The Matter of Plastics." *Journal of Material Culture* 21, no. 1 (December 29, 2015): 1–24.

Liboiron, Max, Manuel Tironi, and Nerea Calvillo. "Toxic Politics: Acting in a Permanently Polluted

World." *Social Studies of Science* 48, no. 3 (2018): 331–349.

Lidskog, Rolf, and Göran Sundqvist, eds. *Governing the Air: The Dynamics of Science, Policy, and Citizen Interaction*. Cambridge, MA: MIT Press, 2011.

Logan, William Bryant. *Air: The Restless Shaper of the World*. New York: W. W. Norton, 2012.

Lyons, Kristina. "Chemical Warfare in Colombia, Evidentiary Ecologies and Senti-Actuando Practices of Justice." *Social Studies of Science* 48, no. 3 (June 2018): 413–437.

> *Vital Decomposition: Soil Practitioners and Life Politics*. Durham, NC: Duke University Press, 2020.

Moore, Jason W. *Capitalism in the Web of Life: Ecology and the Accumulation of Capital*. New York: Verso, 2015.

Murphy, Michelle. "Alterlife and Decolonial Chemical Relations." *Cultural Anthropology* 32, no. 4 (2017): 494–503.

> "Chemical Infrastructures of the St. Clair River." In *Toxicants, Health and Regulation since 1945*, edited by Soraya Boudia and Nathalie Jas, 103–116. London: Pickering & Chatto, 2013.

> "Chemical Regimes of Living." *Environmental History* 13, no. 4 (2008): 695–703.

> *Sick Building Syndrome and the Politics of Uncertainty: Environmental Politics, Technoscience, and Women Workers*. Durham, NC: Duke University Press, 2006.

Nash, Linda. *Inescapable Ecologies: A History of Environment, Disease, and Knowledge*. Berkeley, CA: University of California Press, 2006.

Nguyen, Victoria. "Breathless in Beijing: Aerial Attunements and China's New Respiratory Publics." *Engaging Science, Technology, and Society* 6 (November 10, 2020): 439–461.

O'Neill, Kate. *Waste*. Cambridge: Polity Press, 2019.

Schrader, Astrid. "Responding to *Pfiesteria piscicida* (the Fish Killer): Phantomatic Ontologies, Indeterminacy, and Responsibility in Toxic Microbiology." *Social Studies of Science* 40, no. 2 (2010): 275–306.

Sennett, Richard. "Cities in the Pandemic." *PublicSpace* (blog), May 5, 2020, https://www.publicspace.org/multimedia//post/cities-in-the-pandemic.

Shotwell, Alexis. *Against Purity: Living Ethically in Compromised Times*. Minneapolis, MN: University of Minnesota Press, 2016.

Thorsheim, Peter. *Inventing Pollution: Coal, Smoke, and Culture in Britain since 1800*. Athens, OH: Ohio University Press, Series in Ecology and History, 2006.

Tironi, Manuel. "Hypo-Interventions: Intimate Activism in Toxic Environments." *Social Studies of Science* 48, no. 3 (June 2018): 438–455.

Tsing, Anna Lowenhaupt. *The Mushroom at the End of the World: On the Possibility of Life in Capitalist Ruins*. Princeton, NJ: Princeton University Press, 2015.

Whitehead, Mark. *State, Science & the Skies*. Oxford: Wiley-Blackwell, 2009.

Wylie, Sara, Nicholas Shapiro, and Max Liboiron. "Making and Doing Politics through Grassroots Scientific Research on the Energy and Petrochemical Industries." *Engaging Science, Technology, and Society* 3 (September 28, 2017): 393–425.

Zee, Jerry. "Breathing in the City: Beijing and the Architecture of Air." *Scapegoat* 8 (2015): 46–56.

IMAGES

2.1–2.12
Dust from the Sahara Desert blown over Madrid by Storm Celia, March 2022. Photograph by Marisa González. Courtesy of the artist.

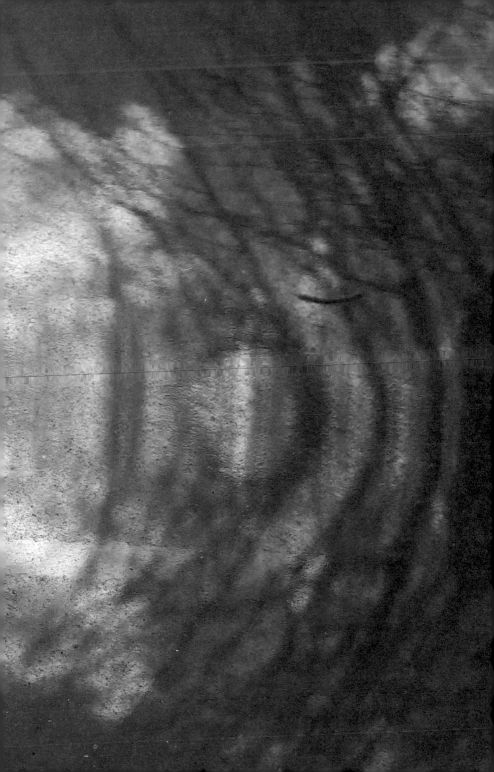

A PAUSE
(ON WRITING
ABOUT PRACTICE)

The following three texts reencounter—see, touch, hold, again and anew—a series of design and spatial design projects developed outside academia and in collaboration with different teams, local governments, and public institutions.

They might read, hit, land differently. I feel like I wrote them differently. They offer retrospective, empirical accounts of things I have done. They draw on what I can remember from my own experience as a designer, builder, and spectator; on repeated and detailed observation of the numerous pictures and videos I have taken, as well as those of collaborators, professional photographers, students, and the public; on the informal conversations I had with participants and visitors during and after the events; and on the slow and unconscious merging of ideas and literature that I was reading at the time. They are an attempt to record an ongoing participatory and sensory ethnography.[1]

I draw on my own projects to actively think through and make sense of the work, to unpack and reorient what a visualization, a material, a construction project, an aerial infrastructure can be while addressing larger theoretical concerns for air, like pollution or the global commons, and attuning to other relations, in the city, on a project. To wonder about what it is we are doing and have done as designers working with a "new" material that models a different kind of design and construction practice. This requires a willingness to be moved by a project, to discover its limits and its possibilities, to air it out, to push it to meet other preoccupations and ideas that may not have been on my mind at the time.

1   Sarah Pink, *Doing Sensory Ethnography* (London: Sage Publications, 2015).

The projects are not meant to be illustrations or examples, let alone solutions, but empirical material to think and revise with. Or, simply put, instances in designing-thinking-making that have contributed to landing, grounding, and suspending ideas; to airing material arrangements or processes, to suggesting other ways of being in the field that undo certain assumptions about architecture and design.

In writing these texts, I was at times asked and tempted to foreground each chapter with "the theory." But together with the editors, we decided to stick to the process by which projects came about, a messy process of thinking-making-designing without a clear beginning or a defined conclusion. Because projects don't end. They change as we change.

SEEING MOLECULES, AFFECTIVE ATMOGRAPHIES

The United Nations Economic Commission for Europe's "Convention on Access to Information, Public Participation in Decision-Making, and Access to Justice in Environmental Matters" (more casually known as the Aarhus Convention) was signed in Aarhus, Denmark, in 1998. As an agreement linking environmental rights to human rights, its aim was to protect citizens' freedom to access environmental information and to guarantee broader public participation in the sustainable development of cities.[1] Its underlying assumption was that information leads to behavioral change and political engagement, both by local authorities and by citizens, so it made measuring and publishing air quality data mandatory for all public administrations across the European Union (EU).

After the Aarhus Convention was adopted, air quality monitoring networks appeared across cities in EU member states and began to make their data public through reports or accessible databases. But due to the lack of public engagement with this air quality data at the time —or, in STS scholar Kristin Asdal's words, the lack of engagement produced by "single numbers"[2]—the EU encouraged its members to communicate air quality through the European Air Quality Index. Air Quality Indexes (AQIs) are conceived as spaces of equivalence; they translate air quality data into its impacts on human health since it is known that relating environmental issues to the body can increase awareness and engagement—although oftentimes fear as well.[3] Intended to produce "action at a distance,"[4] AQIs

127

1   The previous UN international conferences were the Stockholm Declaration on the Human Environment in 1972 and the Rio Declaration on Environment and Development in 1992, among others. The Aarhus Convention became a European directive the same year as the convention, in 1998. You can read the entire agreement here: https://ec.europa.eu/environment/aarhus.
2   Asdal shows how "governing by [single] numbers can fail to work for the environment," which helps us see the limitations of the Convention directives and their understanding of numbers as "agency" and "authority." Kristin Asdal, "The Office: The Weakness of Numbers and the Production of Non-Authority."
3   Karen Bickerstaff and Gordon Walker, "The Place(s) of Matter: Matter out of Place—Public Understandings of Air Pollution"; Sarah Lindley and Helen Crabbe, "What Lies Beneath? Issues in the Representation of Air Quality Management Data for Public Consumption"; Ulrich Beck, *Risk Society*.
4   Or, in other words, intended to influence action or behavior through the communication of only surface-level information. In this case, to make citizens decide on their own whether they can or

communicate this equivalence through a traffic-light color range, from red to green, so that it can be understood without prior knowledge of air quality. AQIs assume that citizens can only understand "simple" information,[5] and are therefore designed to require very little of people—expressing a liberal mode of democracy.[6] Embracing the Aarhus Convention's concern with the "interactions between the public and public authorities in a democratic context," what would a form of engagement with air quality data look like that moves away from liberal democratic modes—where engagement and responsibility is easy, minimal, and individualized—to enhance more collective and sustained forms of engagement with difficult air and environmental issues?

Madrid is an unremarkable EU city, aerially speaking. The city's Air Quality Surveillance System (AQSS), comprised of 24 automated remote stations, first published its data online in 2006 in the form of reports and monthly data sets.[7] It was not until 2008 that real-time data from each monitoring station was made available to citizens in the form of a list searchable only by the monitoring station's name and pollutant. However, this format made it difficult to compare data and to get a more holistic understanding of Madrid's overall air quality. In 2010, the AQSS began presenting real-time data through AQIs superimposed over aerial images of the city. While the city council was following the demands of the Aarhus Convention, making air quality more accessible and understandable to the general public, the council's engagement with air quality stopped there. Accounting for molecules was substituted for actual political action toward

should exercise outdoors. See Bruno Latour and Steve Woolgar, *Laboratory Life: The Construction of Scientific Facts*.

5   Andrew Barry, *Political Machines: Governing a Technological Society*.

6   Noortje Marres, *Material Participation: Technology, the Environment and Everyday Publics*. This book was very important for my understanding of objects' political affordances.

7   The web address at the time of writing is: https://airedemadrid.madrid.es/portal/site/calidadaire, but this has changed over the years.

8   Asdal, "The Office," 6.

9   These gaps between the stations were covered by the climate predictive model CALIOPE, a system

reducing pollution, making citizens self-regulate their own health instead.[8] Furthermore, it was not entirely clear how to interpret the maps provided by the AQSS, or what to do with the information they presented. Although the distribution of data in the map allowed the average AQI across the different stations to be compared, it flattened the different components of the air and only described the aerial conditions of 24 points across the city. What happens in between these stations?[9]

On a warm October morning in 2008, the Visualizar '08: Database City workshop convened around this question at Medialab-Prado. Nine international participants from different backgrounds (an interaction designer, a teacher, an anthropologist, a new media researcher, and some architects) came together for two intense weeks in an effort to make Madrid's air quality visible. This visualization exercise became the starting point of *In the Air*, an ongoing research project.[10] Air quality data

for high-resolution short-term air quality forecasts for Europe developed by the Department of Earth Sciences at the Barcelona Supercomputing Center, and by the models of the Environmental Software and Modelling Group. They are both an effect of the 2008 EU recommendation to model contaminants and produce models to include the local conditions of each territory. These climate predictive models account for risk—instead of measuring concentrations—by putting nature and political management into relation with epidemiological, environmental, and economic research where air is considered a resource. However, the data provided by CALIOPE did not have resolution enough to cover differences within the city. On environmental models and risk, see Steven Shapin and Simon Schaffer, *Leviathan and the Air-Pump*; also see Paul Edwards, "Representing the Global Atmosphere: Computer Models, Data and Knowledge about Climate Change."

10   *In the Air*
Workshop: Visualizar '08: Database City, Medialab-Prado
Curator: José Luis de Vicente
Institution: Medialab-Prado
Design: Nerea Calvillo, with amazing collaborators without whom *In the Air* would not exist: Sandra Fernández, Carlota Pascual, Greg J. Smith, Guillermo Ramírez, Miguel Vidal, Paco González, Raphaël de Staël, and, in particular, Susanna Tesconi and Victor Viña. I cannot thank them enough for their ideas and dedication. We received assistance from the workshop tutors Andrés Ortiz, Fabien Girardin, Juan Freire, and Adam Greenfield. Curator José Luis de Vicente contributed to the definition of the project. Since 2009, the application has been updated several times by Martin Nadal. Due to lack of funding and the continuous changes in the council's data feed, the application is not running live anymore.
Details: 2008, Madrid, intheair.es

had never been spatialized for the public by the Madrid City Council, the project aimed at making Madrid's air visible across the city, to explore which areas were more polluted than others. In other words, it aimed to produce a visualization that would help people make sense of air in relation to the city. By visualizing "official data"—that is, in principle, scientific, accurate—we hoped to "see" the complexity of the urban air. Or more precisely, to see *the air*—real and actual—of Madrid (what I later named Madrid's aeropolis). We assumed that making air visible would help to "fix the problem" of air pollution and lead to environmental justice. As we stated on the project's webpage, the goal was to make the air "visible... for individual and collective awareness and decision making, where the interpretation of results can be used for real-time navigation through the city, opportunistic selection of locations according to their air conditions and as a base for political action."

Looking back, I see now that this was a very mechanistic understanding of accountability and, as far as we know, the application developed at Medialab-Prado has not been used for decision making or political action. While this is a shame, we've also come to understand it differently: individual decision making might be useful for those with the ability and resources to determine their engagement with the city, but not for those who cannot. Many apps and platforms have since been developed to help users navigate a city through low emissions areas

130

In 2009, the application *In the Air* was developed further at Visualizar '09 at Medialab-Prado and adapted to Santiago de Chile (for the Video and Media art biennale of Chile BVAM09, Museum of Contemporary Art of Santiago, Chile) and to Budapest (during a residency at Kitchen Budapest, Hungary). A new visualization, *In the Air São Paulo* was commissioned in 2013 by the European Media Facades Network for the Digital Art Gallery SESI-SP São Paulo, Brazil. Thank you, collaborators, José Luis de Vicente, Valentina Montero, Medialab-Prado, and everyone who made these possible.

or to make air pollution a parameter to assess real estate value, which, again, are only valuable for those who can choose how to commute or where they want to live. These apps and platforms have actually exacerbated urban inequality. But we did not know this at the time, so we kept working.

What were we actually "seeing" on our computer screens? What is 3 mg/m^3 (milligrams per cubic meter) of a gas? And 3 ppm (parts per million) of particles? We wanted to make connections between invisible molecules and larger urban issues but we only had the data from the council, which measured the five gases and particles that cities are required to monitor by EU law to comply with air quality limits—the so-called "pollutants": nitrogen dioxide (NO_2), carbon monoxide (CO), sulphur dioxide (SO_2), particulate matter (PM_{10}) and ozone (O_3). And we wondered: could the same data be presented differently? What exactly did we want to make visible?

We decided to reframe the institutional way of displaying air quality and explore the relationships of the aerial components in time, space, with one another, and the city. To see when and where the air is polluted in relation to its own measurements. Because we soon realized that air is not only gases and particles, but sets of relations, where location and exposures matter. Other than knowing how many pollutants one person breathes at a moment in time, we were interested in the areas most polluted in the city, to identify the areas of environmental injustice. Because toxicity relates not only to emissions, but to exposure too. In Michelle Murphy's, words: "exposures are made to matter" to identify who, what, and when is being exposed, and to eventually link these exposures to larger gendered or racial practices.[11] Only by *situating* air pollution can the segregation that it may be producing be identified. Thus, the possibility of action may be greater and more precise, and the redistribution of life chances, of a livable life, more possible.[12]

DESIGNING AFFECTIVE VISUALIZATIONS

What are the implications of making the environment visible, or representing a truth, as most scientific and policy-making maps claim to do?[13] Can visualizations interfere and induce changes in the world, as feminist scholars of technoscience insist they do?[14] Can they be a form of material ecocriticism?[15] Are visualizations research objects, or can they be research tools too?[16] Can they become collaboration devices, turning audiences into participants?[17]

11 Michelle Murphy, *Sick Building Syndrome and the Politics of Uncertainty: Environmental Politics, Technosience and Women Workers*, 18.

12 This strategy of looking closely at the city may also redistribute the type of engagement, as "the impact and credibility of air quality information may be greater if it is also locally focused." Karen Bickerstaff and Gordon Walker, "Clearing the Smog? Public Responses to Air-Quality Information," 292.

13 Rob Kitchin, Chris Perkins, and Martin Dodge, "Thinking about Maps."

14 Annemarie Mol, *The Body Multiple: Ontology in Medical Practice*.

15 Dana Phillips and Heather I. Sullivan, "Material Ecocriticism: Dirt, Waste, Bodies, Food, and Other Matter."

16 Visualizations have been an ongoing object of research within science and technology studies (STS) since Bruno Latour and Steve Woolgar identified their role in the production of scientific knowledge and followed them in the laboratory. See Latour and Woolgar, *Laboratory Life*; see also Catelijne Coopmans et al., *Representation in Scientific Practice Revisited*; and Regula Valérie Burri and Joseph Dumit, "Social Studies of Scientific Imaging and Visualization."

Digital visualizations as research tools have a tradition in STS as well, where they are used to make visible the networks involved in a certain controversy. See: Albena Yaneva, *Mapping Controversies in Architecture*; Tommaso Venturini, "Diving in Magma: How to Explore Controversies with Actor-Network Theory"; Bruno Latour et al., "A Note on Socio-Technical Graphs." Digitally produced maps, charts, and graphs are also used for sociological research within the wider frame of digital sociology. See Noortje Marres, "The Issues Deserve More Credit: Pragmatist Contributions to the Study of Public Involvement in Controversy."

In addition, visual artifacts are produced by researchers with digital images or video to inquire, sustain, and even present practice-based research outputs in visual sociology. See Nina Wakeford, "Power Point and the Crafting of Social Data."

17 For an incredible example of this, I encourage folks to visit the digital Asthma Files platform by Kim Fortun and colleagues. See also Kim Fortun et al., "Experimental Ethnography Online."

A visualization can do, obviously, many of those things, but its effects, scales, and participants differ enormously. What if, instead of aligning with positivist understandings of information—where knowledge produces individual behavioral change—we pay attention to the collective effects of pollution? This shifts the conventional aims of the visualization from "solving" individual problems to "fussing" air pollution, as a feminist practice where "the very strength of women who make a fuss is not to represent the True, rather to be witnesses for the possibility of other ways of doing what would perhaps be better."[18] Understanding "the relevance of creative practices for inventive modes of registering the materiality of air and atmospheric space," as geographer Sasha Engelmann puts it,[19] I want to highlight the crucial role of design as *the* tool to materialize—both physically and as a matter of concern, in Murphy's sense—*how* things are visualized.[20] Every line or color requires taking a position toward the object of inquiry.[21] Each position determines not only what it is but, most interestingly, what it can be. I have come to name this design process "attentive speculation," a method that departs from a detailed observation of what exists and, instead, speculates on what could become.[22]

The City Council gave us a CD with data for May 2008. We knew nothing about air quality so we started by asking the data some questions: Why are some components measured in parts per million and others in micrograms per cubic meter? Do different gases perform differently? How can they be put together in the same space if they have different units of measurement and different effects?

133

18 Donna Haraway citing philosopher of science Vinciane Despret in Haraway, *Staying with the Trouble: Making Kin in the Chthulucene*, 130.
19 Sasha Engelmann, "Toward a Poetics of Air: Sequencing and Surfacing Breath."
20 Note that everything is designed, even if we have come to think that scientific means objective and therefore not designed or without design.
21 Jonathan Gray et al., "Ways of Seeing Data: Towards a Critical Literacy for Data Visualizations as Research Objects and Research Devices."
22 Nerea Calvillo, "Particular Sensibilities."

We quickly realized that, if we wanted to make the same data visible in a different way, we needed to start making (design) decisions. And, as we wanted to make the visualization more—rather than less—complex, we needed to start differentiating the data as much as we could. We needed to move from the notion of air to airs. Understanding the different concentrations, performances, and spatial and temporal distributions of different components, enabled us to interpolate component topographies in relation to their limit levels (instead of, for instance, their concentrations).[23] In this way the application communicated the relative risk of each component in space and time. We also explored how to differentiate the scale of the actions needed to reduce pollutants, since the impossibility of "seeing" directly the effects of collective citizen actions complicates citizen engagement—moving away from a form of individual citizenship "made easy."[24]

Atmographies

Visualizations *are* storytelling devices. The storyteller chooses which protagonist in the data set is relevant, how to create a narrative out of information or data, and how to do these things to engage with their audiences. But which stories should be told? I have since learned that the prefix *atmo-* ("atmos" in Greek), which refers to vapor or steam, also means to inspire, to blow, to spiritually arouse; and that the suffix *-graphy* names a specific way of describing something (like photography or choreography). Perhaps we need to tell the stories that will move us in some way. So, to move from

---

23   *In The Air* makes visible the five "standard" components: NO_2, SO_2, CO, O_3, PM_{10}.

24   Based on the estimated ecological footprint of a citizen, it was possible to visualize the impacts of a hypothetical action like, for example, 100,000 people cycling instead of driving. This was technically developed for *Budapest In The Air*.

knowing airs to sensing them as affect, I am going to call these air quality visualizations *atmographies*.

> Even though we were using and making visible the City Council's data, we were, by design, simultaneously moving away from precise models of the data (which would focus on the sensing technologies and the reliability of their data as "the truth") and towards a mentally embodied experience, to inspire and stimulate collective action. As opposed to graphs or charts, which require visual literacy, we decided to describe each component through a topographical geo-referenced mesh, like a mountain of data in the air. Because navigating a topography in real time is both intuitive and embodied, and the landscapes of air quality require new visualization strategies that are as much affective as they are actionable.

For geographer Chris Perkins, playing in/on/with maps is an "open ended process of investigation in which new worlds are constructed in overlapping worlds of the imagination, cyberspace, and reality."[25] In other words, playing in/on/with maps is immersive, connecting and activating virtual space with a user's body and subjectivity through imagination: "cartographic practice inherently is learning to make projections that shape worlds in particular ways for various purposes. Each projection produces and implies specific sorts of perspective."[26]

> What was our purpose? What worlds were we shaping? What perspectives were we projecting? Our first visualization objective became to build a virtual space (in 3D) to be inhabited by Madrid airs and the viewer and to do so by avoiding a hegemonic vision of the city and its airs. As Haraway has famously argued, the vantage point is always a problem for visualizations in

---

25 Chris Perkins, "Playing with Maps," 172.
26 Donna Haraway, *Modest_Witness@Second_Millennium: Femaleman_Meets_OncoMouse*, 132.

the way they make claims toward objectivity.[27] Therefore, it was important for us to enable the experience of the data from different points of view. This meant making sure the viewer could get inside the data landscapes, and situate themselves within the city and its airs. The zoom feature in the visualization allowed for the approximation of any point to observe details, or to move away to get a more general perspective; but at the same time, the visualization did not pretend to build a seamless relation between its parts and the whole, as Latour warns.[28] The zoom permitted viewers to "feel" the mesh from above or from below. In addition, the visualization parameters could be customized, to test their effects. So in terms of effort, the immediacy of the topographic mesh facilitated the navigation of the data, but in a different way than "engagement made easy": the information had not been simplified, on the contrary, it had been made more complex.

This complexity allowed for many different types of engagement: from a one-second glimpse of the most polluted areas of the city, to spending time with and learning to decipher its intricacies. Furthermore, by looking at the landscapes of toxicity from a relational perspective we realized that the air is an indicator of the functioning of the city. A year later we learned to read (or re-read) the mesh with the help of newspaper archives, identifying holidays, sale days, football matches, demonstrations, the weather, etc.[29] It was impressive to "see" how particulate matter and nitrogen dioxide are

27 Donna Haraway, *Simians, Cyborgs and Women: The Reinvention of Nature*, 190.
28 Bruno Latour and Émilie Hermant, *Paris Ville Invisible*.
29 This data reading took place at Visualizar '09, again at Medialab-Prado, where *In the Air* was invited to continue its development. Thank you, José Luis de Vicente and Medialab-Prado, for the opportunity.

real-time descriptors of Madrid's daily life, whereas the ozone is slower to react to it.

If some scholars have studied the ways in which the air is felt in the body or through changes in the environment, such as headaches or the color of the sky,[30] could atmographies (like *In the Air*) be an instrument to expand these modes of feeling airs through digital sensation? Could atmographies function as balloons for, as geographer Derek McCormack writes, "doing atmospheric things," or as devices for a "practical aesthetics, in which different qualities of atmospheric spacetimes can be experimented with"?[31] Could atmographies be a form of "airy poetics" that, in the words of geographer Sasha Engelmann, would "require a concerted shift from an affective logic of linear 'flows' to one in which affect condenses, environs, ventilates and dissipates around human and nonhuman bodies and objects?"[32]

We had to keep in mind that while the digital application facilitated an approximation of some of the microscopic or gaseous properties of Madrid's air, it was not its full description. In fact, we realized that we could only see a very small proportion of its "inhabitants." Seeing pollen, volatile organic compounds, formaldehyde, or virus proved almost impossible. Each components' molecules differ in scale. Measuring them requires different units of measurement, different technologies, different institutions, and different time frames. Because sulphur dioxide and pollen, for instance, are totally different "species," but they cohabitate and commingle in the air.

Still, we were not sure what we were actually "seeing" about air quality in Madrid. What the animation of the

30 See, among many others: Timothy K. Choy, "Air's Substantiations"; Nicholas Shapiro, "Attuning to the Chemosphere: Domestic Formaldehyde, Bodily Reasoning, and the Chemical Sublime."
31 Derek P. McCormack, "Devices for Doing Atmospheric Things," 106.
32 Engelmann, "Toward a Poetics of Air," 441.

historic data made clear was the large variability of gas and particle concentrations in just one hour and across nearby stations. Mesmerized, we began calling the air we were tracking Madrid's *breath*. If an aerograph is an instrument for mechanically recording the frequency and extent of respiratory movements, *In the Air* could be read as an aerograph of Madrid's breath.

Affective Atmographies

To expand our understanding of Aeropolis's inhabitants, some years later I developed *Pollen In the Air* for the Laboral Centro de Arte y Creación Industrial in Gijón.[33] I had just read Carla Hustak and Natasha Myers's work on "affective ecologies," which was eye opening.[34] They explain how plants and insects have interactions beyond productivity, where they communicate and help each other in multispecies relations, which include bodily (and eventually pleasant) interactions:

> It is in encounters between orchids, insects, and scientists that we find openings for an ecology of interspecies intimacies and subtle propositions. What is at stake in this involutionary approach is a theory of ecological relationality that takes seriously organisms as inventive practitioners who experiment as they craft interspecies lives and worlds. This is an ecology

33 *Pollen In the Air*
    Exhibition: Datascape
    Curator: Benjamin Weil
    Institution: Laboral Centro de Arte y Creación Industrial
    Design: Nerea Calvillo
    Programming: Martín Nadal
    Collaboration: Marina Fernández, Sección de Vigilancia Epidemiológica (Dirección General de Salud Pública de Gijón)
    Details: 2014, Gijón, Spain, €2,500, intheair.es
34 Myers's work and attitude has been a source of constant inspiration since I first encountered it. Carla Hustak and Natasha Myers, "Involutionary Momentum: Affective Ecologies and the Sciences of Plant/Insect Encounters."

inspired by a feminist ethic of "response-ability" in which questions of species difference are always conjugated with attentions to affect, entanglement, and rupture; it is an affective ecology in which creativity and curiosity characterize the experimental forms of life of all kinds of practitioners, not only the human ones. We will need this mode of ecological thinking in order to do more effective work in challenging the status quo of ecological irresponsibility.[35]

What if, instead of showing a landscape of threat for asthmatic people (as most pollen apps do), the image of Gijón's landscape was one of exuberant plant reproduction? What if we moved away from a human-centered and harm-based understanding of pollen, making it visible as a reproductive entity that serves as food for bees, that pollinates plants, that flies with the wind—and makes some of us sneeze?

In the resulting visualization *Pollen's atmography* positions the city upside down, inverting the human-centered aerial perspective. From this vantage, the user floats with bees or pollen particles. Whilst providing the data about pollen grain predictions that asthmatic people need, pollen was visualized through the trees in the city. As a result, users could observe that when pollen activates, it means that different vegetable species are blossoming. So pollen's atmography was not the landscape of risk or health prediction, but the landscape of plant, wind, and animal intercourse. As a visualization device we used particle clouds, which replicate particle distribution (again, what matters is not how exactly, and therefore the wind is not included. It is the idea, that matters); where multiple species have physical connections that construct various types of affects

139

35 Hustak and Myers, "Involutionary Momentum," 106.

beyond production and reproduction, enacting the air of queer ecologies.[36]

I wish I had read English professor and author Candace Fujikane's *Mapping Abundance for a Planetary Future: Kanaka Maoli and Critical Settler Cartographies in Hawai'i* at the time. For now I would interpret our intentions as an attempt to map abundance, as a critical and political proposition. Fujikane beautifully argues:

> Cartography as a methodology is critical to growing intimate relationships with 'āina (lands and waters who feed) in ways necessary to our planetary future. In this way, mapping abundance is a refusal to succumb to capital's logic that we have passed an apocalyptic threshold of no return. Kanaka Maoli and critical settler cartographies in Hawai'i provide visual and textual illustrations of flourishing Indigenous economies of abundance. I argue that Kanaka Maoli cartographies foreground practices of ea—translated as life, breath, political sovereignty, and the rising of the people. Such ea-based cartographies teach us how to cultivate aloha 'āina, a deep and abiding love for the lands, seas, and skies through which undercurrents of Kanaka Maoli radical resurgence flow. Mapping abundance is a profoundly decolonial act.[37]

Chemo-ethnographies

Visualizations are often fetishized as tools that have the superpower of opening doors to the unknown (data, invisible entities, complex systems); as magical devices that shed light on knowledge that is otherwise inaccessible. They are also most often valued only as final objects. And yet, this fixation with the "results" of the process, with the visualization itself, might obscure other relations, such as

---

36 Matthew Gandy, "Queer Ecology: Nature, Sexuality, and Heterotopic Alliances."
37 Candace Fujikane, *Mapping Abundance for a Planetary Future: Kanaka Maoli and Critical Settler Cartographies in Hawai'i*, 4.

their capacities or what takes place in their production processes. What I've realized over the years is that making a visualization can be a method of thinking with the environment as opposed to representing it;[38] as well as a form of doing an ethnography on a data set; as well as creating a new image of it that can circulate outside of academic contexts. In rethinking visualizations in all these ways, I borrow anthropologists Nicholas Shapiro and Eben Kirksey's concept of "chemo-ethnography," a term they coined to refer to the work of anthropologists inquiring after life with/in chemicals:

> Chemo-ethnographers are starting to conduct research on economic, personal, political, and sentimental relationships that have emerged with modern chemistry. Departing from critical studies of carcinogenic toxics and biomedical cures, this collection also considers chemical relations in more-than-human realms. Anthropologists are starting to characterize corrosive atmospheres and the play of onzymes, alleuls, and reagents in ooological assemblages.[39]

Instead of exploring human-chemical relations, I suggest the making of visualizations as a form of doing ethnographic work around the socio-technical assemblages that make the toxic polluted air a scientific and policy-making issue of concern. Madrid's atmographies

141

---

38 "Thinking through things" has a long tradition, where objects found throughout research are used as heuristics to develop theories. See Amiria Henare, Martin Holbraad, and Sari Wastell, *Thinking through Things: Theorising Artefacts Ethnographically*; and McCormack, "Devices for Doing Atmospheric Things." There are also researchers who think by making things. See Carl DiSalvo, *Adversarial Design*; Matt Ratto and Megan Boler, *DIY Citizenship: Critical Making and Social Media*; Alex Wilkie and Alvise Mattozzi, "Learning Design through Social Science"; Anthony Dunne and Fiona Raby, *Speculative Everything: Design, Fiction and Social Dreaming*; Public Lab, "Public Lab"; among many others. Their practices are heterogeneous and have different aims and claims, ranging from critical design to critical making or citizen science, yet they share with this chapter an underlying challenge: how to relate research and making. Here, the focus will be not on what the object can do for research but on how the making of an object (a digital visualization) can be a research method, to explore the materiality of environmental issues, engaging with their socio-technical assemblages and creating new imaginaries.

39 Nicholas Shapiro and Eben Kirksey, "Chemo-Ethnography: An Introduction," 482.

of toxicpolluted airs made experienceable in real time the phar-makon capacity of airs—their capacity to benefit or harm human bodies via their toxic concentrations.

When designing *Pollen In the Air* we had to identify who published the pollen data and how frequently. As we were unable to find the data on the City Council's website, we had to contact the measuring institution, the regional health institute AsturSalud. This institute publishes graphs in PDF format, under the assumption that pollen concentrations are not needed in real time. Obtaining the data set in a programmable format required institutional collaboration and a long email exchange, revealing who manages pollen monitoring and how. Through our conversations with them, we not only obtained five months of data, but the Pharmacy Medical School and the Open Data Department of the City Council realized their lack of synchronization and decided to change their protocols. Learning about pollen meant also learning about tree species, Gijón's green areas management, pollinators, glass plates, the wind, and so on. We discovered which institution makes the location of urban trees available online to promote open data. While trying to match these trees with pollen counts, we discovered that the trees we had information on were only the ones taken care of by the City Council. These trees are "singular" species whose pollen is not counted because it is quantitatively irrelevant, while the plants producing the pollen included in the data sets were wild shrubs and grasses located on the outskirts of the city, areas that were not mapped. So, what we thought would be "just" a technical and design task of translating a data set into visual form became something where the object of study forced us to connect with the agents involved (many of the institutions in charge of the management of pollen in the area) and activated connections between them (contributing to a rearticulation of their protocols).

When trying to understand why the data feed from the City Council was not active a week before the opening, following urgent correspondence with different institutions, we learned that there was no actual data because the meter was broken, and given the economic crisis, there was no intention of repairing it. The City Council argued that having one meter in Oviedo (60 km away) was "enough" to comply with regulations (and to satisfy citizens). Thus the publication of the data ultimately was only politically intended to perform as a "transparency device,"[40] where the mere action of publishing data was more important than actually considering how this data could be mobilized, or how these results might affect people's health and everyday lives.

Visualizations *are* a method for conducting chemo-ethnographies. They demand spending time with the chemical and getting to understand it. The agents involved emerge along with their power relations and what is at stake, or to put it bluntly, their politics. Their relations come to the fore through the process, without searching for them. One only needs to start visualizing.

AFFECTIVE ATMOGRAPHIES AS MORE-THAN-HUMAN FEMINIST VISUALIZATIONS

The design process of *In the Air* was far from linear. Questions and objectives shifted throughout the course of the project, which sheds light on a larger problem of sensing and visualizing air. Two

40   Penny Harvey, Madeleine Reeves, and Evelyn Ruppert, "Anticipating Failure: Transparency Devices and Their Effects."

temporalities or conclusions can be drawn from the project: we had an initial approach to visualize air differently, but the working process challenged our initial aims and questions and reframed what it means to intervene in the air. But the process also allowed us to both problematize institutionalized ways of visualizing air quality and to push questions of design research and intervention, its desired outcomes, its process, in different directions. Seeing molecules—as with any visualization—inevitably required a frame with which to understand and construct our new virtual world. Engagement made easy? Pollen as an enemy? Highlighting only pollution? Our frame was unconscious but it determined the questions we asked of the data, the design, and how we approached visualizations more broadly. I considered this frame a feminist sensibility—and I still do.

Hacker mama Catherine D'Ignacio and professional nerd Lauren F. Klein (this is how they present themselves in their book), have drawn upon feminist principles to make visualizations or practice data science from a feminist perspective—which is, as they explain, necessarily intersectional and anti-racist.[41] Their main principles are: examine power, challenge power, elevate emotion and embodiment, rethink binaries and hierarchies, embrace pluralism, consider context (not neutral and objective), and make labor visible, everything *through* the visualization's design.

The affective atmographies of both *In the Air* and *Pollen In the Air* address some of these principles—to elevate emotion and embodiment, consider context or rethink binaries—but they definitely do not comply with all of them. One reason might be that D'Ignacio and Klein's work is mostly human-centric, dealing with women's rights data sets. *In the Air*, instead, was concerned first and foremost with air. Despite these different approaches, in order to broaden the way citizens know about air, to inspire new kinds of

144

41   Catherine D'Ignacio and Lauren F. Klein, *Data Feminism*.

engagements with the air, and to situate *In the Air* politically, I think of it as a feminist visualization. To differentiate it from D'Ignacio and Klein's project and to add specificity, could we think about more-than-human feminist visualizations? If so, through *In the Air* we can maybe contribute to feminist visualizations with three more principles:

Speculation: If D'Ignazio and Klein's visualizations engage with feminist issues, we might also consider feminist practices and methods. One of the most powerful attributes of visualizations as storytelling devices is that they can be tools for speculation, at the intersection of science, art, and activist practices. Following Haraway, we might see "speculative fabulation, speculative feminism, science fiction, and scientific fact"[42] as the only way of engaging with the environment, by creating alternative affective landscapes that connect air concentrations to environmental justice or multispecies urban ecologies.

Knowledge politics: Paying attention to the politics of knowledge production expands the ways, formats, and means by which to think with/about air. In our case, from working with the concentrations of some components—or inhabitants—we learned about the motivations behind and limitations of open data, sensors in the public space, public awareness, and institutional politics. This process also highlighted the relevance of unexpected guests such as bees or worms, rain and the wind when trying to visualize air. There is also the opportunity of giving value to alternative modes of producing knowledge other than science and technology. And the same goes for the devices: we believe, with John Pickles, that countermappings have the same ontological status as scientific ones.[43] They just tell other stories.

In the Air was built collaboratively and not-for-profit by temporal associations among collaborators, with its main

145

42   Donna Haraway, "Anthropocene, Capitalocene, Plantationocene, Chthulucene: Making Kin," 160.

purposes being developing the project and participating in the workshop—and having fun. Mostly freelancers and students, none of us had an environmental background or knowledge on air quality. We had to learn how to be affected by each other, the air, and Madrid, eventually changing our own careers (some of the architects are now experts in programming, a former teacher became a "techno-teacher," and so on). We had to learn to work together, with its joys and its challenges. Through this citizen design collaborative process—drawing a parallel with citizen science—we had to engage in an experimental way of understanding design. First, because we did not share a design methodology, hierarchies fluctuated, and air kept demanding things from us. Second and most importantly, because Medialab promotes the production of prototypes instead of finished outputs. With *In the Air*, we aimed to prototype how to "make a difference,"[44] with the uncertainty of knowing how.

Multiplicity: Against the tendency of focusing on the "best" visualization, *In the Air* as a research project suggests generating more references, more visualizations, more inscription devices (visualizations for public space, domestic sensors, installations, etc.), with the desire that unexpected things about the air will emerge, to allow for other images of the environment, engagement, and knowledge. Overall, inspired by Sasha Engelmann and Derek McCormack, I wish these more-than-human feminist visualizations performed as "alchemies," which

> can help us become sensitive to the expressive, affective, partly unknown or otherwise excessive dimensions of elemental experience. And in doing so, they can provide a critical corrective

43   John Pickles, *A History of Spaces: Cartographic Reason, Mapping and the Geo-Coded World*.
44   Donna Haraway, "A Game of Cat's Cradle: Science Studies, Feminist Theory, Cultural Studies."

to the incessant modes of "capture" that are a feature of efforts to reduce the ontology of elemental lifeworlds through forms of epistemic reductivism.[45]

To challenge common understandings of the elemental as merely molecular, and "become sensitive" to what molecules do and what is around them, materially, affectively, even the things obscured by reductive forms of knowing. To "see" molecules beyond molecules, maybe through affective atmographies.

45   Sasha Engelmann and Derek P. McCormack, "Elemental Worlds: Specificities, Exposures, Alchemies," 14.

3.2

3.3

3.6

14.11.2008 20:25

3.4

14.11.2008 18:18

3.5

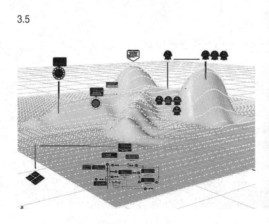

3.7

3.8

3.9

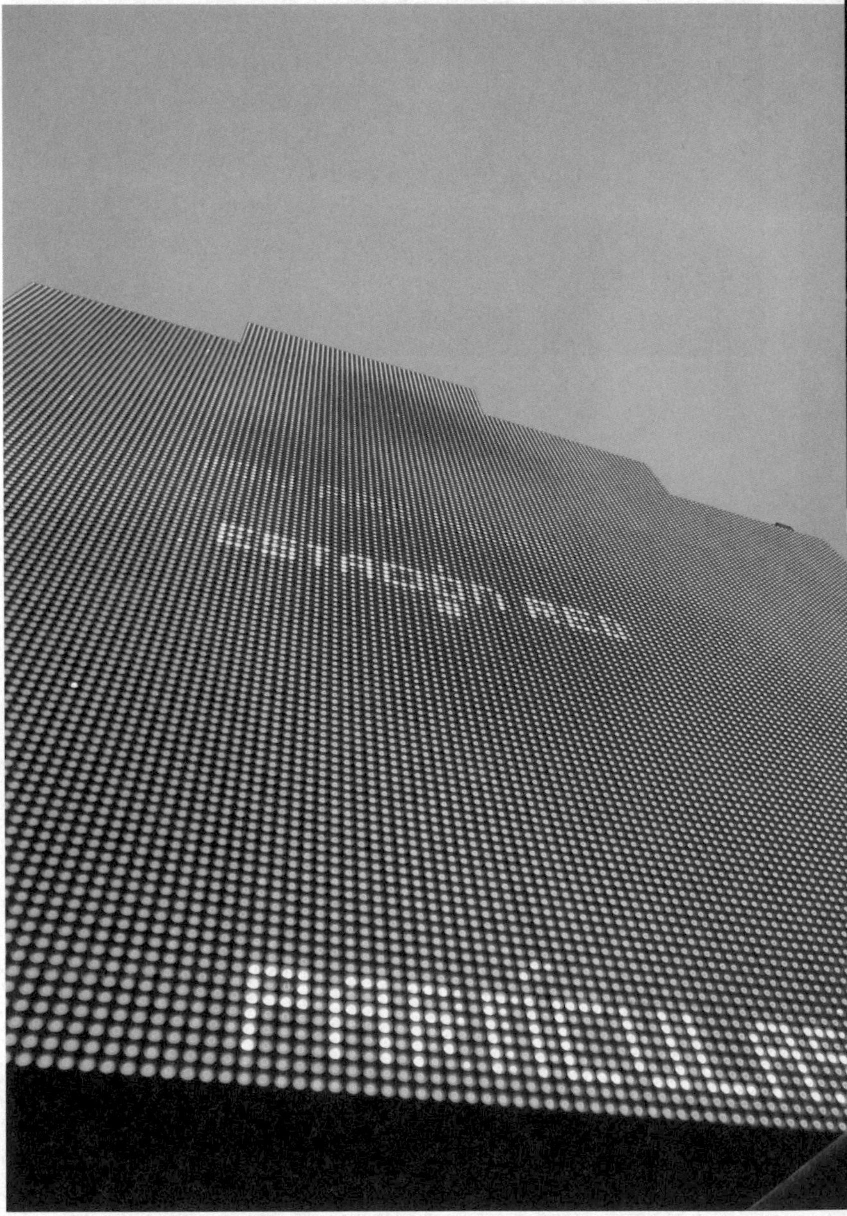

3.10

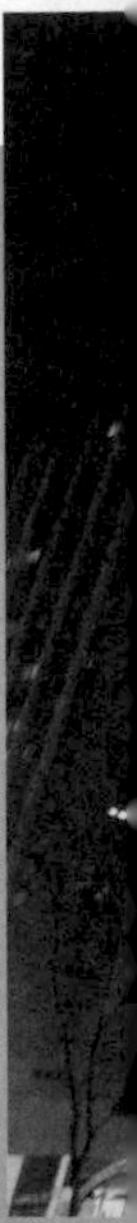

WORKS CITED

Asdal, Kristin. "The Office: The Weakness of Numbers and the Production of Non-Authority." *Accounting, Organizations and Society* 36, no. 1 (January 2011): 1–9.

Axel, Nick, Daniel A. Barber, Nikolaus Hirsch, and Anton Vidokle, eds. *Accumulation: The Art, Architecture, and Media of Climate Change.* Minneapolis, MN: University of Minnesota Press, 2022.

Barry, Andrew. *Political Machines: Governing a Technological Society.* London: Athlone Press, 2001.

Beck, Ulrich. *Risk Society: Towards a New Modernity.* Thousand Oaks, CA: SAGE, 1992.

Bickerstaff, Karen, and Gordon Walker. "Clearing the Smog? Public Responses to Air-Quality Information." *Local Environment* 4, no. 3 (1999): 279–294.

⠀⠀⠀⠀"The Place(s) of Matter: Matter out of Place—Public Understandings of Air Pollution." *Progress in Human Geography* 27, no. 1 (2003): 45–68.

Burri, Regula Valérie, and Joseph Dumit. "Social Studies of Scientific Imaging and Visualization." In *The Handbook of Science and Technology Studies*, edited by Edward J. Hackett, Olga Amsterdamska, Michael Lynch, and Judy Wajcman, 297–317. Cambridge, MA: MIT Press, 2008.

Calvillo, Nerea. "Particular Sensibilities." In *Accumulation: The Art, Architecture, and Media of Climate Change*, edited by Nick Axel, Nikolaus Hirsch, Daniel A. Barber, and Anton Vidokle, 147–157. Minneapolis, MN: University of Minnesota Press, 2022.

⠀⠀⠀⠀"Digital Visualisations to Think with the Environment." In *DigitalSTS: A Field Guide for Science & Technology Studies*, edited by Janet Vertesi and David Ribes, 61–75. Princeton, NJ: Princeton University Press, 2019.

⠀⠀⠀⠀"Slowing." In *Transmissions: Critical Tactics for Making and Communicating Research*, edited by Katrina Jungnickel, 155–172. Cambridge, MA: MIT Press, 2020.

Choy, Timothy K. "Air's Substantiations." In *Lively Capital: Biotechnologies, Ethics and Governance in Global Markets,* edited by Kaushik Sunder Rajan, 121–152. Durham, NC: Duke University Press, 2012.

Coopmans, Catelijne, Janet Vertesi, Michael Lynch, and Steve Woolgar. *Representation in Scientific Practice Revisited.* Cambridge, MA: MIT Press, 2014.

D'Ignazio, Catherine, and Lauren F. Klein. *Data Feminism.* Cambridge, MA: MIT Press, 2020.

DiSalvo, Carl. *Adversarial Design.* Cambridge, MA: MIT Press, 2012.

Dunne, Anthony, and Fiona Raby. *Speculative Everything: Design, Fiction, and Social Dreaming.* Cambridge, MA: MIT Press, 2013.

Edwards, Paul N. "Representing the Global Atmosphere: Computer Models, Data and Knowledge about Climate Change." In *Changing the Atmosphere: Expert Knowledge and Environmental Governance*, edited by Clark A. Miller and Paul N. Edwards, 31–65. Cambridge, MA: MIT Press, 2001.

Engelmann, Sasha. "Toward a Poetics of Air: Sequencing and Surfacing Breath." *Transactions of the Institute of British Geographers* 40, no. 3 (July 2015): 430–444.

Engelmann, Sasha, and Derek P. McCormack. "Elemental Worlds: Specificities, Exposures, Alchemies." *Progress in Human Geography* 46, no. 6 (February 2021).

Fortun, Kim, Mike Fortun, Erik Bigras, Tahereh Saheb, Brandon Costelloe-Kuehn, Jerome Crowder, Daniel Price, and Alison Kenner. "Experimental Ethnography Online." *Cultural Studies* 28, no. 4 (July 2014): 632–642.

Fujikane, Candace. *Mapping Abundance for a Planetary Future: Kanaka Maoli and Critical Settler Cartographies in Hawai'i.* Durham, NC: Duke University Press, 2021.

Gandy, Matthew. "Queer Ecology: Nature, Sexuality, and Heterotopic Alliances." *Environment and Urban Planning D: Society and Space* 30, no. 4 (2012): 727–747.

Gray, Jonathan, Liliana Bounegru, Stefania Milan, and Paolo Ciuccarelli. "Ways of Seeing Data: Towards a Critical Literacy for Data Visualizations as Research Objects and Research Devices." In *Innovative Methods in Media and Communication Research*, edited by Sebastian Kubitschko and Anne Kaun, 290–325. London: Palgrave Macmillan, 2016.

Haraway, Donna. "A Game of Cat's Cradle: Science Studies, Feminist Theory, Cultural Studies." *Configurations* 2, no. 1 (1994): 59–71.

"Anthropocene, Capitalocene, Plantationocene, Chthulucene: Making Kin." *Environmental Humanities* 6 (2015): 159–165.

Modest_Witness@Second_Millennium: Femaleman_Meets: OncoMouse. New York: Routledge, 1997.

Staying with the Trouble: Making Kin in the Chthulucene. Durham, NC: Duke University Press, 2016.

Simians, Cyborgs, and Women: The Reinvention of Nature. New York: Chapman and Hall, 1990.

Harvey, Penny, Madeleine Reeves, and Evelyn Ruppert. "Anticipating Failure: Transparency Devices and Their Effects." *Journal of Cultural Economy* 6, no. 3 (2012): 294–312.

Henare, Amiria, Martin Holbraad, and Sari Wastell, eds. *Thinking through Things: Theorising Artefacts Ethnographically.* London: Routledge, 2006.

Hustak, Carla, and Natasha Myers. "Involutionary Momentum: Affective Ecologies and the Sciences of Plant/Insect Encounters." *Differences* 23, no. 3 (January 2012): 74–118.

Kitchin, Rob, Chris Perkins, and Martin Dodge. "Thinking about Maps." In *Rethinking Maps: New Frontiers in Cartographic Theory*, edited by Martin Dodge, Rob Kitchin, and Chris Perkins, 1–25. London: Routledge Studies in Human Geography, 2009.

Latour, Bruno, and Émilie Hermant. *Paris Ville Invisible.* Paris: Institut Sythélabo pour le progrés de la connaissance, 1998.

Latour, Bruno, Philippe Mauguin, and Geneviève Teil. "A Note on Socio-Technical Graphs." *Social Studies of Science* 22, no. 1 (January 1992): 33–57.

Latour, Bruno, and Steve Woolgar. *Laboratory Life: The Construction of Scientific Facts.* Princeton, NJ: Princeton University Press, 1986.

Lindley, Sarah, and Helen Crabbe. "What Lies Beneath? Issues in the Representation of Air Quality Management Data for Public Consumption." *Science of the Total Environment* 334–335 (2004): 307–325.

Marres, Noortje. *Material Participation: Technology, the Environment and Everyday Publics.* London: Palgrave Macmillan, 2012.

"The Issues Deserve More Credit: Pragmatist Contributions to the Study of Public Involvement in Controversy." *Social Studies of Science* 37, no. 5 (January 2007): 759–780.

McCormack, Derek P. "Devices for Doing Atmospheric Things." In *Non-Representational Methodologies*, edited by Phillip Vanni, 89–111. New York: Routledge, 2015.

Mol, Annemarie. *The Body Multiple: Ontology in Medical Practice.* Durham, NC: Duke University Press, 2002.

Murphy, Michelle. *Sick Building Syndrome and the Politics of Uncertainty: Environmental Politics, Technoscience, and Women Workers.* Durham, NC: Duke University Press, 2006.

Perkins, Chris. "Playing with Maps." In *Rethinking Maps: New Frontiers in Cartographic Theory*, edited by Martin Dodge, Rob Kitchin, and Chris Perkins, 167–188. London: Routledge Studies in Human Geography, 2009.

Phillips, Dana, and Heather I. Sullivan. "Material Ecocriticism: Dirt, Waste, Bodies, Food, and Other Matter." *Interdisciplinary Studies in Literature and Environment* 19, no. 3 (January 2012): 445–447.

Pickles, John. *A History of Spaces: Cartographic Reason, Mapping and the Geo-Coded World.* London: Psychology Press, 2004.

Public Lab. *Public Lab.* https://publiclab.org.

Ratto, Matt, and Megan Boler, eds. *DIY Citizenship: Critical Making and Social Media.* Cambridge, MA: MIT Press, 2014.

Shapin, Steven, and Simon Schaffer. *Leviathan and the Air-Pump: Hobbes, Boyle, and the Experimental Life.* With a new introduction by the authors. Princeton, NJ: Princeton University Press, 2011.

Shapiro, Nicholas. "Attuning to the Chemosphere: Domestic Formaldehyde, Bodily Reasoning, and the Chemical Sublime." *Cultural Anthropology* 30, no. 3 (2015): 368–393.

Shapiro, Nicholas, and Eben Kirksey. "Chemo-Ethnography: An Introduction." *Cultural Anthropology* 32, no. 4 (November 2017): 481–493.

Venturini, Tommaso. "Diving in Magma: How to Explore Controversies with Actor-Network Theory." *Public Understanding of Science* 19, no. 3 (January 2010): 258–273.

Wakeford, Nina. "Power Point and the Crafting of Social Data." *Ethnographic Praxis in Industry Conference Proceedings* 2006, no. 1 (September 2006): 94–108.

Wilkie, Alex, and Alvise Mattozzi. "Learning Design through Social Science." In *About Learning and Design*, edited by G. Camuffo, M. Dalla Mura, and A. Mattozzi, 196–203. Bozen-Bolzano: Bozen-Bolzano University Press, 2014.

Yaneva, Albena. *Mapping Controversies in Architecture*. London: Routledge, 2012.

IMAGES

3.1
Still from *Madrid in the Air: 24h* showing nitrogen dioxide (NO_2) levels at night, Royal Academy of Arts London, 2019. Courtesy of the author.

3.2
In the Air montage for Budapest, Kitchen Budapest, 2009. Courtesy of the author.

3.3
Visualization tests at the Visualizar '08: Database City workshop, *In the Air*, Medialab-Prado Madrid, 2008. Courtesy of the author.

3.4
Visualizar '08: Database City workshop at Medialab-Prado Madrid, 2008. Courtesy of the author.

3.5
Initial sketch of digital application, *In the Air*, 2008. Courtesy of the author.

3.6
Victor Viña, Susana Tesconi, and Miguel prototyping the "diffused façade," *In the Air*, Medialab-Prado Madrid, 2008. Courtesy of the author.

3.7
Still from *Madrid in the Air: 24h* showing Madrid's particulate matter (PM_{10}) levels in the morning, Royal Academy of Arts London, 2019. Courtesy of the author.

3.8
Digital application of *In the Air* for Madrid, Medialab-Prado Madrid, 2008. Courtesy of the author.

3.9
In the Air's adaptation to Medialab-Prado's urban screen, Medialab-Prado Madrid, 2008. Courtesy of the author.

3.10
In the Air projection for São Paulo, Digital Art Gallery SESI-SP, São Paulo, 2013. Courtesy of the author.

3.11
In the Air projection for Santiago de Chile, Museo de Arte Contemporáneo de Chile, 2010. Courtesy of the author.

4.1

TOUCHING PARTICULATE MATTER, ATMOSPHERIC INFRASTRUCTURES

Little is known about the Greek physicist and inventor Ctesibius of Alexandria, though he is called the "father of pneumatics." In the second century BC he used hydraulic and steam power to create mechanical singing birds, bursts of flame, and moving statues; he created the first vending machine, automatic door, and wind-powered organ; he wrote prolifically. Across the few books that survive, the ancient inventor explores the concepts of automata or war machines. But his most famous work, known collectively as *Pneumatica*, chronicles his early exploration of steam and hydraulic power and his invention of the aeolipile, considered the world's first steam engine.[1] Centuries would pass until 1698, when its cousin machine—the steam engine patented in Britain—turned air in its vapor state into an energy infrastructure, transforming societies and landscapes, including the aerial one.

The Industrial Revolution put air to work as the engine of "progress" and capitalism by burning the coal that fed steam engine furnaces, which filled the air as well as the soil and the lungs of humans and other living bodies with coal particles. This man-made pollution made visible that air is itself infrastructure, because air, which we breathe, makes possible (most) life on earth. And yet, for many years, the steam engine won over breath. Rapid progress and industrialization were deemed more important than clean air. In 1992, however, the United Nations (UN) declared the atmosphere a "global commons." That is, it designated the atmosphere as a limited resource needed by all humans but overused by some (at the expense of others) and, therefore, as something that needed to be governed by all nations.[2]

---

1 I bring up this reference to keep in mind that not all air-related issues began with the Industrial Revolution but centuries before, and to remind us that the first known air infrastructures come from Alexandria (in today's Egypt). See https://www.popularmechanics.com/science/energy/a34554479/heron-aeolipile.

But the very idea of the commons is unruly. First, I mean this definitionally: The concept can refer to a specific piece of land (like the English Commons, or the Spanish *dehesas*), to different forms of collective management, to valuable entities that need to be preserved (a monument, a language, a ritual, a dish). The commons can be cultural, social, technical, material. However, they are typically associated with joint management of resources. As the UN designation "global commons" suggests, this governance has geopolitical consequences, and one of the difficulties of relating the concept of the commons to the management of resources is that the discussion ends up being dominated by questions of economy and cost—questions that do not take into consideration the human and environmental effects of governance, of producing and deploying infrastructure that is and has been a crucial instrument for ongoing colonization and extraction.

Second, I mean this in terms of the commons' potential to disrupt the world as we know it. For feminist literary scholar and cultural theorist Laurent Berlant the commons refers to the ways in which a world—or many worlds?—is and could be cohabited, as

> a powerful vehicle for troubling troubled times. For the very scenes in which the concept attains power mark the desire for living with some loss of assurance as to one's or one's community's place in the world, at least while better forms of life are invented and tried out. The better power of the commons is to point to a way to view what's broken in sociality, the difficulty

2   According to the United Nations Environment Programme (UNEP), the "global commons" refer to resource domains or areas that lie outside the political reach of any one nation-state: the high seas, the atmosphere, Antarctica, and outer space. They are resources that no one owns but all life relies upon and are therefore under the care of all nations. These resources are both economic and geopolitical. When detailing them as resources they include the atmosphere and land, the oceans and ice sheets, a stable climate and abundant biodiversity, the forests, the gigantic flows of carbon, nitrogen, water, and phosphorus, and more. The role of the UNEP has been to define boundaries, tipping points, and so on. See Silke Helfrich, *Genes, Bytes y Emisiones: Bienes Comunes y Ciudadanía*; Naomi Klein, *This Changes Everything: Capitalism vs. the Climate*.

of convening a world conjointly, although it is inconvenient and hard, and to offer incitements to imagining a livable provisional life... [to] learning to live with messed up yet shared and ongoing infrastructures of experience.[3]

I find Berlant's approach particularly exciting to think with because she reorients the term away from managing an object, resource, or action and toward living in/with the contradictions of "troubled times." Berlant's proposition isn't any less pragmatic. It takes the difficult context of our worlds as the point of departure and provides a framework to imagine the interventions that would be desirable, possible, and needed to establish better forms of life—what she calls "infrastructures for troubling times." She proposes the commons as a troubling concept—and therefore orients us away from solutions—which acknowledges the need to learn to live with the "messed up and yet shared and ongoing" and the difficulty and effort of imagining a shared world. For Berlant, the concept is productive because it affirms a desire to live without the certainty of belonging to a community, at least while other (not newer, better) forms of life are tested; and is a provocation to desire a livable life, which can only be provisional. Furthermore, the commons orient us toward "what's broken in sociality" to start wondering how to intervene in it.

What if, with Berlant, we shift our understanding of airs as the matter we breathe toward an atmospheric infrastructure that sustains our breath? Which is to say, what if we consider global commons as infrastructures? This is a change of scale as well as an ontological one. Because a resource "can" be extracted, but an infrastructure needs to be cared for and requires budgets, organizations, negotiations... And what if when that infrastructure is broken, we do not simply maintain the current order of things but "generate [alternative] form from within the brokenness beyond the

---

3   Lauren Berlant, "The Commons: Infrastructures for Troubling Times," 395.

exigencies of the current crisis"?[4] From this perspective, what could an infrastructure of a global commons—an infrastructure of an infrastructure, so to speak—mean or look like? And what about those related to toxicpolluted air?

INFRASTRUCTURES FOR AIR AS A COMMON

Filters are the most common and distributed infrastructures for toxicpolluted air. They establish what is let in—into a building, a car, your lungs—and what needs to be released or kept out. They are made of fabrics, meshes, glues, metals. Filters are porous membranes of all sizes that cover almost everything in a city's aeropolis: they are chimneys, masks, windows...

Other air infrastructures manage air quality to explore the air's composition, like the automated and networked technologies that populate urban environments and the skies (ground monitoring stations, satellites) to monitor the distribution and concentration levels of gases and particles for policymaking and regulation. Other infrastructures are designed to "clean" pollutant concentrations. Large geoengineering projects branded as sustainable solutions are developed in scientific institutes and tech, oil, or construction corporations, to purify urban air or sequester carbon in the deep layers of the earth.[5] But—even if these projects were successful—the effectiveness of these interventions in reducing pollutants is minimal compared to the scale of the issue. And most importantly, these projects sustain the economic system that causes the pollution in the first place—considering that many of the proponents of these infrastructures are the corporations and nation-states that pollute most. So, if the large, expensive (and polluting) engineering infrastructures that we know are unfit—and if the new ones (like sequestration through

164

4   Berlant, "The Commons," 393.
5   For instance, the air-purifying tower built in Xi'an, China, and Quest, the partnership between Shell, Canada Energy, and Chevron to capture, transport, and store CO_2 deep underground.

regenerative agriculture, afforestation, biochar, etc.) that appear to "reform" pollution are really just in service of capital expansion—which other infrastructures are needed?[6]

To be clear: the only way out is to stop polluting. But moving from a cleaning approach toward a nonpolluting one—and therefore to a scenario in which the commons are protected—requires more than (clean) infrastructures. It requires deep structural, cultural, political, energetic, and economic changes. Changes that are hard to enact and possibly even harder to imagine. The urgency becomes more pressing every day. So, while working on the structural changes, the present—understood as a moment in transition—also requires attention. As Berlant argues,

> To attend to the terms of transition is to forge an imaginary
> for managing the meanwhile within damaged life's perdurance,
> a meanwhile that is less an end or an ethical scene than
> a technical political heuristic that allows for ambivalence,
> distraction, antagonism and inattention not to destroy
> collective existence.[7]

Forging this imaginary is an opportunity—and a responsibility, according to Berlant—for experimentation. Then how else could we imagine the infrastructure of air as a global commons?

For techno-science, infrastructures are material devices to solve specific problems in the most efficient way. Science and technology studies have shown that they are much more: socio-technical assemblages composed of hard, soft, human, and nonhuman entities, situated and networked in different ways.[8] Artist Natalie Jeremijenko has

6   To meet the climate change targets, scientists and policy makers are debating whether, in addition to emissions reductions, geoengineering projects are needed to remove the pollution that is already there. For a great discussion on the state of the art of geoengineering projects, their challenges and opportunities, see Holly Jean Buck, *After Geoengineering: Climate Tragedy, Repair, and Restoration.*
7   Berlant, "The Commons," 394.
8   Stephen Graham and Simon Marvin, *Splintering Urbanism: Networked Infrastructures, Technological Mobilities and the Urban Condition*; Susan Leigh and Geoffrey Bowker, "How to Infrastructure";

challenged the goals, materiality, and scale of engineering infrastructures through her "lifestyle experiments": small interventions that put to work living entities in an attempt to understand how complex systems work (hurricanes, flooding, species extinction, etc.), and to test the design of infrastructures that take this complexity into account.[9] Jeremijenko's lifestyle experiments have multiple and overlapping aims, entangled at various scales. Most importantly, they are not conceived as silver bullets that "solve the problem" but rather as ways to get a better (and closer) understanding of the specificities of each site. In Berlant's words, to experiment to find out what's broken and to trouble troubled times.

With Jeremijenko, I am interested in expanding what infrastructures can do, to consider their different scales, temporalities, and experimental capacities. I am particularly interested in reflecting on the potential of the infrastructures that manage the "terms of transition that alter the harder and softer, tighter and looser infrastructures of sociality itself."[10]

AIR INFRASTRUCTURES FOR THE COMMONS

Jeremijenko proposes that we evaluate an infrastructure's success in relation to its contributions to human and environmental health—instead of how it relates to the economy and costs.[11] In other words, how can an infrastructure *of* a common (the air) also be an

Lea Schick and Brit Ross Winthereik, "Making Energy Infrastructure: Tactical Oscillations and Cosmopolitics"; and Susan Leigh Star, "The Ethnography of Infrastructure."

9   For instance, in the project "Cross [X] Species Construction," a sandcastle competition in the Rockaways after Hurricane Sandy, Jeremijenko "discovered" that, to replenish the beach after the hurricane, the Army Corps of Engineers had used sand from a nearby riverbed full of nutrients, which did not belong to the seaside ecosystem, creating algae bloom. In Jeremijenko's words: "This small-pocket experiment demonstrated that these actions taken by the Army Corps and the politicians in the so-called public interest, were not." See Delia Hannah and Natalie Jeremijenko, "Natalie Jeremijenko's New Experimentalism," 205. Jeremikenko's work has been a constant inspiration.

10 Berlant, "The Commons," 394.

11 And I would add that we evaluate this success in relation to its contribution to social and environmental justice, too.

infrastructure *for* the common, one that addresses other ways of being together? Infrastructures for the commons acknowledge a broken world but they also trigger new ways of living in it. How do we start thinking about infrastructures to deal with airs in our context of industrial toxicity, financial insecurity, and permanent war in ways that enable other forms of cohabitation?

For Berlant, the commons often reinforce an idea of the collective based on agreement and belonging (to a community or a state, for instance). Considering the challenges that these idealistic approaches imply in terms of who belongs to those commons and how—inspired by non-sovereign critiques and decolonial theory—I follow Berlant in her proposal to imagine being in common by being with, holding space for, and actively (and intimately) feeling difference as opposed to a unified (dissident or not) collectivity or sense of belonging. That is, in Berlant's words:

> the disturbance of being close without being joined. And without mistaking the other's flesh for one's own or any object world as identical to oneself. Nonsovereignty is not here the dissolution of a boundary. It's the experience of affect, of being receptive, in real time.[12]

But how can this common be achieved, and if so, designed? Philosopher Marina Garcés proposes moving from a "what to do" mentality to one that focuses instead on changing our modes of dealing with things, with each other, and with the world.[13] To do this, Garcés proposes that we shift from modes focused on representation and action—like the Greenpeace campaigns of past decades, where banners were hung from offshore oil platforms to make visible the responsible actors of environmental disasters and the work of LGTBQI+ communities during the AIDS/HIV epidemic—

167

12   Berlant, "The Commons," 402.
13   Marina Garcés, *Un Mundo Común*.

toward attention and treatment. For Garcés, this means to pay closer attention to what surrounds us and understand what those surroundings require us to do, and to think about how to treat things, the world, and ourselves. Thus, paying attention to existing air infrastructures and unpacking their material, social, and political assemblages might provide an idea of what is at stake, how certain narratives are being articulated and, eventually, the effects of certain design decisions.

TOUCHING DATA

To explore these questions in practice, let's look at *Yellow Dust*, a project commissioned for the Seoul Biennale of Architecture and Urbanism 2017 titled "Imminent Commons."[14] *Yellow Dust* was a mist canopy that measured, made visible, and partially remediated the particulate matter suspended in a courtyard of Donuimun Museum Village, one of the venues of the Biennale. In line with Garcés, *Yellow Dust* was conceived as an infrastructure to deal with the toxic air in a common world; an infrastructure that acknowledges a broken world but might trigger other ways of living in it. Instead of asking what to do with polluted air, it tested modes of paying attention to it; instead of cleaning polluted air, it aimed to explore other forms of treating, engaging, and sensing it, physically, emotionally, culturally, poetically.[15]

14 *Yellow Dust*
   Exhibition: Seoul Biennale of Architecture and Urbanism 2017
   Authors: C+arquitectos/*In the Air* (Nerea Calvillo with Raúl Nieves, Pep Tornabell, Toby Chai, Emma Garnett, Marina Fernández), with the collaboration of Victor Viña
   Details: 2017, 12 m², Seoul, $35,000
   Images: Daniel Ruiz and Nerea Calvillo
   Support: Acción Cultural Española and an impact ESRC IAA grant from the University of Warwick and the Economic and Social Research Council (ESRC)
   Thank you to Raúl, Pep, and Toby for being there for adventures and making them happen.
15 I refer to *Yellow Dust* as an infrastructure (instead of an installation, for instance) to focus on its performative capacity, to look and think about what it does or can do—instead of what it looks like, for example—and to reinforce its transformative capacities and multiple agencies.

Designing Atmospheric Infrastructures

Studies on the impact of air pollution data on citizens have demonstrated that information does not necessarily produce behavioral changes. In fact, quite often it creates indifference and eventually fear.[16] Maybe one of the reasons is that data requires interpretation, and scientific visualization formats require a certain visual literacy. Artistic or architecture projects like artists Andrea Polli's *Particle Falls* or *The Living's Living Light* have worked on creating more seductive encounters with data in public spaces. Yet all these cases reinforce vision as *the* primary way of knowing. What if instead of making data visible, we make it sensible?

One challenge is that in scientific visualizations, temperature, precipitation, or particles in the air, for instance, are described on the same graphs or pie charts with a label as the only differentiator. The material properties of these elements are never represented, becoming only abstract entities. What if we pay attention to the material properties of pollution and play that out? What if visualizations perform like the objects they're supposed to represent? For instance, artist Olafur Eliasson, in his work *Green river*, dyed rivers with uranine, a nontoxic water-soluble dye. Eliasson acknowledges how "this act of dying a river green has been used by others for a number of reasons—by scientists tracing water currents, by the city of Chicago to celebrate St. Patrick's Day, and by activist organisations like Extinction Rebellion, to name a few."[17] Following in this tradition, *Yellow Dust* aimed to make the air visible in order to register "the constantly changing, yet overlooked agencies, that make up our natural-cultural environment." It was an experiment to test whether, instead of seeing information about air pollution, collectively sensing it—sensing as "feeling"—would produce other responses and affects.

16 Andrew Barry, *Political Machines: Governing a Technological Society*.
17 Olafur Eliasson, *Green river*, 1998.

Materiality poses resistance to ideas. And this is why having to build a project—and not just think about it—is such a fascinating exercise. Air's fluidity and constant transformation became an opportunity to explore alternative ways of getting to know toxicity.

In 2008, I visited an atmospheric scientist at my former university. When I asked her how to "taint" the air to make it visible, she responded furiously that I had no idea what I was talking about, that it was not only absurd and difficult, but also illegal to release gases or particles into the air (I have since then wondered how factories get around this). This encounter lingered. It shaped how we would come to realize the prototype that became *Yellow Dust* years later—in that we thought there were no materials to work with. Until water came to mind. What if we intensified one of the air's most abundant components, water vapor, to create a mist?[18]

Of all the gases and particles that compose the air, which ones should be made evident? Components with the highest concentrations, or the most controversial? Local emissions or transboundary ones? Paying attention to what matters about pollution and which particles and gases (and effects) are made visible is a form of making air pollution a matter of concern, of airing the issue of pollution. What if we take the chance to air not only pollution's concentrations but also its politics and affects?

With *Yellow Dust* we decided to pay attention to particulate matter. Particulate matter concentrations are usually high in Seoul, but the government and the media attribute them to *hwangsa* (yellow dust in Korean),

18 This was not new. Diller & Scofidio had built the Blur Building, a large fog building created for Expo 2002 in Lausanne, Switzerland. The architects, inspired by *Fog Sculpture*, created by artist Fujiko Nakaya for the Pepsi Pavilion (Osaka, 1970), were interested in the blurring capacity of fog: "Blur is not a building, Blur is pure atmosphere, water particles suspended in mid-air. The fog is a dynamic, phantom mass, which changes form constantly. Blur is a constant battle between artificial and real weather forces." Elizabeth Diller and Ricardo Scofidio, *Blur: The Making of Nothing*, 325.

transboundary fine soil particles carried by the wind from Mongolia and northern China mostly during the spring—bringing with them other types of industrial pollutants. Although there are frequently high levels of particles created by local sources, the notion of *hwangsa* creates a sense of matter out of place.[19] Of a nonhuman invasion that reinforces the distinction between local and foreign air, which triggers legal and political international conflicts. What forms of intervention could be opened up so as not to get trapped in colonial biases and forms of dealing with "the other"?

Yellow Dust aimed to unsettle the idea of the yellow dust as a foreign entity. During the months when *hwangsa* did not happen, *Yellow Dust* showed how there was still particle pollution in Seoul's atmosphere, to help visitors identify and locate themselves within aerial conditions that are simultaneously local and planetary. In reference to *hwangsa*, the mist of *Yellow Dust* was colored with yellow light to put this cultural bias to work, with the idea that when *hwangsa* arrives, *Yellow Dust* disappears, emerging only with local emissions. During the design process we realized that this decision did not comply with the assumption that all air pollution visualizations correspond to the air quality index—the color gradient that correlates particle concentrations with their effects on human health. The reason for avoiding this relation was to find other modes of attending to the air beyond human health.[20] This was not to imply that human health does not matter. On the contrary, it took into consideration that every body—human or more than human—reacts to pollution, only differently. So, to

19   Marie Douglas, *Purity and Danger: An Analysis of Concepts of Pollution and Taboo.*
20   David Shooter and Peter Brimblecombe, "Air Quality Indexing."

account for all these diverse sensitivities, *Yellow Dust* did not address any specific body, and focused on what touches the collective, the social implications of pollution. In an exhibition space adjacent to *Yellow Dust*, we mapped Seoul's main particulate emitters. The public was touched to see the impact of barbecue restaurants and saunas, central to celebrations and communal gatherings, in the quality of the airs they breathed.

The soft mist of humidity that is possible when working with water vapor turns data into something that can be felt tickling the skin, opening the nostrils, freshening the lungs. It makes data permeable, democratizing the perception of air pollution and highlighting the unevenness of its effects. Only sensitive bodies sense pollution, but it is likely that more bodies sense humidity.

On days with high particle concentrations (*hwangsa*-related or not), several modes of sensing *Yellow Dust* overlapped: one could see (the color of pollution, the color of the mist), one could touch (through the moisture of humidity and the temperature of the mist), and one could feel in the nose, eyes, or lungs (for particle-sensitive bodies). Water vapor sometimes alleviates the symptoms of asthma, so the infrastructure may also have served as a relief to some. Overall, it produced an overlapped—and even excessive—sensorial experience. Thus, the de-coding of air pollution was not immediate, and it may have taken time for passersby to be able to compare particle concentrations with earlier hours or previous days. *Yellow Dust* moved away from speed-of-information tropes, and it required time to get to know it, and for bodies to become trained to sense the different atmospheric intensities.

Adding moisture to polluting particles is literally wetting data. It transforms the temperature and humidity of the air, which can be useful in acclimatizing the outdoors space during the dry seasons of autumn and spring (during the wet season, as there is normally no air pollution, there would be no water vapor). And as water deposits particles, the mist might reduce concentrations of polluting particles in that specific location. What if an infrastructure monitors, makes visible, and remediates at the same time?

By wetting the data, *Yellow Dust* also wet the city, helping remediate particulate matter concentrations in Donuimun. Therefore, by adding a second sensor, we turned *Yellow Dust* into an experiment in remediation. *Yellow Dust* grew and moved with the wind, making visible the density of suspended particles as well as meteorological conditions. Experiencing *Yellow Dust*, it was not possible to distinguish between the technology and the matter upon which it acted. The water vapor conjoined with the air. So, not only did the infrastructure become atmospheric, but it made the air infrastructural, too—by being the support of its own data, literally making itself visible. *Yellow Dust* was both sensible and inapprehensible, intensifying its experiential potential to create atmospheric attunements with the toxic air: encounters registered beyond reason, collective, difficult to explain?

It could be argued that *Yellow Dust* created a kind of atmospheric media that brought together technologies and urban conditions below the threshold of sensing.[21] Media and the air became the same thing: they became elemental conditions.[22] Conditions that, as geographer Derek McCormack suggests, act like a chemical interaction, as a milieu, and as an environment.[23]

21   Nigel Thrift, "Remembering the Technological Unconscious by Foregrounding Knowledges of Position."
22   Derek P. McCormack, "Elemental Infrastructures for Atmospheric Media: On Stratospheric Variations, Value and the Commons."
23   Derek P. McCormack, *Atmospheric Things: On the Allure of Elemental Envelopment.*

Within infrastructures and built environment research, building as a social-material process is rarely paid attention to. The fixation on the origin story (a sketch, an inspiration) and on the finished (built) project hides everything beyond those glorified moments. However, the construction phase is a messy process where economies, politics, affects, exclusions, techniques are done—or undone; where certain bodies (usually the migrant, ethnic minority, socially vulnerable) are put at risk; and where the material and social contexts create friction and resistance to change. Construction demands touch, by and across many people. We can consider construction as being in touch—and more often than not, this kind of coming into contact is conflictive, not unproblematic. At the same time, touching is a matter of care, as feminist author María Puig de la Bellacasa writes:

> Standing here as a metonymic way to access the lived and fleshy character of involved care relations, the haptic holds promises against the primacy of detached vision, a promise of thinking and knowing that is "in touch" with materiality, touched and touching. Yet the promises of this onto-epistemic turn to touch are not unproblematic. If anything, they increase the intense corporeality of ethical questioning.[24]

Puig de la Bellacasa's ethical questioning detaches touch from an exclusively phenomenological approach, and its beautiful "intense corporeality" brings ethics to the material realm. Who, why, and how do touch interactions take place? What is gained, learned, or rejected?

> When producing and assembling *Yellow Dust*—between Barcelona and Seoul—we (the design and construction team) came into contact with other commons, other forms

24 María Puig de la Bellacasa, "Matters of Care in Technoscience: Assembling Neglected Things," 95.

of collectivity, other understandings of infrastructures. We had to get acquainted with water vapor and its own technical infrastructure. We had to spend time testing (at two collaborators' workshop and home in Barcelona) how to create mist—and not water droplets. To train our eyes to the different densities of the mist. To attune our skin to sense intensities of wetness. Instead of trying to control the air we had to train our bodies to be touched, physically and symbolically, by the mist. Even when we did not want it. Even when it was inconvenient and the summer heat too oppressive.

Due to multiple unknowns, the structure was bought and assembled in Seoul, which, together with the setting-up of the sensors, assembling the different components, testing the system, and getting access to water, Wi-Fi, and electricity, required more experimentation than we had expected. We had to explore other forms of treating each other. We had to establish alliances and new rhythms with everyone on-site, as everyone's work seemed to depend on others: the team, the local contractor, the curators, the contractor's representative on-site, a translator. This was a daily negotiation. Our needs as designers always seemed misaligned or ahead of everyone's capacities to meet them. We also had to learn to communicate with the salespeople of the materials shops, who did not speak English and could not be bothered for a couple of screws—understandably so.

We encountered strong resistance: from the air, which evaded being measured, to intense weather conditions. I had never lived through a monsoon before, never felt air so saturated with water. Water did not leave my skin. I felt like my body would end up dissolving in the air. As Garcés and many feminist thinkers have claimed for decades, without noticing it, we had to put our bodies in the air and in the experiment: to build, to sweat, to argue, to test, to get touched. And again, coming into contact with water meant coming into contact with other people.

Air and water were confronted as a commons in a challenging way. Due to the delays in the restoration of the village we were provided water only a few days before the opening from a hose connected to the courtyard of another pavilion. The tap leaked, and the participant located in that pavilion refused to have the tap open. Coincidentally, their project was about water management in California. So, droughts on the West Coast of the United States were confronted alongside air pollution in Seoul. One common against another. We had to keep in touch with water. This conflict, as with many other tensions that emerged, was not sorted out through deliberations and consensus. Temporary alliances, compromises, back-and-forths, provisional solutions, and a lot of stress enabled everyone and everything to cohabit the same space, just being next to each other, as a form of commoning.[25]

"Commoning" Infrastructures

It is widely known that infrastructures tend to be hidden, often buried underground. From the sewage tunnels of the nineteenth century to the service basement of Mies van der Rohe's Barcelona Pavillion, as architect Andrés Jaque has made visible.[26] They are

176

25 Nerea Cavillo, "Involvement as an Ethics for More than Human Interdependencies."
26 See: Andrés Jaque, *Mies y La Gata Niebla: Ensayos Sobre Arquitectura y Cosmopolítica.* Many other projects by Jaque/The Office of Political Innovation are a key reference for this. I still remember the excitement I felt when I saw the project *12 Actions to Make Peter Eisenman Transparent* (2010),

the spaces, materials, technologies and practices required for other systems to function, and air infrastructures are no different. Scientific and policy-driven air monitoring infrastructures tend to be invisibilized as well. They are black boxed—literally, steel boxes with no indication of their purpose camouflaged in public space—focused on gathering the most accurate and stable data. One of the problems with these widespread systems is that their invisibility reduces the possibilities of people understanding their performance, and therefore limits our potential to intervene.[27] Sociologist Fernando Dominguez Rubio and architect Uriel Fogué argue that urban infrastructures can do more than manage urban resources: they can make the resources participate in public life and can propose different forms of citizenship.[28] What if we make not only the air visible, but also the infrastructure itself? What are the limits of visibilizing an infrastructure? Can this process be a form of commoning, and if so, how?

> *Yellow Dust* revealed its own infrastructure: the steel cable supporting the water vaporizers, the sensors, the cables that channeled the water, the LED lights... and also all the devices required for this infrastructure to function: the water pump, the microcontrollers, the Arduino... From an ecosystemic perspective, it also made visible what it takes to monitor and display air pollution information, through small water and energy meters that displayed their own consumption. The project engaged with the toxicity of the city by revealing the monitoring process, making the infrastructure's performance visible, as—in

177

which, by providing different colored helmets to the workers of different construction companies, made visible the complex logistics involved in building a singular project, Cidade da Cultura in Santiago de Compostela.

27 Anne Galloway, "Intimations of Everyday Life: Ubiquitous Computing and the City."

28 Fernando Domínguez Rubio and Uriel Fogué, "Technifying Public Space and Publicizing Infrastructures: Exploring New Urban Political Ecologies through the Square of General Vara Del Rey"; on infrastructures and visibility see also: Uriel Fogué, "Ecología Política y Economía de La Visibilidad de Los Dispositivos Tecnológicos de Escala Urbana Durante El Siglo XX Abriendo La Caja Negra."

the words of Dominguez Rubio and Fogué—a way of politicizing it.

We also aimed to make *Yellow Dust* replicable. Diagrams explaining the hardware installation were made available to render the project not only an infrastructure of the common air but also an infrastructure for an expanded idea of the commons, one that addresses alternative ways of being together. To this day we don't know if any group or grassroots organization has restaged *Yellow Dust*. Against rhetoric entrenched in makers or open source communities, it has become clear that sharing the "how-to" is not enough. Because an infrastructure requires materials—and therefore budgets—and material changes—and therefore labor. A huge effort is needed to mobilize an infrastructure in other contexts.

Unexpected common socialities did emerge. Through an ethnography conducted by anthropologist Emma Garnett we later realized how, instead of creating a space for discussion about air pollution, the collectivity that took place under the mist was much closer to Berlant's proposal of the commons: people were next to one another, engaged in different activities: asking questions about air pollution, playing, resting, chatting, meeting other people, taking selfies... With Garnett we have argued that this form of collectivity was articulated through "molecular intimacies," where a sense of intimacy and belonging was achieved through molecular exchanges between air particles, water droplets, and humans' breath and skin.[29] *Yellow Dust* did not create a parliament where humans and more-than-humans come together. It created

29 Nerea Calvillo and Emma Garnett. "Data Intimacies: Building Infrastructures for Intensified Embodied Encounters with Air Pollution."

a blurry space of cohabitation where intimacy could also take place, to echo Berlant's words, closer to the idea of proximity and of being receptive, of being in the same place without distinctions in relation to citizenship or sovereignty.

Yellow Dust engaged with air as a global commons not by cleaning its pollution but by making Seoul's pollution sensible, as a form of asking questions about shared responsibilities. What gets touched by particulate matter? Who makes the air untouchable? *Yellow Dust* moved away from framings of air pollution as an individual health risk to consider it a common issue that affects public health (and the health of animals, plants, buildings, and so forth); public budgets; corporations' responsibility (and lack thereof); forms of energy production; and social and environmental inequality, among others. Overall, *Yellow Dust* was a speculation—and an experiment, in line with Jeremijenko—of what air design can do to engage with the urbanisms of the air, what it can mean to treat the environment, and more specifically air pollution, differently. And it was a fragile, precarious, and temporary experiment on how to have better airs, as well as on how to (better) live in a shared world; a fragile, precarious, and temporary experiment on touching infrastructure. Like geographer Sasha Engelmann and visual researcher and designer Sophie Dyer's fascinating Open Weather project, where they consider how long-distance satellite signals touch landscapes, bodies, and atmospheres while imagining what a more equitable planetary radio might sound like.[30]

Just to be clear, I am not arguing that proposals like *Yellow Dust* will "solve the problem" of air pollution, as I am often asked. To solve the problem of air pollution, at the very least, stopping economic growth and radically changing the ways in which energy, food, and manufactured products are used and produced are needed.

30   Sasha Engelmann, "Planetary Radio."

Yellow Dust was a step toward change, or as Berlant suggests, a step toward materializing a provisional infrastructure: One that would, as philosopher of science Isabelle Stengers has so vividly invited us to do, contribute to "repopulating the devastated desert of our environmental imaginations."[31] One that would imagine other relations with our urban ecologies. One that would propose a more common prototype for public space and the air.[32] One that would fundamentally ask whether, by staying in the mist as a form of being in and with the problem, we could come up with other possible futures and engage with air pollution differently.

4.2

31 Isabelle Stengers, *In Catastrophic Times: Resisting the Coming Barbarism*, 132.
32 Alberto Corsín, "The Right to Infrastructure: A Prototype for Open Source Urbanism."

4.3

4.4

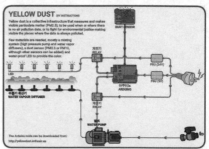

YELLOW DUST DIY INSTRUCTIONS

Yellow dust is a collective infrastructure that measures and makes visible particulate matter (PM2.5), to be used when or where there is no air pollution data, or to fight for environmental justice making visible the places where the data is always polluted.

Few materials are needed, mostly a misting system (high pressure pump and water vapor diffusers), a dust sensor (PM2.5 or PM10, although other sensors can be added) and water-proof LED to provide the color.

The Arduino code can be downloaded from:
http://yellowdust.infinoia.us

4.5

4.6

4.7

4.8

4.9

4.10

4.11

WORKS CITED

Barry, Andrew. *Political Machines: Governing a Technological Society*. London: The Atholone Press, 2001.

Berlant, Lauren. "The Commons: Infrastructures for Troubling Times." *Environment and Planning D: Society and Space* 34, no. 3 (2016): 393–419.

Buck, Holly Jean. *After Geoengineering: Climate Tragedy, Repair and Restoration*. New York: Verso, 2019.

Calvillo, Nerea. "Air Infrastructures for the Common." In *Imminent Commons: Urban Questions for the Near Future*, edited by Alejandro Zaera-Polo and Hyungmin Pai, 54–59. Barcelona: Actar, 2017.

"Involvement as an Ethics for More than Human Interdependencies." In *Ecological Reparation: Repair, Remediation and Resurgence in Social and Environmental Conflict*, edited by Dimitris Papadopoulos, María Puig de la Bellacasa, and Maddalena Tachetti, 137–152. Bristol: Bristol University Press, 2023.

Calvillo, Nerea, and Emma Garnett. "Data Intimacies: Building Infrastructures for Intensified Embodied Encounters with Air Pollution." *The Sociological Review Monographs* 67, no. 2 (2019): 340–356.

Corsín, Alberto. "The Right to Infrastructure: A Prototype for Open Source Urbanism." *Environment and Planning D: Society and Space* 32, no. 2 (April 2014): 342–362.

Diller, Elizabeth, and Ricardo Scofidio. *Blur: The Making of Nothing*. Harry N. Abrams, 2002.

Domínguez Rubio, Fernando, and Uriel Fogué. "Technifying Public Space and Publicizing Infrastructures: Exploring New Urban Political Ecologies through the Square of General Vara Del Rey." *International Journal of Urban and Regional Research* 37, no. 3 (2013): 1035–1052.

Douglas, Mary. *Purity and Danger: An Analysis of Concepts of Pollution and Taboo*. Classics Series. London: Routledge, 1966.

Engelmann, Sasha. "Planetary Radio." *The Contemporary Journal*, no. 3 (March 2021).

Fogué, Uriel. "Ecología Política y Economía de La Visibilidad de Los Dispositivos Tecnológicos de Escala Urbana Durante El Siglo XX Abriendo La Caja Negra." *E.T.S. Arquitectura*, Universidad Politécnica de Madrid, 2015.

Galloway, Anne. "Intimations of Everyday Life. Ubiquitous Computing and the City." *Cultural Studies* 18, no. 2/3 (May 2004): 384–408.

Garcés, Marina. *Un Mundo Común*. Barcelona: Ediciones Bellaterra, 2013.

Graham, Stephen and Marvin, Simon. *Splintering Urbanism: Networked Infrastructures, Technological Mobilities and the Urban Condition*. London: Routledge, 2009.

Hannah, Delia, and Natalie Jeremijenko. "Natalie Jeremijenko's New Experimentalism." In *Anthropocene Feminism*, edited by Richard Grusin, 197–220. Minneapolis, MN: University of Minnesota Press, 2017.

Helfrich, Silke, ed. *Genes, Bytes y Emisiones: Bienes Comunes y Ciudadanía*. Mexico: Fundación Heinrich Böll, 2008.

Jaque, Andrés. *Mies y La Gata Niebla: Ensayos Sobre Arquitectura y Cosmopolítica*. Barcelona: Puente Editores, 2019.

Klein, Naomi. *This Changes Everything: Capitalism vs. The Climate*. New York: Simon & Schuster, 2014.

Leigh, Susan, and Geoffrey C. Bowker. "How to Infrastructure." In *The Handbook of New Media*, edited by Leah A Lievrouw and Sonia Livingstone, 230–245. London: Sage, 2006.

McCormack, Derek P. *Atmospheric Things: On the Allure of Elemental Envelopment*. Durham, NC: Duke University Press, 2018.

"Elemental Infrastructures for Atmospheric Media: On Stratospheric Variations, Value and the Commons." *Environment and Planning D: Society and Space* 35, no. 3 (2016): 1–20.

Puig de la Bellacasa, María. "Matters of Care in Technoscience: Assembling Neglected Things." *Social Studies of Science* 41, no. 1 (January 2011): 85–106.

Schick, Lea, and Brit Ross Winthereik. "Making Energy Infrastructure: Tactical Oscillations and Cosmopolitics." *Science as Culture* 25, no. 1 (January 2016): 44–68.

Shooter, David, and Peter Brimblecombe. "Air Quality Indexing." *International Journal of Environment and Pollution* 36, no. 1/2/3 (2009): 305.

Star, Susan Leigh. "The Ethnography of Infrastructure." *American Behavioral Scientist* 43, no. 3 (January 1999): 377–391.

Stengers, Isabelle. *In Catastrophic Times: Resisting the Coming Barbarism*. Translated by Andrew Goffey. London: Open Humanities Press, 2015.

Thrift, Nigel. "Remembering the Technological Unconscious by Foregrounding Knowledges of Position." *Environment and Planning D: Society and Space* 22, no. 1 (2004): 175–190.

IMAGES

4.1–4.11
Unless otherwise noted, all images are from *Yellow Dust*, C+arquitectas/*In the Air*, Seoul Biennale of Architecture and Urbanism 2017. Photographs courtesy of the author.

4.1
Building *Yellow Dust*.

4.2
The installation. Photograph by Daniel Ruiz.

4.3
Raul Nieves building *Yellow Dust*'s data processor and interaction system.

4.4
Testing *Yellow Dust*'s water vapor system in ▮ʋɾʋʋɩʋɾɩɑ, ⌐ʋ⊺⌐.

4.5
DIY instructions to replicate *Yellow Dust* provided on postcards.

4.6
Builders trying to fix *Yellow Dust*'s water supply, Seoul, 2017.

4.7
Yellow Dust PM_{10} sensor detail. Photograph by Daniel Ruiz.

4.8
Testing *Yellow Dust*.

4.9
Monsoon rain, Seoul, 2017.

4.10
Women in traditional costumes at the opening in front of *Yellow Dust*.

4.11
Sensors. Photograph by Daniel Ruiz.

HOLDING HELIUM AND NITROGEN, AIR DESIGN

Security smoke released to capture robbers. Women's March in Leicester Square. Auschwitz. Protests in Taksim Square. Mosquito fumigation. The Electric Circus. The Haitian Revolution. Wildfires. Weather modification in China...

How does air serve certain ends? How does one work with the material composition of particles and gases? How does one design airs? What does it mean to speculate with/in airs in the physical world?

These are not hypothetical questions. Everyone and everything is in a constant exchange with airs: absorbing, releasing, accumulating gases and particles. In and out. We breathe. Plants breathe. Factories breathe. Cities breathe. And some industries and institutions ("security" departments, entertainment companies, weapons industries, etc.) design machines, devices, and infrastructures where airs are put to work, where airs are designed to carry out various (geopolitical) projects.

One of the ways airs are put to work is by using them as a vehicle for other substances. Chemical laboratories collaborate with the military to develop weapons that release deadly gases, like the yellow gas bombs used by the Germans in World War I. Cultural theorist Peter Sloterdijk writes that this was the starting point of what he calls "air design"—where mass destruction was, for the first time, conducted by poisoning the environment instead of individuals directly.[1] This warfare technique was further developed during World War II. The Germans released Zyklon B into gas chambers to kill over one million people—the poison gas was produced, perversely, with the slave labor at Auschwitz and other concentration camps. With the development of cyanide-based pesticides, these chemicals were used after the war to fumigate crops on a large scale, to kill "invasive" insects, thus becoming a fundamental technology in the propagation of monocrop agriculture. More recently, cyanide

1   Peter Sloterdijk, *Terror from the Air*.

bombs have been *planted* by the thousands by a public agency in the United States to kill coyotes and other animals that cause problems to private agricultural interests.[2] Another form of aerial warfare has been conducted against insects like mosquitoes, where large territories are fumigated to kill these vectors of deadly malaria, dengue, and other diseases. After more than seventy years, insecticide and herbicide companies have become multibillion-dollar corporations operating around the world, hand in hand with the development of GMO species. This is all happening despite how consistently it has been proven that these chemicals are responsible for the slow deaths of humans and other-than-humans, for poisoning the land, reducing biodiversity, slowly damaging certain organs, and economically suffocating the poor.[3] Conversely, air has also been put to work in warfare by removing some of its components, oxygen in particular, like the "vacuum bombs" that Russia has been reported to use in its invasion of Ukraine since March 2022.[4]

Taking the notion of "air design" literally—that is, to change air's composition with a specific purpose, although not necessarily to kill—sheds light on an even wider range of implicated practices, technologies, and bodies. Again, to be clear, the aim of looking through the weaponization of air is not to undermine the brutality of

2   "If you haven't heard of the US agency that placed the bomb, you're not alone. Its name is Wildlife Services, and for years it has operated in relative obscurity, with limited oversight from Congress or the American public. Housed in the Department of Agriculture, the agency primarily works on behalf of private ranchers and farmers, killing coyotes, wolves, bears, birds and other creatures that cause problems for agricultural interests. In 2018, it exterminated nearly 1.5 million native animals, and a huge number of invasive animals as well." Jimmy Tobias, "The Secretive Government Agency Planting 'Cyanide Bombs' across the US."

3   Vandana Shiva, *One Earth, One Humanity vs. the 1%*.

4   "The thermobaric weapon, also known as an aerosol bomb or fuel air explosive, is a two-stage munition. The first-stage charge distributes an aerosol made up of very fine material—from a carbon-based fuel to tiny metal particles. A second charge ignites that cloud, creating a fireball, a huge shock wave, and a vacuum as it sucks up all surrounding oxygen. The blast wave can last for significantly longer than a conventional explosive and is capable of vaporising human bodies. Such weapons are used for a variety of purposes and come in a range of sizes. Hellyer says what we may see in Ukraine is Russia using them in a 'bunker-buster' role to destroy defensive positions. Extremely large, air-launched versions are designed to destroy caves and tunnel complexes." Virginia Harrison, "What Are Thermobaric Weapons and How Do They Work?"

this bloodless and often invisible form of mass destruction—which is, because of its apparent brutality, most often publicized. Instead, it is to connect us to other questions, histories, techniques, responsibilities, politics, affects, and effects mobilized through less visible air design practices and their impacts.

Air design is used to reproduce urban inequities through forms of capture and control, intimidation, and dispersal. I still recall the violence of the tear gas grenades used in 2013 by the police at Taksim Square in Istanbul to disperse protesters, and the rage and frustration that this "touch-less" form of police brutality sparked. There are other forms of air design that are less directly harmful but still violent in the way they affectively attempt to remake individuals. I am thinking, for instance, of how the gambling industry entraps visitors by pumping particular scents into casinos; of how addiction is encouraged in an industry that is already aimed at disenfranchising low-income folks;[5] or, on the other end of the spectrum, of how brands like Abercrombie and Fitch aggressively use scent to construct the interiors of their stores, a tactic that would literally mark anyone coming and going as a customer with a particular smell. While targeting different audiences, air design is an engine of consumerism to uphold the ordering logics of capitalism, where airs are used to furnish specific worlds that either ensnare or entice, rooted in and reinforcing preexisting class divisions.

Air design is also used to produce scientific knowledge, like open-air gas attack tests. Here, air is both the vehicle and the rehearsal stage for air design. These design techniques are being tested in the actual city, not in a laboratory or a so-called "empty" site like the desert where geography, architecture, infrastructure define air, and vice versa. As architect Paulo Tavares notes,

> During field trials, scientists equipped with small bottles
> filled with some kind of volatile liquid release a gas into the

5   Natasha Dow Schüll, *Addiction by Design*. Thank you, Joanna, for this reference.

atmosphere. At specific points, they collect air samples to measure levels of concentration, trying to trace the patterns of dispersion of the element across the urban environment. This atmospheric-mapping procedure relies on a sophisticated network of sensors installed throughout the built fabric of London. Because those tiny electronic filters are hyper-sensible, it is possible to conduct open-air trials releasing only very small, non-harmful concentrations of a determined gas. Despite its low intensity, however, the operation through which knowledge about air is produced is similar to a violent act to which air is the medium, because it is the design and the rehearsal of a "non-harmful attack" that makes possible to estimate the potential spatial impacts of an exceptional situation. In other words, the knowledge produced about the behaviour of air corresponds to the techno-ecological power of intervening in the atmosphere.[6]

This case raises a fundamental question: who is allowed to release stuff to the air and where? What is deemed an acceptable amount to release? On what grounds? With what kind of responsibility?

What if air design is the often unexpected and unwanted result of other forms of design? Let's think about wildfires, for instance, which are occurring with increasing frequency across the world due to climate change and global warming—the result of large-scale deforestation, urbanization, ecocide, among other factors. It could be argued that the smoke produced from these fires is a form of air design, the result of centuries of (by design) extractive, racist, colonial capitalism. Considering wildfires as air design poses another useful question: How "conscious," "voluntary," or "visible" does the design process have to be, and how traceable or identifiable do its designers (as agents) have to be to parse their responsibility and accountability?

---

6   Paulo Tavares, "General Essay on Air: Probes into the Atmospheric Conditions of Liberal Democracy."

As with accountability, it is often difficult to evaluate the benefits of altering the composition of airs. For instance, some carbon sequestration projects capture atmospheric CO_2 to transform it into energy, or compact CO_2 to create ink or construction bricks. They might reduce some CO_2 from the atmosphere, but their construction and functioning consume energy, water, sand, and other resources, often polluting water bodies, depleting mines, and so forth. And, of course, the benefit of CO_2 reduction is not evenly distributed. Large companies (often petrochemicals) design airs to profit off their own pollution—with the aim of "cleaning" them.

I'd like to reorient "air design" toward other kinds of practices; to explore the resistant or liberatory potential of air due to its ingraspability and its capacity to shift conditions of transparency and visibility. In their introduction to "Smoke: Figures, Genres, Forms," media studies scholar Michael Litwack, artist Rosa Aiello, and Black and media studies scholar Nataleah Hunter-Young recall how arson was an important strategy of insurrection on the plantations during the Haitian Revolution. Smoke "came to materialize a symbol and a technology of Black and anti-colonial uprising, as well as a medium that transmitted the message of revolt" while also operating as a signal of death and danger for the colonizers.[7]

Today, this symbolic quality of smoke is put to work in demonstrations and parades, where colored smoke is used to visually represent the collective struggle of the demonstrators, where "air becomes a turbulent urban agent, virtually incontrollable and hard to police."[8] A few years ago I marched in London in a pink cloud in a rally for pensions and working conditions organized by the UCU union, surrounded by purple and red smoke for International Women's Day, and amid yellow bubbles in a demonstration organized by Fridays for Future. For Litwack, Aiello, and Hunter-Young,

---

7   Michael Litwack, Rosa Aiello, and Nataleah Hunter-Young, "Smoking Out: An Introduction," 7.
8   Tavares, "General Essay on Air."

in an age of neoliberal cooptation and capture, when activists, artists and critics increasingly respond to the regulatory coercions and encroachments often elicited through the invitation to visibility, it is no surprise that smoke and its cognates have emerged as compelling rubrics to imagine alternative political tactics and forms of life.[9]

Air design can open up other forms of being together, and designers can contribute to this. And they have.

During the twentieth century, the air, not in its chemical but in its physical conditions, was taken up as a structural element to create inflatable structures. The lightness, ephemerality, transparency, and transportability of new plastics enabled the creation of completely new types of enclosures. Against the solid, permanent, and mostly opaque enclosures of traditional buildings, inflatable structures were colorful and transparent, soft and reactive to touch and wind, cheap, and easy to install. These "practical" conditions were seen to blur the limits between interior/exterior, encourage more collective forms of gathering, and engage with popular culture, as well as modes of political resistance.[10]

Beyond violent acts of destruction, environmental management and forms of demonstration or resistance, air design is also part of the everyday. In fact, the built environment was born *through* air design, stratifying indoor and outdoor air to protect and provide shelter. Buildings are intense air metabolizers, and architecture is deeply implicated in this process. Air's movement through buildings has been designed—usually by engineers—to create comfort or permit inhabitation in the first place.[11] Today, due to the high levels of air pollution

9   Litwack, Aiello, and Hunter-Young, "Smoking Out," 10.
10   For the cultural and political implications of inflatables, see: Marc Dessauce, *The Inflatable Moment: Pneumatics and Protest in '68*; Sean Topham, *Blow Up: Inflatable Art, Architecture and Design*.
11   For an elaboration on indoors air and architecture, see Daniel A. Barber, *Modern Architecture and Climate: Design before Air Conditioning*; Jiat-Hwee Chang, "Thermal Comfort and Climatic Design in the Tropics"; David Gissen, *Manhattan Atmospheres: Architecture, the Interior Environment, and Urban Crisis*.

across the world, the built environment has become organized around what anthropologist Jerry Zee names "architectures of air":

> Air design has become an everyday practice, especially through the transformation of domestic spaces into protected airspaces. In Chinese medical classics, freedom from the wind was a deliverance from chaos itself. Similarly, the architecture of air in Beijing seeks a final autonomy of airs from one another through a technological extrication, and especially a fracture from the "great air" (daqi) of the city.[12]

This autonomy of architecture from the (polluted) open air—managed through purifiers, filters, technologies of all sorts developed in the early twentieth century—reinforces traditional separations and architectural binaries between inside and outside. Filters *build* "architectures of air":

> Filter technologies begin from the problem of indoor air rather than air quality writ large, especially the suspicion, borne out through pocket-sized air quality measurement devices, that even indoor air is not safe. As such, filters operate at the much more concrete interface between the body and its highly localized breathing environment, and aim to create intermittent pockets of clean air. Rather than clearing the entire atmosphere, they allow for the multiplication of smaller breathing spaces carved out one room at a time, to create a breathing space that surrounds the body as a microsphere hugging close to the mouth and nose. They transform rooms into containers and, without the fan-driven forcing of air through filters, bodies are unsafe even in the deep interiors of unfiltered domestic space. Where the air threatens, the human body itself takes on the characteristics of a compromised airspace: it extends past the porous wall of

12 Jerry Zee, "Breathing in the City: Beijing and the Architecture of Air," 53.

the skin. Filtered air and filtered airspaces promise, then, an escape from the environment in which one must live, a small re-establishment of the body as a hard inside delivered from particulate exposure.[13]

Architectures of air might serve or support a kind of neoliberal individualism in which "pockets of clean air" exist for *a* body—but not the social body. Architectures of air stratify breathers by income, and therefore race, class, gender. For example, the wealthier you are, the "cleaner" or "purer" the airs you can inhabit are—even if that inhabitation is temporary. Is it surprising that a distinctive factor of luxury hotels in Shanghai is to have "pure air" rooms? That the hospitality industry is able to capitalize on the qualities of its air? It shouldn't be surprising, but it is. Breathing clean air becomes something that only a few can afford. Because as long as there is a "solution" for it, the cause of such pollution does not need to be addressed.[14] As a consequence, the open, outdoor air evidences these inequalities. The thicker the walls, the more sophisticated the filters and the more powerful the air-conditioner units indoors, the worse the air quality is outdoors. Who has not smelled and felt the heat released into the street by air-conditioner heat pumps on a summer afternoon? And yet, cleaning the open air is—at least for now—not a solution. The only "solution" is to stop polluting through a systemic change. In the meantime—or in parallel—it might be useful to explore alternative and multiscalar forms of air design and intervention with/in it beyond solutionist approaches.

What might air design be in Aeropolis? How might it be mobilized to rethink designing *with* air and designing *the* air? This distinction highlights the multiple roles that air can have in "air design."

198

13   Zee, "Breathing in the City," 55.
14   As a recent newspaper article reported: "Tech billionaires are buying up luxurious bunkers and hiring military security to survive a societal collapse they helped create, but like everything they do, it has unintended consequences." Douglas Rushkoff, "The Super-Rich 'Preppers' Planning to Save Themselves from the Apocalypse."

And it points in different directions. When I speak about designing *with* air, air is put to work as a construction material, to build something else. When I refer to designing *the* air, air itself is the object of design.

DESIGNING *WITH* AIR

In 2014, curator Iván Lopez Munuera commissioned C+arquitectos to design the exhibition "Fan Riots," as part of the SOS4.8 music festival. The brief for the show (which was focused on music fandom) was complicated: we were asked to visually transform a 700-square-meter space within a convention center without touching the existing building (not even with a screw!); to condition the space to host art installations, performances, and roundtables; to "attract" partygoers whose main interest when attending a festival may not actually be art; and to do all this with a limited budget and limited time (two days to setup and five hours to dismantle).

The outcome, which we eventually called *Polivagina*,[15] was an unpredictable exploration of how to use air and helium as the main materials for construction. Helium has lifting power, which meant that by designing *with* it we could create a self-sustaining structure.

15 *Polivagina*
Exhibition: Fan Riots
Curator: Iván López Munuera
Institution: Festival de música, cultura y arte SOS 4.8
Design: C+arquitectos (Nerea Calvillo with Marina Fernández)
Construction: Workshop with architecture students from the Universidad de Alicante, directed by Miguel Mesa del Castillo: Vicent Ibi, Rebeca Férez, Gloria Herranz, Irene Corcoles, Maria Cabañero, Andrea Montoya, Martín Carballo, Jesús M. Saorín, Isabel Blanco, Rosa Villaescusa, José Miguel Asencio, Carlos Sanjuán, Jose Diaz, Beatriz Antón, Marta Navarro, Mercedes Muela, Rafael Hernández, Vicente Llinares, Jesús Cases, Viviana Bey, Elisabeth Ferrando, Carlos Lidon, Mark S. Hamaoka, Carlos E. Pérez, Alberto Navarro, Carlos Paternina, and volunteers from the Universidad de Murcia.
Details: 2014, 650 m², Murcia, Spain, €35,000
Images: Imagen Subliminal
My greatest appreciation to Iván for his trust, open-mindedness, and creativity; and to the enthusiastic construction team, who rocked it.

Compared with bricks, stone, or concrete, helium is fluid; it can move, change, and react. To create a self-sustaining structure we enclosed helium with ordinary objects: polyamide balloons. But working with balloons-as-containers added an extra dimension of complexity and technical difficulty. As balloons are not used in architectural construction, the manufacturers do not provide technical specifications stating how balloons should perform (their lift capacity, for example). There are no building codes or regulations covering their usage, and there is little to no expertise in how to assemble balloons at such a scale. In the absence of this system of rules, we collected stories, experiences, and expertise about helium from domains outside architectural construction.

We consulted corporate conference designers, decorators, and wedding catalogues; we drew on our own memories of childhood birthday parties. We tested small prototypes in the office, recording weights and lifting times, trying out ways of sticking, attaching, gluing, or tying them together. Tied up and holding balloons, we tried to feel, understand, attune ourselves to three interrelated and processual aspects of all aerostatic things: envelopment, inflation, and buoyancy.[16] Our arms became more sensitive to the very small changes in the amount of helium in each balloon; we could sense the tension of stretching polyamide; we were moved by the unexpected choreography of balloons in response to the subtle currents of breeze through the balcony window.

Designing with helium demanded we shift our spatial design practices. If a building project requires documenting how materials come together through drawings, budgets, and specifications—for economic and legal reasons—designing with air transformed the process into an experimental one.

200

16   Derek P. McCormack, "Aerostatic Spacing: On Things Becoming Lighter Than Air."

There were too many unknowns. There was no way to really draw and control the shape of 4,000 units, for instance. Instead of outlining every construction detail, we defined the conditions of experimentation. This meant shifting the type of documents needed to materialize *Polivagina*: away from producing drawings and towards setting up protocols.[17]

Reflecting on designing these protocols and conditions of experimentation, I am reminded of geographer Steve Hinchliffe's Stengers-inspired notion of a "cosmopolitical experiment," which in some ways describes our design and construction process with helium and balloons:

> We learn to add field observation to field observation—to discuss, to collaborate, to corroborate, to build a sense... Sensitivity to minor differences may or may not prove fruitful. But it seems to us that, as with other scientific endeavors, this openness to difference, which is borne out of a looser kind of sense, a knowing around rather than a knowledge of, is a vital means to allow for nonhuman knowledgeabilities.[18]

201

17 This makes me think of the kind of compositional and instructional shift proposed in the 1960s by the art collective Fluxus, specifically of Mieko Shiomi's "Music for Two Players II" from 1963, for instance: "In a closed room
pass over 2 hours
in silence.
(They may do anything but to speak.)"
The score was conceived by the artist as a set of instructions. With the parameters of the work, a performer could realize it at any time. Fluxus artists often used language as opposed to musical notation, so that anyone could carry out the instructions. See https://www.moma.org/magazine/articles/407.

18 To protect an urban site, Stephen Hinchliffe and collaborators had to prove the existence of animal life, and water voles, as protected species, seemed a good objective. However, water voles are very difficult to see, as they avoid humans. They realized that instead of trying to "capture" water voles it was more ethical—and practical—to explore alternative methods to register the existence of water voles. Similarly, we had to accept that we could only "know around" helium, by sensing the small differences of the gas's properties and attributes when inside polyamide balloons. Steve Hinchliffe et al., "Urban Wild Things: A Cosmopolitical Experiment," 653.

In designing the *Polivagina*, we traded "knowledge of" for "knowing around," control for uncertainty—and risk. As a consequence, the project became a performative and emergent practice that blurred the limits between design and construction. We had to accept that we would not be able to completely control the shape, structural conditions, or finishes of the project. So what we designed were a few construction guidelines, like the number of balloon arches, as guiding references, to allow for flexibility in the filling, distribution of time and labor. And we had to accept that some sort of failure, even though stressful and painful, was part of the process. This experimental setting was less connected to a scientific laboratory and more to what geographer Derek McCormack has named "atmospheric fieldwork":

> The balloon, as an unstable platform of experience and experiment, provides an important way of rendering atmospheres explicit via a range of practices and procedures: ascension, immersion, envelopment and release. But it also discloses atmospheres as fields not just measured by extent or qualified through intensity. Rather, atmospheric fields also become a matter of densities—densities disclosed and reworked through the felt relations within and between atmospheric bodies. And atmospheric fieldwork becomes a deliberate attempt to attend to, experience and experiment with these relations.[19]

The materiality of air configured a specific form of designing, building, and relating.[20] I describe this configuration as a requirement from air, as we had to, unexpectedly and under a lot of stress,

---

19 Derek P. McCormack, "Devices for Doing Atmospheric Things," 47.
20 Which, at a completely different scale, resonates with cultural anthropologist Christine Folch's account of the role of water in the construction of the world's second-largest renewable energy power plant on the border of Brazil and Paraguay: "Our relationship to the environment is a form of cultural

unlearn what we knew and had planned for and relearn how to listen and feel the air just by holding it. Only then could we design and build *with* it. Paying attention retrospectively to the physical, social, and emotional interactions between the participants, designers, collaborators, students, publics, air, helium, and balloons showed what the material itself requires and what is at stake when design-building *with* air.

Bodies and Balloons, Building *with* Airs

Once on-site, there was a constant push and pull between the material, the corporeal, the logistical, and the regulatory demands of the project. Helium required certain things of us and of the balloons, and I, as an individual body, but also the collective body and a team of participants/collaborators, had to adjust to accommodate the needs of the material.

The strong, unpredictable lifting capacity of helium made us realize that we needed counterweights. Because air is heavier than helium, we started filling balloons with common air, until we achieved an equilibrium between the two gases. Our bodies became mediators between them, since the balloons did not respond to our instructions or needs. We had to learn to build *with* air. If "the materiality of things becoming lighter than air is generative of distinctive modes of experiencing—or sensing—aerostatic space,"[21] the sensing experience of being *with* air was more intimate, non-representational, and embodied. Echoing the specific movements that

production, which, in turn, inflects political, economic, and social structures. That is, narratives, values, and aspirations mark and emanate from electricity. Understanding the dam requires the dual intervention of political ecology, which analyses both how human interventions shape environment and how the shaping of nature in turn affects human communities." The materiality of the Paraná River configured specific forms of politics, controversies, and understandings of the land. See Christine Folch, *Hydropolitics: The Itaipu Dam, Sovereignty, and the Engineering of Modern South America*, 4.

21 McCormack, "Aerostatic Spacing," 27.

early-twentieth-century skyscraper construction workers developed to keep their own equilibrium when they were suspended in midair without protection,[22] we developed our own movements, not for being *in* the air, but for being *with* airs: holding them with our arms, pushing them with our knees, displacing them with our chest. Practices of material assemblage were substituted by practices of soft material care.

Working with airs and balloons posed further construction challenges. The estimates we received from contractors were terribly high, as the balloons needed to be handled individually. So, with our students from the architecture school of Alicante University and joined on the last day by student volunteers from all disciplines from Murcia University, we transformed the construction site into a student workshop.[23] Again, helium and air required changes in the social structure of the construction process. Helium's strong lifting capacity destroyed our dome-like assemblages every night. Due to time constraints and our inability to control the balloons, the team had to readjust through a redistribution of power and decision-making. We— the architects—were no longer the ones explaining what and how to build, not even coordinating tasks. We broke down into small self-organized and ever-changing teams to experiment, make decisions, and share findings spontaneously.[24]

204

22 Derek P. McCormack, "Atmospheric Choreographies and Air-Conditioned Bodies."
23 The line between unpaid labor and learning is very fine and difficult to navigate.
24 These reformulations of design and construction may resonate with practices of collaborative design, participatory design, or co-design. But the *Polivagina* became a different process: there was neither a shared understanding among the various stakeholders of what was taking place, nor was there an awareness of the organizational contexts in which this form of cooperative design was enacted. Furthermore, we were not designing with future users in mind, as in co-design or participatory design. In this cosmopolitical experiment, decisions were not negotiated or agreed upon. It became

The fact that the team became a group of "makers" as well as mediators with the air affected the construction technique itself. Instead of hitting, breaking, and assembling materials with tools as when building a house, for instance, our bodies became the main instrument to build with. We caught, blew, inhaled, lifted, hugged, tugged with the help of scissors, tape, and string. We had to learn to be affected by gases.[25] The sound of our voices changed from inhaling helium, the occasional higher-pitched frequency vibrating out from behind and under metallic surfaces. Instrumentalizing the body was needed to understand, for instance, how much a 45cm balloon lifts depending on its shape, in a similar fashion as the bodies of the chemists of the nineteenth century were epistemic instruments.[26] We didn't need to be particularly strong or agile; we didn't need to conform to the bodily stereotype of the construction industry. On the contrary. Young, old, queer, non-normative bodies took command of the installation. While we were catching, blowing, inhaling, lifting, hugging, tugging, I thought of all those bodies typically excluded or included, expected or unexpected, at construction sites, and the ways in which laboring bodies who tend to be migrant, precarious, and racialized are disproportionally included in this form of labor.[27]

a distributed, difficult to trace decision-making process, with no time for agreements or discussions, and included aggressive moments, tears, and a lot of stress. Arguably, and if we think of this project in terms of involvement-in-design and human/nonhuman participation, we co-designed *with* helium and air. See Thomas Kvan, "Collaborative Design: What Is It?"; Lucy Suchman et al., "Back to Work: Renewing Old Agendas for Cooperative Design"; Elisabeth B.-N. Sanders and Pieter Jan Stappers, "Co-Creation and the New Landscapes of Design"; Alex Wilkie, "Regimes of Design, Logics of Users."

25 Bruno Latour, "How to Talk about the Body? The Normative Dimension of Science Studies."

26 Chemists smelled, touched, breathed substances. Their senses were basic tools for knowledge production and experimentation. Celia Roberts, "The Death of the Sensuous Chemist: The 'New' Chemistry and the Transformation of Sensuous Technology."

27 Kadambari Baxi, Jordan Carver, and Mabel O. Wilson, "Who Builds Your Architecture?"

Gases also required a shift in forms of governance once *Polivagina* was installed. The elevating force of helium, its resistance to being confined, and its overall recalcitrance[28] caused the biggest conflicts and controversies. The balloons, very slowly, pulled the whole structure up, until the top of the domes reached the point where they triggered a laser detector installed in the ceiling, which activated the fire alarm. This incident, three hours before opening, triggered an institutional conflict, bringing together the building's security guards, institutional representatives of the cultural complex, the balloons, the festival promoters, and us. The City Council technicians proposed technical solutions to lower the structure, but the balloons had reached an equilibrium and we had lost control over them. They could not be brought down without dismantling the overall structure. Another option, bursting the bigger balloons, although acceptable from our side, was rejected by the promoters, who prioritized the aesthetics and decided to push for an administrative solution. After two hours of phone calls and meetings, the issue—how to meld safety, aesthetics, budget, and time—escalated to the municipal authorities, then the regional ones.

The solution adopted was to temporarily replace the laser smoke detector with a whole crew of firefighters, who became responsible for the building, the event, and the installation. Interestingly enough, this did not only redistribute power relations, as now the firefighters could decide what would and would not take place, but the air transformed the newly arrived representatives of control and power into members of the public themselves, where

206

---

28 Manuel Tironi and Nerea Calvillo, "Water and Air: Territories, Tactics and the Elemental Textility of Urban Cosmopolitics."

firefighters were taking selfies, listening to the round-tables, and watching the video art pieces. Conflict can trigger other forms of temporary sociality and temporary publics as well, expanding the agents involved by making people from different contexts come together and discuss issues such as public event regulations, institutional security protocols, and firefighter budgets.

Polivagina triggered ephemeral socialities and publics, as well as affective atmospheres. Feminist anthropologist Kathleen Stewart's notion of "atmospheric attunements" accounts for the temporary, sometimes conscious and sometimes unconscious, adaptations and transmissions of effects, not only between humans but also with nonhumans. Opposed to overt forms of communication (verbal, visual, bodily, etc.) that can be heard and made sense of, for instance, Stewart's atmospheric attunements describe tuning into connections and affects, all the subtle and ephemeral conditions that are difficult to pinpoint in our immediate environment. Connections and affects that configure specific atmospheres that can only grasped through a kind of bodily openness and material sensitivity. Atmospheres where "things matter not because how they are represented, but because they have qualities, rhythms, forces, relations and movements."[29] Stewart's concept is useful for the way it helps reveal the socialities and affects created by the air and the space, by humans, balloons, and works of art, and how each of these entities was relevant for everyone involved (audience, artists, firefighters) not because of what they symbolized but because of how they performed altogether.

Under the *Polivagina*, due to the unstable equilibrium achieved with air and helium, the balloons moved, crashed, came unstitched. *Polivagina* was alive, producing strangeness and fragility, constructing an atmosphere of attention and a collective sensation of participating in

29   Kathleen Stewart, "Atmospheric Attunements," 445.

something ephemeral and not fully finished, a space in transition, holding the tension of a structure just about to be disassembled on its own before the spectators' eyes. Yet this collective and indeterminate attunement with gases is precisely why "proliferating little worlds of all kinds that form up around conditions, practices, manias, pacings, scenes of absorption, styles of living, forms of attachment (or detachment), identities, and imaginaries" could be sensed.[30]

My own attention to the liveliness and world-making capacity of the air has, until now, left another materiality unattended: the balloon and more specifically, its polyamide. Being attuned to this light film—with its mechanical strength, barrier properties, and reflective silver finish—seemed to determine how people came together and how they engaged with the exhibition's themes.[31]

The metallic, mirrored surface was kaleidoscopic. It diffused the limits of the space, refracted light, hid furtive hugs, distorted smiling faces; it multiplied Michael Jackson's fans to infinity, reminded someone of Warhol's Factory, made us desire Warhol's Silver Clouds. WThe silver color seemed to attract the attention of the festivalgoers and music fans. The installation was identified as a "cool" place to take a selfie, becoming a site for both self-representation and collectiveness, spreading by word of mouth and bringing people in. This effect was designed and planned, as a sort of *practical aesthetics*, "engaged in thinking about and devising modes of sensory and affective apprehensions of the world," and as "possible sites for experimenting with experience."[32]

30 Stewart, "Atmospheric Attunements," 446.
31 For me, this resonates with Stewart's account of the different ways in which the color red played a role in material, affective, and symbolic New England. Kathleen Stewart, "New England Red."
32 McCormack, "Devices for Doing Atmospheric Things," 105.

The intention was that, once inside, visitors would engage with the art pieces and join roundtable discussions and performances. All of which happened. Visitors who had never been exposed to such contexts not only listened but engaged in the debate. The strangeness of the space— very different to a museum or art gallery—and the fact that they inhabited it in their own ways—coming and going, taking pictures, chatting—empowered them. As one of the visitors mentioned, they felt at ease to ask, question, and speak their minds.

To some extent, thanks to the polyamide, visitors, festivalgoers, cleaners, firefighters, technicians, and guards formed "new collaborative spacetimes of experimental togetherness, new forms of association."[33] This, of course, did not result in the constitution of a sort of "parliament." This attunement took place at specific moments, without possible control, and through temporary and fragile engagements. And yet, the experimental setting or atmospheric fieldwork also became a site for experimenting with experience, which required a form of suspension of assumptions and dis- belief,[34] to allow the process and the space to rearrange in different possibilities.

DESIGNING *THE* AIR

A year later, Iván López Munuera was, again, appointed to curate the arts section of the SOS music festival. This time the exhibition, *The Dark Side of the Party*, explored the hidden or invisible aspects of music parties and the displacements and violence they can cause. We were commissioned for the exhibition design and, familiar with the constraints of the space (the building, the schedule, the budget), decided to work with air again. But this time

33   McCormack, "Devices for Doing Atmospheric Things," 105.
34   Timothy K. Choy and Jerry Zee, "Condition—Suspension."

we approached it differently: without a container, to test how to design *the* air *with*—loose—airs. Without a form of containment, how does one work with a kinetic material that is in between a thing and an event, "much less discrete, much more atmospheric"?[35] What are its constraints, challenges, and opportunities?[36]

As the curatorial project required differentiated spaces, an invisible change in the aerial conditions—altering its temperature or humidity conditions, for instance—would not have been enough. So, to design the air we decided to add new particles and gases to it. And to call the project *Sticky Airs*.[37] We introduced smoke and fog, at high and low densities, to create different, shifting spatial configurations. Designing the air with smoke machines is certainly not new: it is common practice in nightclubs, theaters, fashion events, art, and military installations.[38] But we could not find references for how to do it at this scale, so we had to start learning again. Fortunately, not from scratch. Designing and building *the* air—*with* air—shared some processes and challenges that we encountered when designing *with* it in *Polivagina*.

35 McCormack, "Aerostatic Spacing."
36 Some of these questions are the result of conversations with anthropologist Javier Lezaun for our joint presentation, "Smoke-Filled Rooms: Atmospheric Matters and the Legibility of Encounters," at the seminar "Horizons of Movement: Interdisciplinary Encounters in Kinesthetic Thinking" at the Institute of Science, Innovation and Society, Oxford, September 2019. I am grateful to Lezaun for his generosity and support on conceptual and practical academic matters.
37 *Sticky Airs*
    Exhibition: The Dark Side of the Party
    Curator: Iván López Munuera
    Institution: Festival de música, cultura y arte SOS 4.8
    Design: C+arquitectos (Nerea Calvillo with Marina Fernández and Ana Melgarejo)
    Construction: Workshop with architecture students from the Universidad de Alicante directed by Miguel Mesa del Castillo: María José Abellán, Mari Ángeles Aracil, Isabel Blanco, Maria Elena Carrión, Ester de Juan, Anabel de la Torre, Jose Alberto Esteve, Joan Fernández, Alicia Fernández, Cristian Francés, Rosa Gómez, Paula González, Rebecca Guilabert, Esperanza Jurado, Antonio López, Begoña López, Manuel López, Eva Martín, David Martínez, Nuria Martínez, Agustín Morazzoni, Israel Pastor, Rosa Pérez, Mariana Tomás, Alejandra Vallejo.
    Details: 2014, 650 m², Murcia, Spain, €25,000
    Images: Imagen Subliminal
38 Iván López Munuera, "HIV and AIDS Kin."

We had to design the experimental setting, this time without the possibility of testing due to the high rental price of the machines. Instead, we investigated the material properties of different types of smoke: dry smoke, fog, or liquid nitrogen, among others, and we had to imagine their effects. On-site, we used machines that liquefy, solidify, atomize, vaporize... by releasing new materials to the existing air: water, mineral oil, CO_2, nitrogen. To gain spatial resolution and control smoke densities we used fans and water vapor to direct flows.

Designing air rearticulated traditional architectural elements. Without walls, for instance, to curate movement, to hang or enclose works of art, to locate emergency exits, how would we differentiate or help folks navigate the space? "Walls" instead became a combination of technologies and atmospheres, in Stewart's sense. Smoke, machines, pallets, illumination lamps, metal stairs. The visitors' circulation was configured through the distribution of the art pieces, through LED lights and photoluminescent stickers on the floor. Fire exits were signaled through plasma screens. The location of smoke machines and the density of smoke each released created areas with different conditions of visibility, which allowed visitors to navigate the space intuitively. This redefinition of building elements challenged the contemporary exhibition-space typology of the "white—or black—cubes": the space was full of stuff. Art, smoke, light, noise.

Once on-site, we were able to briefly test times, densities, conditions of visibility and security with our bodies, pen, paper, and a chronometer. The smoke was theatrical—staging and restaging the artwork.[39] The artists, unexpectedly, appreciated the setup, as they noticed that in the company of fog other spatialities, contours,

39   Uriel Fogué, "Ecología Política y Economía de la Visibilidad de los Dispositivos Tecnológicos de Escala Urbana Durante el Siglo XX: Abriendo la Caja Negra."

contrasts, intimacies emerged. The smoke made you feel like it was just you and the art, on your own and isolated from the world except for the unsynchronized artificial breathing of the machines that spoke out in varied pitches and intensities and the soft smell that emanated from the oil-based machines. Pshhhhhhhhhhh... tiiiiiiiiiiiiiishhhhhhh... push-push-push.

Designing *the* air in *Sticky Airs* evidenced what happens when air becomes visible: bodies and space co-constructed each other.[40] The lack of visibility sharpened other senses.[41] Both water and air conditioned the space—and visitors could sense the temperature as they moved through it. This mobilized other forms of navigating the exhibition space and of interrelating with others. The thickness of the air dissolved everyone's physical features, de-individualizing visitors. Gender, race, age, and presentation seemed to blur, becoming one out-of-focus picture. We had to learn to identify friends and colleagues through gestures and gait, through physical contours, through voices. We had to relearn to encounter each other, producing situations of unexpected intimacies; celebratory encounters ("Hey! It's you!"); coziness in the "auditorium," which had an air of togetherness, of concentration, of isolation from the rest of the festival. In sum, the different airs stuck to our bodies, reminding us that the air impacts not only human health but also how we relate to each other, making visible, as the tear gas weaponized in demonstrations, that air is social.

40   In a context where the air outdoors is never as polluted as in Beijing, for example.
41   Making the air nontransparent demanded that the photographers unlearn what "good" art or installation photography is. Because all the parameters that constitute a "good picture"—depth of focus, for instance—did not apply. As everything was blurred, the images and videos looked too similar to each other, as the camera barely captured the small differences in density, visibility, and change that our bodies could sense. Which poses an interesting question: What medium best captures atmospheric change?

Designing with/the air transforms design: from an attempt to control the capacities of a future building and regulate its inhabitants, to an experimental setup that embraces uncertainty. Design—understood broadly to encompass space, object, graphics, environment—is no longer only about deciding how to create a shape and assemble components. It is also a practice concerned with how to design the construction process as an experiment. It is concerned with how we design and build. So, to work with airs, we need to learn to be affected. Because we cannot see it, therefore we need to feel it, holding, sensing, putting the body in. Because the air requires its own practices, which force (us) humans to adapt. The air unsettles what we know, and silently demonstrates that the design and building tools we have been using until now to deal with wood or stone might no longer be adequate.

I have come to describe *Polivagina* and *Stisly Aire* as environmental mediations. They are technically not buildings nor installations; they are environments themselves that at the same time mediate *with* the environment. In both projects, the agency of air demanded not only different recombinations of matter and humans but different practices to do so because it was not about changing the order of materials (as in other accounts of architecture). In fact, the air made visible or brought to the fore that design is no longer a process that ends with the construction of a structure, but a constant reassembly of materials, humans, ideas.[42] The agency of air not only shifted the order in which humans participate (as in practices of co-design, where users also participate in the initial design phases). It became also about finding new practices of construction and inhabitation, such as horizontal and self-organized construction teams or playful spectatorship.

213

---

42 Michael Guggenheim, "Building Memory: Architecture, Networks and Users"; Albena Yaneva, *Made by the Office for Metropolitan Architecture: An Ethnography of Design*.

Thus, designing with/the air through environmental mediations opens up other types of affects with material entities, like atmospheric attunements. But most importantly, it offers the possibility of designing desirable socialities with political and/or transformative capacities. Building with air calls for feminist or queer construction practices where anybody can contribute, and practices of assembly are substituted by practices of care.

Gases Are Not Dogs

To better understand this relationship between more-than-humans and socialities, I would like to propose one last speculation: that the cosmopolitical experiment may be read better as a process of conviviality, as a temporary cohabitation with more-than-humans. What if, akin to Donna Haraway's *Companion Species Manifesto*,[43] we imagined that helium and air became our companion species?

Sure, gases are not dogs. They are not conventional companion species. But thinking about them through Haraway's framework may help us engage with two propositions. The first one is to think of our relationship with the air—a composition of gases and particles (and any other material, for that matter)—not as something out there to be managed, but as material with which we have intimate bodily and affective attunements. The second one is to see how in architecture there can be ways of engaging with more-than-humans other than control and domestication, processes of mutual training and learning to be affected, yet without expectations. Because, as Haraway claims in her dog–human co-habitation, "dog's value and life does not depend on the human's perception that the dogs love them. Rather, the dog has to do his or her job,"[44] which is precisely what the helium balloons did. Even though we established some sort of physical and chemical affect, some sort of "animacy"[45] with

43   Donna Haraway, *The Companion Species Manifesto: Dogs, People and Significant Otherness.*
44   Haraway, *The Companion Species Manifesto*, 38.
45   Mel Y. Chen, *Animacies: Biopolitics, Racial Mattering, and Queer Affect.*

the helium balloons, they did not respond to our care but carried on lifting, destroying the installation. And yet temporary, fragile, brief moments of equilibrium can be achieved by constantly looking at what emerges from the relationship, which can challenge modes of sociality precisely because we are not used to them. Everyone needs to learn how to engage, and in this process, new or different relationships can emerge. The question, paraphrasing Haraway, is: "How might an ethics and politics committed to the flourishing of significant otherness be learned from taking [air–human] relationship seriously"[46] while, as social scientist and design researcher Laura Forlano warns, always keeping in mind "the ways things [dogs, air] are always entangled with bodies and subjectivities" such as experiences, histories, and oppressions?[47]

46   "Dog-human" in the original. Haraway, *The Companion Species Manifesto*, 3.
47   Laura Forlano, "Posthumanism and Design," 28.

5.3

5.4

5.7

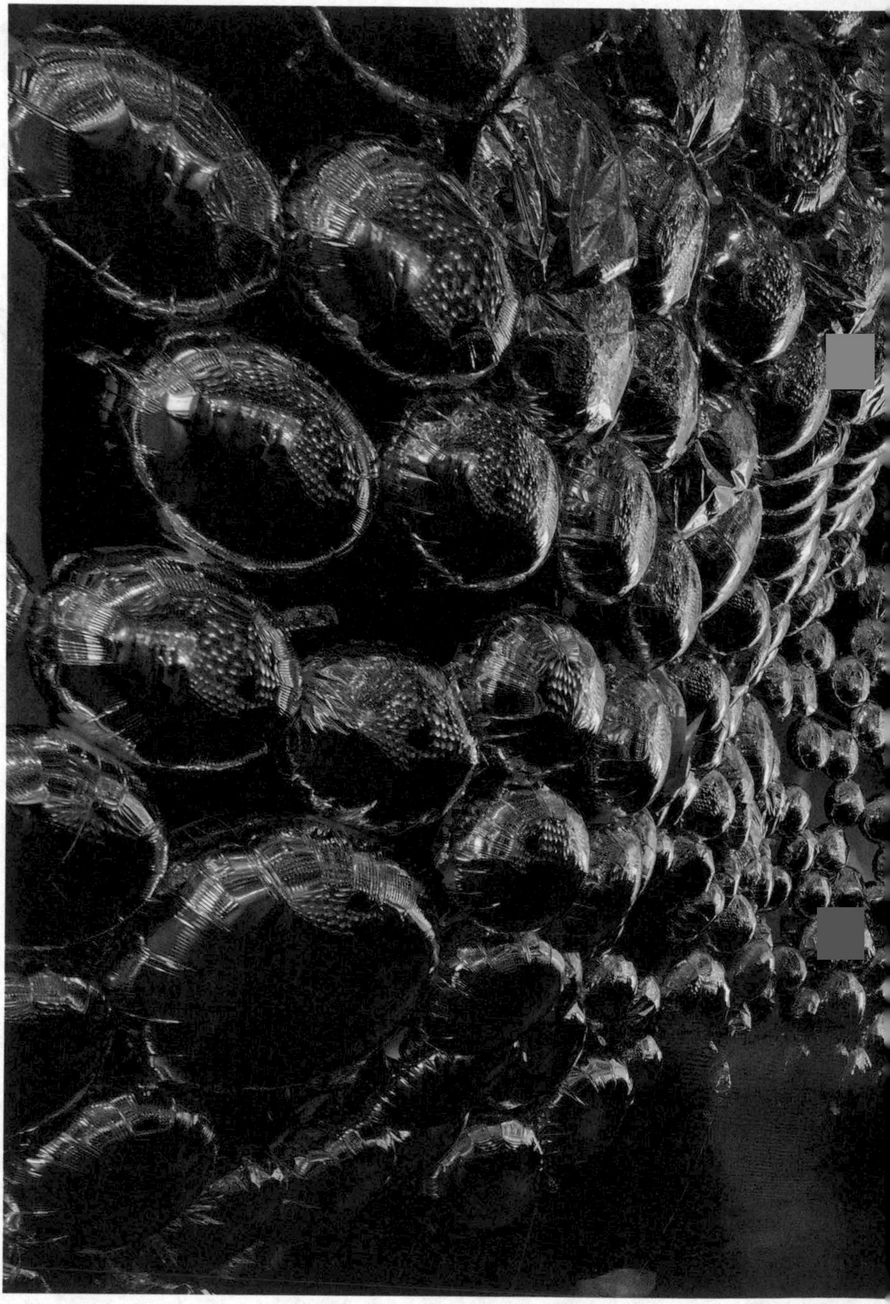

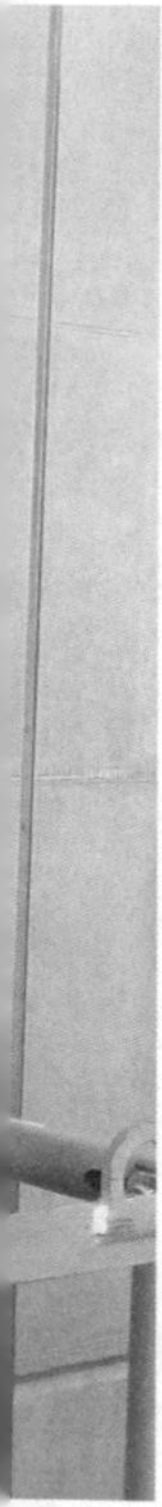

5.11

5.12

5.13

5.14

5.17

WORKS CITED

Barber, Daniel A. *Modern Architecture and Climate: Design before Air Conditioning.* New York: Princeton University Press, 2020.

Baxi, Kadambari, Jordan Carver, and Mabel O. Wilson. "Who Builds Your Architecture? An Advocacy Report." *e-flux Journal*, no. 66 (October 2015). https://www.e-flux.com/journal/66/60751/who-builds-your-architecture-an-advocacy-report.

Calvillo, Nerea. "Inviting Atmospheres to the Architecture Table." In *Inventing the Social*, edited by Noortje Marres, M. Guggenheim, and Alex Wilkie, 41–64. Manchester: Mattering Press, 2018.

Chang, Jiat-Hwee. "Thermal Comfort and Climatic Design in the Tropics: An Historical Critique." *Journal of Architecture* 21, no. 8 (November 2016): 1171–1202.

Chen, Mel Y. *Animacies: Biopolitics, Racial Mattering, and Queer Affect.* Durham, NC: Duke University Press, 2012.

Choy, Timothy K., and Jerry Zee. "Condition—Suspension." *Cultural Anthropology* 30, no. 2 (2015): 210–223.

Dessauce, Marc. *The Inflatable Moment: Pneumatics and Protest in '68.* New York: Princeton Architectural Press, 1999.

Dow Schüll, Natasha. *Addiction by Design.* Princeton, NJ: Princeton University Press, 2012.

Fogué, Uriel. "Ecología Política y Economía de la Visibilidad de los Dispositivos Tecnológicos de Escala Urbana Durante el Siglo XX: Abriendo la Caja Negra." *E.T.S. Arquitectura*, Universidad Politécnica de Madrid, 2015.

Folch, Christine. *Hydropolitics: The Itaipu Dam, Sovereignty, and the Engineering of Modern South America.* Princeton, NJ: Princeton University Press, 2019.

Forlano, Laura. "Posthumanism and Design." *She Ji: The Journal of Design, Economics, and Innovation* 3, no. 1 (March 2017): 16–29.

Gissen, David. *Manhattan Atmospheres: Architecture, the Interior Environment, and Urban Crisis.* Minneapolis, MN: University of Minnesota Press, 2013.

Guggenheim, Michael. "Building Memory: Architecture, Networks and Users." *Memory Studies* 2, no. 1 (January 2009): 39–53.

Haraway, Donna. *The Companion Species Manifesto: Dogs, People, and Significant Otherness.* Chicago: Prickly Paradigm Press, 2003.

Harrison, Virginia. "What Are Thermobaric Weapons and How Do They Work?" *The Guardian*, March 1, 2022. https://www.theguardian.com/world/2022/mar/01/what-are-thermobaric-weapons-and-how-do-they-work.

Hinchliffe, Steve, Matthew B. Kearnes, Monica Degen, and Sarah Whatmore. "Urban Wild Things: A Cosmopolitical Experiment." *Environment and Urban Planning D: Society and Space* 23, no. 5 (2003): 643–658.

Kvan, Thomas. "Collaborative Design: What Is It?" *Automation in Construction* 9, no. 4 (2000): 409–415.

Latour, Bruno. "How to Talk about the Body? The Normative Dimension of Science Studies." *Body & Society* 10, no. 2–3 (January 2004): 205–229.

Litwack, Michael, Rosa Aiello, and Nataleah Hunter-Young. "Smoking Out: An Introduction." *Public* 29, no. 58 (Fall 2018): 6–21.

McCormack, Derek P. "Aerostatic Spacing: On Things Becoming Lighter Than Air." *Transactions of the Institute of British Geographers* 34, no. 1 (January 2009): 25–41.

    "Atmospheric Choreographies and Air-Conditioned Bodies." In *Moving Sites: Investigating Site-Specific Dance Performance*, edited by Victoria Hunter, 79–94. London: Routledge, 2015.

    "Devices for Doing Atmospheric Things." In *Non-Representational Methodologies*, edited by Phillip Vanni, 89–111. New York: Routledge, 2015.

Munuera, Iván López. "HIV and AIDS Kin: The Discotecture of Paradise Garage." *Thresholds*, no. 48 (April 2020): 133–147.

Roberts, Lissa. "The Death of the Sensuous Chemist: The 'New' Chemistry and the Transformation of Sensuous Technology." *Studies in History and Philosophy of Science* 26, no. 4 (1995): 503–529.

Rushkoff, Douglas. "The Super-Rich 'Preppers' Planning to Save Themselves from the Apocalypse." *The Observer*, September 4, 2022. https://www.theguardian.com/news/2022/sep/04/super-rich-prepper-bunkers-apocalypse-survival-richest-rushkoff.

Sanders, Elizabeth B.-N., and Pieter Jan Stappers. "Co-Creation and the New Landscapes of Design." *CoDesign* 4, no. 1 (March 2008): 5–18.

228

Shiva, Vandana. *One Earth, One Humanity vs. the 1%*. Oakland, CA: PM Press, 2019.

Sloterdijk, Peter. *Terror from the Air*. Cambridge, MA: MIT Press, 2009.

Stewart, Kathleen. "Atmospheric Attunements." *Environment and Urban Planning D: Society and Space* 29 (2011): 445–453.

"New England Red." In *Non-Representational Methodologies*, edited by Phillip Vanni, 19–33. New York: Routledge, 2015.

Suchman, Lucy, Janette Blomberg, and Randall Trigg. "Back to Work: Renewing Old Agendas for Cooperative Design." In *Computers and Design in Context*, edited by Morten Kyng and Lars Mathiassen, 267–287. Cambridge, MA: MIT Press, 2003.

Tavares, Paulo. "General Essay on Air: Probes into the Atmospheric Conditions of Liberal Democracy." *Meusite* 1, 2008. https://www.essayonair.online/pagina-inicial.

Tironi, Manuel, and Nerea Calvillo. "Water and Air: Territories, Tactics and the Elemental Textility of Urban Cosmopolitics." In *Urban Cosmopolitics: Agencements, Assemblies, Atmospheres*, edited by Ignacio Farias and Anders Blok, 207–224. London: Routledge, 2016.

Tobias, Jimmy. "The Secretive Government Agency Planting 'Cyanide Bombs' across the US." *The Guardian*, June 26, 2020. https://www.theguardian.com/environment/2020/jun/26/cyanide-bombs-wildfire-services-idaho.

Topham, Sean. *Blow Up: Inflatable Art, Architecture and Design*. London: Prestel, 2002.

Wilkie, Alex. "Regimes of Design, Logics of Users." *Athenea Digital* 11, no. 1 (March 2011): 317–334.

Yaneva, Albena. *Made by the Office for Metropolitan Architecture: An Ethnography of Design*. Rotterdam: 010 Publishers, 2009.

Zee, Jerry. "Breathing in the City: Beijing and the Architecture of Air." *Scapegoat* 8 (2015): 46–56.

IMAGES

5.2–5.7
Unless otherwise noted, all images are from *Polivagina*, C+ arquitectos, SOS 4.8 Music Festival, Murcia, Spain, 2014. Photographs courtesy of the author.

5.1, 5.8–5.17
Unless otherwise noted, all images are from *Sticky Airs*, C+ arquitectos, SOS 4.8 Music Festival, Murcia, Spain, 2015. Photographs courtesy of the author.

5.1
Detail of *Sticky Airs*. Photograph by Imagen Subliminal.

5.2
Construction detail.

5.3
Setup crisis: 90 cm balloons pulling so hard they broke the dome.

5.4
People taking selfies during the music festival.

5.5
Setup.

5.6
Helium canisters.

5.7
View of the performance area. Photograph by Imagen Subliminal.

5.8
Setting up and infrastructure testing.

5.9
Setup tests. Photograph by Imagen Subliminal.

5.10
Fog machine.

5.11
Different kinds of smoke.

5.12
Setup tests. Photograph by Imagen Subliminal.

5.13
Tests. Photograph by Imagen Subliminal.

5.14
Tests.

5.15
Performance area setup with Maria Jerez rehearsing. Photograph by Imagen Subliminal.

5.16
Sticky Airs during the festival. Photograph by Imagen Subliminal.

5.17
People taking selfies during the music festival. Photograph by Imagen Subliminal.

6.1

QUEERING POLLEN (AND URBAN POLITICAL ECOLOGIES)

Miss Casandra: What took you so long?
Maya: I had a beautiful dream!
Miss Casandra: A dream? But Maya, bees never dream!
Maya: One day I'll tell you what I dreamed. I had so much fun!
Miss Casandra: Maya, we bees weren't born to spend the day talking, but to work!

Every time I hear the word pollen, *Maya the Bee* comes to mind.[1] As a child, I was fascinated by this chatty and inquisitive cartoon character. Maya joyfully defied the norms of the beehive—driving Miss Casandra, the newborn bees' caretaker, crazy.

Miss Casandra: It's dangerous out there, you must be very careful!
Maya: What would happen if you didn't stay at home, Miss Casandra?

Maya was meant to be another "soldier," restricted to collecting pollen for the colony. But she was drawn to the whole ecosystem beyond the hive—playfully rebelling against her assigned productive and reproductive life to venture into the unknown. Looking back, I think it was Maya's curiosity and nonconformity that I enjoyed most; her constant questioning of what was taken for granted; her desire to fly away or flee the roles assigned to her in the hive.

Maya: Why is it naughty for me to want to see the outside world? Next time I'll be clever and run away when nobody is looking...

233

---

1 Particularly the original German-French cartoon from 1975, which was aired and dubbed on the Spanish public television station some years after its initial release. The dialogue is taken from the first episode, when Maya is born. Just one caveat: I do not agree with some of the values expressed in the cartoon, nor with the views of the author of the original book. I cite Maya because, having been born and raised in a big city, she contributed to shaping my—very limited—idea of pollen, bees, and "nature."

From spring to fall, the wind carries enormous amounts of micro-scopic pollen particles—a different grain for each plant species—to fertile plants near and far. Despite their near-invisibility, each pollen grain challenges binaries between "good" and "bad," "healthy" and "harmful," as they produce multiple, and diverse, effects. Pollen is both reproductive (for some plants) and allergenic (for some human bodies). It is organ and dust; pleasure and irritation; (super) food and toxin all at once. Pollen challenges the western scientific paradigm of reproduction as a functional monogamous and effi-cient process because plants need others—insects or the wind—to reproduce. Wind-pollinated plants, flowers, and trees need to produce and release billions of pollen grains to ensure that at least some of them reach their female counterparts. Thus pollen signals a form of multispecies reproduction that is inefficient and exces-sive, based on chance and multiplicity.

Pollen travels. It can alter breathing conditions, cause asth-ma, irritate throats, water eyes. For botanists, it is a key element in plant ecosystems; for urbanites, a seasonal nuisance or even danger. For urban design it is what architecture theorist David Gissen has termed "subnature"—all those natures considered primitive, filthy, fearsome, or uncontrollable.[2] Pollen is often considered pollution too. Technically, because the size of a pollen grain is similar to that of other suspended particles—like sand or heavy metals—air quality sensors register pollen grains as Particulate Matter (PM_{10}).[3] Which is to say, pollen is literally counted as air pollution. But airborne pollen cannot be air pollution—it cannot be matter out of place—because it is meant to travel through the air. So why is pollen still considered pollution? Why do people speak about "pollen offenders"

2 Gissen recognizes how architecture has focused on "good natures," the desirable ones such as the sun, trees, and rivers; as opposed to the "subnatures," the forms of nature categorized as "bad," like mud, dust, weeds, insects, and gas. David Gissen, *Subnature*.

3 Most PM_{10} sensors use the light-scattering method to detect and count particles with density 0~1000ug/m³, but it does not identify their chemical composition. Therefore, the sensors count all sorts of particles, including fungus spores, pollen, ashes, sand, and so on.

or "pollen danger" when pollen is central to biodiversity?[4] Where did this repulsion and disdain for pollen came from, and why does it matter?

FROM POLLEN GRAINS TO TERRITORIAL TRANSFORMATIONS

Let us suspend ourselves, this time in New Orleans, around 1870. The causality between pollen and hay fever had just been established.[5] Writing on hay fever and its prevention, physician and asthmatic William Scheppegrell studied the morphology of different pollen grains and figured out that "the only pollens which can cause hay fever are those which are carried by the wind, and are therefore in the air."[6] Scheppegrell and colleagues tried to find a cure for hay fever by intervening in their patients' bodies, without success.[7] So they turned to intervening in their patients' environments.

Notions and assumptions about pollen's capacity for triggering asthma symptoms were thus transferred from the small floating grains to the plants that produced them. Scheppegrell classified the different asthma-inducing pollen types according to whether it came from grasses, trees, or weeds. Weeds produced autumnal hay fever, which accounted for "the large majority of cases" in the

---

4   These terms are used in the media and in asthma tracking apps. See "Pollen Library: Plants That Cause Allergies," *Healthline*, https://www.healthline.com/health/allergies/pollen-library; "GE-R-3: Information on Pollen," Umwelt Bundesamt, https://www.umweltbundesamt.de/en/topics/climate-energy/climate-impacts-adaptation/impacts-of-climate-change/monitoring-report-2019/indicators-of-climate-change-impacts-adaptation/cluster-human-health/ge-r-3-information-on-pollen#ge-r-3-information-on-pollenv.

5   While symptoms of a seasonal asthma described as "summer catarrh"—or "hay fever" as it was commonly called—had been documented since the 1820s, it was not until 1873 that the link between pollen and hay fever was proven by English doctor Charles Harrison Blackley.

6   William Scheppegrell, "Hay-Fever: Its Cause and Prevention," 707.

7   As Oren Durham, one of the most prominent pollen researchers at the time, wrote in 1936: "Being non-fatal and funny, like sickness, ha(d) not been a matter of much concern to anyone except the sufferers themselves and to the patient-medicine men" throughout the nineteenth century. Sufferers would change climate, have operations on their noses, follow chiropractic diets, drink whisky, take quinine, snort cocaine, grow mustaches, wear goggles while outdoors, take baths... Oren C. Durham, *Your Hay Fever*, 13.

United States. On the long list of hay fever–causing weeds, ragweed was found to be responsible for about 85 percent of autumnal hay fever. As a result, weeds—and ragweed in particular—were targeted as the main source of pollen pollution in cities, framed (and fought against) as an enemy of public health and the (only) target of intense plant eradication campaigns. As Scheppegrell noted:

> The warfare against weeds, even from an agricultural standpoint, has been considered of so much importance that many States have enacted laws to control them. So difficult was the task of fighting these weeds individually, and so onerous from the standpoint of labor and expense, that the legislative power of the State was invoked to assist in their eradication. In many cases this has been entirely successful, as the weeds against which this special legislation was directed have practically been eradicated.[8]

That these eradication campaigns gained such significance and support was reflective of a social atmosphere where the biological response to pollen was thought to be divided by class and race. Because hay fever was considered an "aristocratic disease." Only ruling upper-class (white) men—doctors like Scheppegrell, the clergy, and later businessmen, lawyers, and other urban professionals—were thought to be susceptible and sensitive to hay fever:

> if it was not "almost wholly confined to the upper classes of society, it was rarely, if ever, met with but among the educated"; rarely did it seem to afflict the rural working class.[9]

According to this upper class, weeds were no longer nuisances but indicative of larger "sanitary, safety and moral problems."[10]

---

8   Scheppegrell, "Hay-Fever," 709.
9   Mitman citing Blackley in his seminal 1873 treatise, "Experimental Research on Hay Fever." Gregg Mitman, "Hay Fever Holiday: Health, Leisure, and Place in Gilded-Age America," 18.
10 Zachary J. S. Falck, *Weeds: An Environmental History of Metropolitan America*, 28.

The "educated" thus mobilized "the legislative power of the State" to "protect" their own bodies from these asthma-producing plants. But the subsequent eradication campaigns—the largest starting in New Orleans in 1913 and spreading later to Chicago and New York—were not as successful as Scheppegrell claimed. Weeds simply grew back (due to the sturdiness of their roots, the resilience of their seeds, and the impact of urbanization on soil aeration). Most campaigns attempted to root out weeds by hand, but after World War II, using chemicals developed during the war, New York City embarked on chemical eradication campaigns. They were unsuccessful for the same reasons, ultimately leaving the areas subject to these campaigns desolate.

This is a story of a techno-scientific "solution" to pollution "gone wrong." What fascinates me about it is how it connects particles in the air with cities and geographies of illness, and more specifically, with urban interventions. In Scheppegrell's diagnosis and prescription, we see how harm, fear, and risk around pollen move from particles to plants, wind to weeds, air to ground; how aerial matters are terrestrial matters. Morals facilitated public acceptance: weeds represented everything but the ideal of the new world, which was to be controlled, clean, white. The advantage of having a single enemy—weeds—was that the solution could also be singular. The eradication campaigns were conducted under the fantasy that, just by removing weeds, cities too would become safe, clean, "good." So I wonder: what is done in the name of air pollution, how are spaces transformed in the process, and what are their social, cultural, and political motivations and consequences?

QUEERING URBAN POLITICAL ECOLOGIES

The field of urban political ecology explores how urban natures are produced by social and technological processes imbricated in complex systems.[11] With a strong commitment to environmental justice, urban political ecology pays special attention to how the development of some environments comes at the expense of others, both internal and external to the city—where "nature" is often considered a resource and rarely a polluted environment.[12] While there is a large body of urban political ecological work on water—as a resource, a recreational feature, or a source of energy production—urban airs and their "warmed-up cocktails of gases" have received little attention, let alone attention from a critical perspective:

> Much work thus remains to be done to explicate the political ecologies and politics of the materiality of urban air in the context of rapid urbanisation and global climate change. Such a project needs to make explicit the systematic anthropogenic and machinic manufacture and material conditioning of both "good" and "bad" air, through design, technoscience, capitalist industrialism, militarism, warfare, commodification, consumerism and so forth.[13]

There are, of course, exceptions to this. Take environmental humanities scholar Irma Allen's feminist approach to air, which reinforces its intimate and relational embodied condition—renaming air as "air-and-breathing-bodies";[14] or geographer Matthew Gandy's call for the need to queer (wild) urban natures.[15] Gandy asks: "How far can queer theory be usefully or meaningfully extended beyond the

11 For an introduction to urban political ecology, see the keystone book Nik Heynen, Maria Kaika, and Erik Swyngedouw, *In the Nature of Cities: Urban Political Ecology and the Politics of Urban Metabolism*.

12 See Erik Swyngedouw, "Metabolic Urbanization: The Making of Cyborg Cities," in *In the Nature of Cities*; Wendy Harcourt and Ingrid L. Nelson, *Practising Feminist Political Ecologies: Moving Beyond the "Green Economy."*

13 For a review on urban political ecology and air, see Stephen Graham, "Life Support: The Political Ecology of Urban Air," 193, 195.

14 Irma Allen, "Thinking with a Feminist Political Ecology of Air-and-Breathing-Bodies," 7.

15 Matthew Gandy conducts a useful and comprehensive review of interdisciplinary projects that connect queer theory and urban ecology to identify how queer sex, urban nature, spatial theory, and politics intersect in different ways. Although Gandy's approach addresses queering from a

realm of sexuality to the study of complexity, indeterminacy, and new models of scientific explanation more generally?"[16]

It seems to me that the answer should be, "Far." Aeropolis proposes that we think about air's complexity and its indeterminacy by bringing queer theory and urban political ecology together. Because queer theories are well equipped to engage with the "invasive," the "foreign," or the "deviant," and to detect how these adjectives have material and affective impacts. For instance: the notion of "foreign" assumes a framework of preconceived definitions of what needs to be protected or eliminated, left out or let in, removed or kept, that evince certain biases; regardless of whether that term is applied to a particle of metal in the air, a flower, a plant, a river, a human, or whole ecosystems. Because as queer (with feminist, Indigenous, Black and brown, and critical theory) scholars and activists have demonstrated, people who suffer these forms of "othering" are the ones who bear the consequences of neoliberal racial capitalism, genocide, ecocide, and the climate crisis.

Queering urban political ecologies asks us to "look much more queerly at the understandings of nature," to "unsettle normative thinking about environmental status quos."[17] Queering urban political ecologies is to examine natural processes through multiple scales of space and time and to recognize the importance of what is often taken for granted—like the sand particles from the Sahara Desert, which are carried by the wind to the Amazon Rainforest, creating water clouds and soil conditions that keep the rain forest alive.[18] Therefore, queering urban political ecologies is also a practice

non-identitarian sexuality perspective, I'm interested in how "the intersection between queer theory and urban ecology also raises questions in relation to conventional categorizations of urban nature so that distinctions between design and 'nondesign' become unclear, the connection between 'wild nature' and landscape authenticity is radically attenuated, and the idea of pleasure in nature is extended." Matthew Gandy, "Queer Ecology: Nature, Sexuality, and Heterotopic Alliances," 740.

16 Gandy, "Queer Ecology," 742.
17 Catriona Mortimer-Sandilands, "Whose There Is There, There? Queer Directions and Ecocritical Orientations," 63.
18 William Bryant Logan, Air: The Restless Shaper of the World.

concerned with fighting for environmental and social justice and ecological queerness; it is also "a domain of responsibility for and to unruly actors," those who are considered matter of displacement or matter out of place.[19]

In Aeropolis, queering is both a verb and a practice.[20] *To queer* as a mode of estranging ourselves from our own assumptions, in this case, about air, nature, and urban spaces. To consider urban airs as urban natures. To embrace the complexity of airs and their relations—toxic or not—with other entities, and to see connections where they have been denied. Because if air is commonly pictured as an inanimate (and often toxic) gaseous entity, queering it brings to the fore the whole world of animate and invisible entities that are part of it. Viruses, bacteria, spores, fungi, microscopic wasps, and pollen coexist with gases and inert particles: whole microscopic ecologies that create and decompose biological life, from small insects to centuries-old trees. To pause when air is referred to as clean, pure, dirty, or polluted; not to negate the existence of harming and deadly human and nonhuman interactions, but to unpack what counts and what is excluded when these terms are used. To pay attention to the ways in which the effects of air in human bodies are physical and affective. To stay with what is deemed abject, to embrace uncertainty, to explore opportunities. Queering as an analytical tool for radical politics: a tool of survival, a way to think with care,[21] "a collection

19 Darren J. Patrick, "The Matter of Displacement: A Queer Urban Ecology of New York City's High Line," 921.
20 Queering is at the same time a conceptual framework and a practice, a form of understanding—or, better, challenging—established views about nature, bodies, technology, politics, and the city itself. What matters for queer practice and politics is not identities per se, but their naturalization as fixed categories, as "the norm." What matters is to understand what is at stake when categories are used and mobilized, to pay attention to the forms of oppression and exclusion that they produce, to what does not fit in them. To pay attention to what they sustain and what they forbid or eliminate, and to recognize the power relations that emerge or are consolidated through those categories, to acknowledge and embrace multiplicity and diversity. In addition, through gender analysis queer theories have demonstrated how, in practice, categories are not fixed biological or social constructions. They are fluid and might (or might not) change over time.
21 In María Puig de la Bellacasa's definition, to recognize and appreciate invisibilized things material and discursive. María Puig de la Bellacasa, *Matters of Care: Speculative Ethics in More Than Human Worlds.*

of methodologies to unpick binaries and reread gaps, silences and in-between spaces,"[22] to validate more or alternative ways of doing things, more or alternative modes of being, knowing, and sensing beyond the established, normative ones.

Queering Pollen

Pollen is a useful particle to think with in Aeropolis. Its role in this complex, entangled, and always evolving world that is air is easier to imagine because it can be seen and felt—and it is taught in school!—and yet its ambivalence, its being "good" and "bad" at once, exposes the need to queer it.

To queer pollen is to look at the "outside world" the way Maya did. Maya's curious, joyful, inquisitive pollination challenges the role of pollen described by (militarized) science—which describes biological processes with a warlike vocabulary,[23] like Scheppegrell's "warfare against weeds." To queer pollen is to pay attention to how plants and insects collaborate for plant reproduction and seduce and attract each other, displaying colors and releasing chemicals or waves into the air like smell, movement, or sound, bringing flesh, lust, and desire to nature—and, as we will see, transform urban and nonurban territories.[24] Queering pollen is a form of imagining futures or world-making that brings desire, multispecies reproduction and interactions, excess, and ambiguity to Aeropolis.

To queer pollen is also a tool for seeing the various ways in which pollution has never actually been a condition of matter but has and continues to be put to work to "do" things. Thus to grasp the world-making potential of sensing and living with pollution differently, it is first necessary to unravel the broader social, political, and

22 Myra J. Hird and Noreen Giffney, *Queering the Non/Human*, 5.

23 Emily Martin, *Flexible Bodies: Tracking Immunity in American Culture from the Days of Polio to the Age of AIDS*.

24 For the role of desire in architecture, see: Uriel Fogué, "Architectura Amandi: Hacia Una Cosmopolítica del Deseo"; Uriel Fogué, *Las Arquitecturas del Fin del Mundo: Cosmotécnicas y Cosmopolíticas Para un Futuro en Suspenso*.

ecological processes that pollen engages. It is also necessary to unravel the processes that have delimited its effects and relationships as they touch down and transform our environments, keeping in mind that in every history there are many others not accounted for or told. These "exceptions" to the storied "rule," which run counter to the dominant narrative, open new ways of doing things.

"NATURE" PUT TO WORK FOR "PURE AIR" (AIR DESIGN)

Let us now return to the United States' rapidly developing cities around the turn of the twentieth century. Much has been written in architecture discourses on the construction of parks as "green lungs" in urban environments, one of the key strategies of the hygienist movement.[25] Through urban parks, nature was put to work as a healer, offering a breath of fresh air to offset the filthy carbon smoke that inundated cities.[26] What is less known to readers of architectural history is that between the 1880s and the 1930s, pollen and its "polluting" capacity was also mobilized to intervene in and create new typologies of "green areas." Empty lots became areas of concern while hay fever resorts and national

242

25   For an interdisciplinary history of the hygienist movement and its effects on architecture and urban design, see Giovanna Borasi and Mirko Zardini, *Imperfect Health: The Medicalization of Architecture.*

26   In response to the rapid industrialization and growth of the main harbor cities of the East Coast, since the early nineteenth century, middle-class elites promoted, managed, and designed urban parks in collaboration with landscape designers like Frederick Law Olmsted (and his sons)—who designed most of the central parks of US cities. Urban parks functioned not only as "lungs," they were also an ideological and political project. The parks were designed for social control, to keep working-class bodies fit in order to increase factory production, and to homogenize the morals of the wide variety of immigrants who constituted the labor force of industrialization and the construction of cities. To achieve this disciplining, Olmstead and his collaborators opted to re-create the pastoral landscape of England—calm, quiet, orderly. The plants and trees for these parks were imported from Europe, but they were not considered "foreign" or "invasive," possibly because they were brought in by the landscape designers themselves—who had been trained in Europe. It is also surprising that the only pollen that was accounted for (and fought against) was that of weeds, without considering the pollen released by the newly planted grasses and trees—or that the guano and human waste from nearby neighborhoods that were used as fertilizers went unnoticed. Through the design of public parks, that air too becomes entangled within these systems of control and discipline. Dorceta E. Taylor, "Central Park as a Model for Social Control"; Jane Hutton, "Inexhaustible Terrain."

parks were subsequently designed to prevent hay fever symptoms (and therefore pollen in the air); vegetation was "put to work" for "pure air" (which meant removing pollen from it). What is powerful about examining empty lots, hay fever resorts, and national parks together is how they reveal the different ways in which some forms of nature—pollen, weeds—were positioned socially and spatially in opposition to others—trees, gardens, forests. Thus, notions of pollen and the green areas designed to prevent its spread co-constructed each other.

Understanding the different entanglements between air, pollen, pollution, society, health, and so forth through these green typologies, and their implications, requires parsing a new set of relationships:

In order to scrutinize, and ultimately move beyond, the conceptualization of "nature" as a resource for human well-being and quality of life, we need to consider what counts as "good" or "bad" nature in these spaces.

In order to identify the social and cultural atmosphere that the ruling class had to create to mobilize budgets, infrastructures, logistics, and regulations in service of these spaces, we need to understand what the ruling class considered pollution and how they intended to "solve" it.

In order to explore how "solutions" bring with them political motivations and forms of exclusion,[27] we need to ask what forms of "othering" were constructed through "green areas" and the public space.

In order to identify within and against the power relations at play in forms of world-making and resistance, we need to interrogate who or what benefited from otherness or exclusion.

243

---

27 As French West Indian psychiatrist and political philosopher Frantz Fanon points out, colonial space is configured through boundaries, and space itself is used to keep the colonized and the queer in their place. Following Fanon, it could be argued that each of the green areas, by forming new spatial boundaries, was meant to clean the air and to segregate various groups of people, reproducing colonial relations and environmental injustice. Frantz Fanon, *The Wretched of the Earth*.

Empty Lots and the Fight against the Invasive

Throughout the second half of the nineteenth century and the first half of the twentieth, and growing at the same speed as cities, weeds grew everywhere: on private property, in sidewalks, roads, parks, and (with much exuberance) empty lots. As the leftovers of rapid urbanization in industrial cities, empty lots came to represent uncontrolled and uncontrollable space. Dirty and impure, they challenged the clean image of development. They did not have real estate value. They were too small to accommodate housing and too small to be turned into public space. Empty lots were unwanted and abandoned, deemed unproductive and infertile. They were regarded as polluted and polluting spaces at once: wasteful and crime ridden, corrupting the atmosphere, morals, and aesthetics of city life. They were what sociologist Alice Mah has termed "wasted places," frustrating the voracious appetite of capital.[28] In places like empty lots, "violence comes to be seen as endemic to particular forms of neglected urban nature, leading policy-makers as well as scientists to approach ecological change as a matter of social control rather than as an environmental concern."[29]

From a queer urban political ecologies perspective, it is not a coincidence that the solution to hay fever was the elimination of weeds. Weeds were considered invasive and foreign species, reproducing the fictions and ideologies of difference and estrangement underlining settler colonial projects.[30] A St. Louis police court judge described weeds in 1899 as "the witches' cauldron into which much of the loathsome filth and offal of a great city is cast to stew and simmer."[31] They were also viewed negatively for reproducing in excess with a "discouraging fertility," as Chicago pollen collector Oren Durham described, and for not conforming to stereotypical

28 Alice Mah, *Industrial Ruination, Community, and Place: Landscapes and Legacies of Urban Decline.*
29 Nate Gabriel, "Urban Political Ecology: Environmental Imaginary, Governance, and the Non-Human," 40.
30 Ros Gray and Shela Sheikh, "The Wretched Earth: Botanical Conflicts and Artistic Interventions."
31 Zachary J. S. Falck, "Controlling the Weed Nuisance in Turn-of-the-Century American Cities," 613.

standards of plant beauty.[32] Defined as "a plant in the wrong place," a "plant growing where it is not wanted," weeds were spatially determined and thus bound up with all the other racialized systems and biases underpinning the environment. Weeds often grow and live in the cracks, in liminal and unexpected places, which has always created a sense of un-belonging, but their very classification is inconsistent, contingent, unruly. For a weed to be a weed it is dependent on the place where it grows. The same plant species might be considered a weed in one location and not in another. Thus, the cultural meaning and material reality of weeds refuse the imperialist need for control (of humans and otherwise), making their unruliness a threat to knowledge, power, and authority.

The social, political, and ideological threat weeds posed to the project of urban order was so significant that weeds also became a metaphor for some humans who were themselves targets of significant social campaigns at the time. Throughout the nineteenth century, the ruling class called migrants, the poor, homeless, and criminals "human weeds" because, in their eyes, they were physically weak and unproductive, and were seen as outsiders to the accepted norms of social and economic life.[33] This dehumanizing process deemed the lives of the poor, like weeds, disposable.[34] Based in Darwinian notions of species competition and aligned with the competitive capitalist economy of the time, the notion of "human weeds" was strongly wielded by the eugenicist movement, which proposed population control through sterilization and incarceration.[35] But where the eugenicists regarded the "human weeds'" lack of physical and mental fitness to be the consequence of their biology, reformists, on the other hand, attributed this to the effects of pollution, poor

32 Durham, *Your Hay Fever*.
33 The term "human weeds" was widely used at the time, when the eugenicist movement, motivated by race and control of property, was incredibly violent. Falck, *Weeds*.
34 This resonates with what political theorist Achille Mbembe has pointed out, that Indigenous life was considered animal life by the colonizers and was therefore "disposable." Achille Mbembe, *Necropolitics*.
35 Falck, *Weeds*.

housing, and other environmental conditions. In fact, in many cities, "human weeds" were used as free labor for the weed-eradication campaigns, which became for the reformists a strategy to control both the air and society at the same time.

These eradication campaigns were deployed by policymakers to remove weeds—and the pollution, people, and activities thought to come with them—from public land, especially from empty lots. By removing the unwanted plants, policymakers designed the air by clearing everything in an attempt to go back to the land's "original" state—empty, pre-polluted, and ready for development. However, what was not taken into consideration was that while one single solution (removing weeds) could temporarily mitigate symptoms of hay fever, it did not address its root causes—soil disturbance— nor did it account for the polarizing social effects of urbanization. Empty lots set the stage for a civic, aesthetic, and moral project that ultimately deepened social, health, and urban divisions in the name of "reform."

This episode demonstrates how notions of "foreign" and "invasive" do not necessarily map onto what is endemic and productive ecosystemically, but to the *dominant* attitudes, ideas, morals, and political ambitions of those who were privileged to "design the air." However, against this prevailing diagnostic tendency, there were botanists who were curious about weeds and offered a different narrative. For New York–based botanist Roger Wodehouse, who studied the taxonomy and ecological cycles of weeds, weeds were not invaders but—in his words—"pioneers" that could prevent erosion, attract pollinators, and regenerate the soil. Wodehouse even went so far as to invert weeds' supposed responsibility for pollution: because weeds grow in removed soil, they are actually the product of urbanization. Consequently, Wodehouse concluded that hay fever was in fact a human-made disease, and not the consequence of a "polluted or invasive nature."[36]

While the eradication campaigns were taking place in cities, the war on weeds expanded into rural areas. In *Breathing Space: How Allergies Shape Our Lives and Landscapes*, historian of science Gregg Mitman offers a fascinating account of the entanglement between pollen and place in the United States at the turn of the twentieth century. He recounts how, in the 1870s, wealthy men left the pollen (and coal) polluted cities on the East Coast and the Midwest, in particular New York and Chicago, in search of "pure air" to alleviate their hay fever symptoms.[37] They traveled to remote destinations—like the White Mountains in New Hampshire, the Great Lakes, or the desert settlement of Tucson—on "hay fever holidays." Luxurious hay fever resorts were built to host these men during the pollen season, which could last from April to November. These resorts were cultural and commercial spaces, where "consuming nature [and 'clean air'] for health and leisure went hand in hand."[38]

"Purity" is, of course, a construction that requires differentiating what is pure and what is not. Hay fever resorts were defined by this forced opposition between polluted urban nature (which included pollen that triggered hay fever) and unpolluted rural nature (exploited as a refuge, as the space of pure air). This distinction was also sustained by beliefs about what constituted life in the city (busy, noisy, dirty) and life in nature (calm, quiet, and clean)—contributing to the narrative that nature provided a safe escape for wealthy men. An escape from the mess that they, paradoxically, had created and benefited from in the city:

> Hay fever became the prided malady of the summer residents who had escaped the nervous energies of the city to breathe more deeply and freely in the relaxed setting of cultured nature.[39]

247

36 Roger P. Wodehouse, "Hayfever, A Man-Made Disease." Running counter to conventional science at the time, Wodehouse demonstrated that ragweed, for instance, was native to North America.

37 Gregg Mitman, *Breathing Space: How Allergies Shape Our Lives and Landscapes*.

This romanticization sublimated breathing (deeply and freely) as both an aesthetic experience and a privilege.[40] Hay fever "became a favored American pastime... it drew upon and contributed to a flourishing tourist industry that catered to an educated elite largely centered in the urban and industrial East."[41] Again, according to the early stages of hay fever research, men were the only ones considered sensitive to pollen—and so for many years women were not even allowed in hay fever resorts. In fact, the US Hay Fever Association only provided full membership to males:

> The US Hay Fever Association was overwhelmingly composed of physicians, judges, lawyers, ministers, merchants, and other educated male professionals for whom a six-week vacation away from business and family, costing anywhere from six to twelve months of a laborer's wage, was little problem.[42]

Hay fever came to be regarded as "the price of wealth and culture, a part of the penalty of fine organization of indoor life."[43] It was then also a mark of, perhaps, not needing to work outdoors. Hay fever resorts were thus productive in other ways: They became spaces for decision-making, career promotion, and cultural exchange for the privileged, the gathering place for all those men who legislated, controlled, determined, and policed the city to enforce the "natural" order of things.

The success of hay fever resorts was so great that more hotels were built, roads and railway networks kept expanding. These

---

38 Mitman, *Breathing Space*, 45.
39 Mitman, "Hay Fever Holiday," 614.
40 This idealization of life in nature was elaborated through the US and European artistic and cultural style of Romanticism, which glorified through literature and painting the natural sublime, the heroic encounter between man (always masculine and usually alone), and a mysterious and uncontrollable nature. Getting lost in the forests, breathing pure air, sublimated breathing as an aesthetic experience. But access to "pure air"—and purity in general—was a gender, race, and class privilege.
41 Mitman, "Hay Fever Holiday," 609.
42 Mitman, "Hay Fever Holiday," 621.
43 Mitman, "Hay Fever Holiday," 601.

works created dust and moved soil, inviting more weeds to grow, and, consequently, "polluted" the "pure" air sanctuaries with pollen grains. Once these places were no longer oases from hay fever—and with the development of antihistamines—the elite escaped elsewhere, abandoning the hotels and towns they had so much enjoyed and pushing them into decline. Here, again, through hay fever resorts, we see how constructed binaries between "good" and "bad" nature—weeds and pollen opposed to rural landscapes—rather than actually contending with the true catalysts of pollution ultimately serve to maintain the political, social, and economic status quo.

Hay fever resorts are thus a good example of what a capitalist and colonial strategy toward land, nature, and pollution does: it colonizes, extracts, pollutes, and leaves, to start over again in a new location, leaving the burden to those who cannot afford to leave. However, the departure of some leaves space for others. The local and seasonal Jewish population of Bethlehem, New Hampshire—the largest town in the White Mountains—had not been able to afford the luxurious hotels during the hay fever seasons. They eventually took over some of the decaying hotels and created the Hebrew Hay Fever Relief Association, which offered relief from hay fever and a possibility of leisure to nonaffluent visitors, helping the local economy recover.[44]

National Parks and the Construction of Wilderness

After seeing with their eyes and feeling with their lungs the speed at which the spaces they had "discovered" became atmospherically ruined, the US Hay Fever Association sought to protect "untouched" natural areas from development. In the 1890s, the association campaigned to establish a federal forest reserve in the White Mountains, to preserve "the original" landscape and the

44   Michael Hoberman, "How Strange It Seems: The Cultural Life of Jews in Small-Town New England."

purity of its air—initiating the practice of forest preservation. But the federal protection of a large piece of land to preserve its air was unprecedented, so scientific, managerial, and cultural shifts were required to generate significant support for the project. First, atmospheric purity had to be scientifically defined. To demonstrate the difference between hay fever–free air and polluted air, the association commissioned a study in 1888 to find scientific evidence of "pure air," as there were no prior references.[45] However, purity of air was not enough to mobilize resources for the project, so the association had to demonstrate that these lands were unfit for agriculture, pasturing, and settlement, and, perhaps most significantly, lobbied for the protection of large areas of land as a matter of national importance.[46] As a young nation lacking a built heritage, a source of national identity was found in the sheer scale of the North American landscape, like Niagara Falls or Yosemite, which were unmatched in Europe.[47] Thus what became national parks protected the so-called wilderness, "untouched" edenic landscapes, over landscapes that had been transformed by humans—and therefore had lost their air purity—through deforestation, agriculture, and urbanization.

This idea of wilderness became crucial to the federal protection of forests against pollen, air pollution, and other effects of development. In *Wild Things*, English and Gender studies scholar

45   As Mitman accounts: "Enlisting the support of laymen, [naturalist and hay feverlte Samuel Lockwood] endeavored to gather meteorological records of temperature, wind velocity and direction, humidity, and barometric changes, along with microscopic analysis of atmospheric particles and experiences of patients under their local influence, to arrive at 'trust-worthy' results 'on the line of comparative pathology.'" Half a century later, Oren Durham conducted, due to popular interest, a systematic study of pollen in national parks. Mitman, "Hay Fever Holiday," 632; Oren C. Durham, "Air-Borne Allergens in the National Parks."
46   H. Duane Hampton, "Opposition to Natural Parks."
47   This had institutional and infrastructural effects. For historian Denise Meringolo, national parks redefined the American landscape as a public resource, bringing together science, business, and government. Meringolo argues that the development of a new discipline, public history, was needed to define national parks as history, along with institutions to preserve them. Denise Meringolo, *Museums, Monuments, and National Parks: Toward a New Genealogy of Public History*.

Jack Halberstam explains that "the binary logics that set the wild in opposition to the modern, the civilized, the cultivated, and the real" were coined at the same time by naturalist writers like Thoreau,[48] where "the wild" was framed through racial, gendered, and colonialist understandings of nature.[49] The wilderness, as "untamed" and "available" nature, became a symbol of freedom for the same elite who managed the parks and enjoyed the hay fever resorts, and was built up as tourist destinations for travelers in search of picturesque "untouched" vistas. What is left out of these national narratives are the earlier histories of Indigenous settlement in these landscapes and their subjection to the violence and displacement of US settler colonialism. When accounting for these histories and developments, national parks, and thus narratives of pollution, can themselves be read as a protracted form of social control through the land. As Indigenous scholar Brenda J. Child has noted:

> The experiences of Ojibwe people in the Great Lakes suggest that the creation of national parks in their homeland was part of a broader colonial history of appropriating Indigenous lands and resources, and extended the damaging policies of the Indian assimilation and allotment era farther into the twentieth century.[50]

Thus, calling places like the White Mountains "wild" was a means of mystifying the persistence of colonial violence. Because "the nostalgia for a lost Eden, an idealized space outside of human time, is closely connected to displacing the ways that colonial violence disrupted human ecologies."[51] Even the desire for wilderness was classed, racist, gendered, as the number of non-European

48 Jack Halberstam, *Wild Things: The Disorder of Desire*, ix.
49 For Mortimer-Sandilands, "Parks were born from a gendered and racialized view of nature, and were also used to impose gendered and racialized relations on nature." Catriona Mortimer-Sandilands, "Unnatural Passions?: Notes Toward a Queer Ecology."
50 Brenda J. Child, "The Absence of Indigenous Histories in Ken Burns's *The National Parks: America's Best Idea.*"
51 Elisabeth DeLoughrey and George B. Handley, *Postcolonial Ecologies: Literatures of the Environment*, 9.

immigrants living in cities, women entering the workforce, and the growing working and middle class motivated "the need for 'clean' spaces for white folks."[52]

Even though parks were designed to preserve "good air," to represent the glory of the newly born country, and serve as landscapes for public leisure, they also became spaces of contestation. While the tourism campaigns for national parks promoted conventional American ideals like self-sufficiency and family values, these landscapes were also used as sites to escape from these norms. For example, during the 1960s youth counterculture movements, Yosemite became a camping place where people could form and re-form communal living situations overnight.[53] These anecdotes are important, not because they demonstrate total relief from life under capitalism, or its defeat, but because they illuminate its weaknesses, cracks, fissures. They illuminate that it is not a totalizing project, that different forms of life and coming together are possible and do exist. They provide optimism in a violent and unequal world and are places to think with and learn from when imagining other possible worlds.

CONCLUDING THOUGHTS ON AEROPOLIS AS A QUEER(ING) TERRITORY

We have seen how perceptions of health go hand in hand with conceptions of the natural environment, how these narratives can scaffold the legacies of colonialism and capitalist development.[54] Attributing polluting sources, either in the environment or in human bodies, has major consequences for different groups, either extending their privileges or increasing their dispossession. This

52   Mortimer-Sandilands, "Unnatural Passions?"
53   Guy McClellan, "Hippies in the Park: Yosemite and the Counterculture in the Sixties American West."
54   See Linda Nash, *Inescapable Ecologies: A History of Environment, Disease, and Knowledge.*

tendency also requires that attention be paid to what else is done in the name of "cleaning" the environment, and to who does the cleaning.

Unsurprisingly, the battle against pollen and weeds is far from over. The number of asthma sufferers throughout the world grows every day, as insects' pollination decreases. While efforts to re-populate forests and green cities increase pollen concentrations in the air, the distinction between what is a toxin (natural) and a toxicant (anthropogenic) becomes less clear, as pollen is becoming, in many places, toxic.[55] The battle against weeds is still promoted by multinational herbicide corporations, who need the "existence" of weeds to sell their products. Others profit from weeds by letting them grow, reducing the value of properties and creating the opportunity for speculation.[56] Forcing marginalized people to solve our most threatening environmental problems is a common practice that persists today. For instance, in California, every summer prisoners are sent to fight deadly wildfires for a fraction of minimum wage. The COVID-19 pandemic has reproduced and exacerbated these contradictions and processes. It is the most vulnerable who are not only more susceptible to infection (because they can't afford to stay home, for example) but also more integral (as frontline workers at hospitals, care homes, etc.) to sustaining daily life in the city.

These contradictions suggest the impossibility of finding simple solutions to pollen, weeds, or asthma, so it is surprising how practices of escaping, protecting, or cleaning pollution are still proposed today.[57] Thus, knowing the historical account of pollen's

55 Due to the increase of anthropogenic pollution in the air, pollen particles stick to heavy metals. They form larger particles—becoming toxin and toxicant at once—spiking respiratory problems and creating pollen storms that travel long distances. As with other forms of pollution, they damage more than respiratory organs and can have other forms of deadly effects. One example of this is the pollen produced by GMO plants. GMO pollen is toxic for bees and has detrimental effects on human life. As it travels with the wind it germinates in organic fields, contributing to the precariat of large communities of farmers who see their livelihoods destroyed by their forced dependency on the multinationals that create the fixed markets of GMO seeds. Vandana Shiva, *One Earth, One Humanity vs. the 1%*.

56 Cooking Sections, *The Empire Remains Shop*.

transformation from a valuable grain to a threat to human health and its consequences is crucial for understanding the problems of techno-scientific solutions. But beyond simply knowing, queering aspects of these historical accounts provides other questions, lines of work—sometimes dead ends—and inspiration to do things differently for more livable presents and futures. To open and construct, conceptually and physically, other worlds. As environmental humanities scholar Nicole Seymour argues,

> With a queer ecological perspective attuned to social justice, we can learn to care about the future of the planet in a way that is perhaps more radical than any we have seen previously: acting in the interests of nameless, faceless individuals to which one has no biological, familial, or economic ties whatsoever. This kind of action operates without any reward, without any guarantee of success, and without any proof that potential future inhabitants of the planet might be similar to the individual acting in the present—in terms of social identity, morality, or even species, if some doomsday predictions are to be believed. It is invested in the ends (survival of the non-human alongside the human) but emphasizes the means (caring for the non-human alongside the human).[58]

One way to explore other possible futures is to challenge—to queer—the way that certain concepts of nature—the invasive, the pure, and the wild—were mobilized against other forms of nature in empty lots, hay fever resorts, and natural parks. Queering the

254

57 For instance, the superrich are building bunkers and isolated and insulated areas in preparation for a climate disaster; after decades of planting male trees in cities to avoid the fruits of female trees, which raised pollen counts, this practice is now being reversed; and herbicide companies are still profiting from weed eradication, even though some are trying to find less toxic "solutions." Thomas Leo Ogren, "Botanical Sexism Cultivates Home-Grown Allergies"; Matt Blois, "Following Several Fallow Decades, Herbicide Companies Are Searching for New Modes of Action"; Douglas Rushkoff, "The Super-Rich 'Preppers' Planning to Save Themselves from the Apocalypse."
58 Nicole Seymour, *Strange Natures: Futurity, Empathy, and the Queer Ecological Imagination*, 11.

"invasive" invests in "non-productive" spaces, like empty lots, not so much to make them productive but to open up counteropportunities.[59] It means acting in the interest of "spaces in which the imperative of capitalist redevelopment is suspended long enough so that we might genuinely engage alternative modes of being," such as the abandoned and overgrown High Line in New York City that was a safe space for cruising before its redevelopment into a commercial park.[60] Nonproductive spaces have the potential to be reinvented, to become something different, possibly outside the marketization of land, to improve social well-being and life. The suspension of conventional or commercial aesthetic values can clear the way for spaces to perform differently, like hiding in plain sight whilst being with others outside the codes of heteropatriarchy.

When thinking about what it means to queer purity, cultural theorist C. Riley Snorton's articulation of the "transitive" is productive:

> "Transitive," not only as a term that articulates the quality of "passing into another condition, changeable, changeful; passing away, transient, transitory," but also in terms of the mechanics of grammar, in which the transitive refers to the expression of an action that requires a direct object to complete its sense of meaning... Transitive modes of differentiation in which difference is neither absolute nor binaristic but changeable.[61]

Snorton mobilizes the transitive to trace "the circulation of "black" and "trans" (as matter and metaphor) as they are brought into the same frame by the various ways they have been constituted as fungible, thingified, and interchangeable, particularly within the logics of transatlantic exchange."[62] Perhaps queering purity means

59   Jack Halberstam, *In a Queer Time and Place: Transgender Bodies, Subcultural Lives*.
60   Patrick, "The Matter of Displacement," 936.
61   C. Riley Snorton, *Black on Both Sides: A Racial History of Trans Identity*, 5.
62   Snorton, *Black on Both Sides*, 6.

thinking of "purity" as a transitive condition instead of a fixed category. What if what differentiates the pure from the impure is an action, something transient and changeable? In particular, I find useful here Snorton's reading of the Snaky Swamp as an inhabitable space for humans, where "blackness-as-fungible engenders forms of nonrecognition,"[63] permitting an ungendered body to live and escape. What forms of life and death are possible in thinking about the landscapes and atmospheres of the White Mountains as passing into another condition or substance, transitory, and even passing away?[64]

To queer the wild, I take inspiration from Halberstam, who proposes that

> wildness can escape its function as a negative condition and can name a form of being that flees from possessive structures of governance and remain opposed to so-called normal humanity... I try to offer another account of wildness within which it functions as a form of disorder that will not submit to rule, a mode of unknowing, a resistant ontology, and a fantasy of life beyond the human.[65]

This understanding of wildness can shed light on ecologies that might not look threatening—or spectacular, or untouched—but that threaten what an ecology worth protecting is. I am thinking of peatlands or marshes, for instance, which have been regarded for a long time as empty and "useless" nature to be eradicated— whose transient and undefinable water-land conditions have in many instances been removed, either by draining for urban or agriculture

---

63 Snorton, *Black on Both Sides*, 71.
64 For example: a swamp located on the border of Virginia and North Carolina became the refuge of fugitive slaves. "These self-extricated communities, which were in complex relations with other slaves, indigenous peoples and colonial administrations, established self-reliant communities as they removed themselves from violent captive enslavement." Dimitris Papadopoulos, *Experimental Practice: Technoscience, Alterentologies, and More-Than-Social Movements*, 100.
65 Halberstam, *Wild Things*, 8.

development or as soil factories to nurture lawns and gardens. To consider the opportunities in protecting the uncategorical, the empty, and the "useless" like peatlands or marshes, we must unlearn what we know of them and recognize the lives beyond the human (animal, plant, gaseous) that they contain and are part of.

Aeropolis as Queer(ing) Territory

Framing Aeropolis as a queer urban political ecology permits us to unpack how particles and gases in the air—including so-called pollutants—harm *and* transform humans and environments: materially (darkening, eroding, growing, reproducing, killing) and conceptually (configuring ideas of nature and having material effects in the air, humans and urban spaces). It permits us to see how pollution disproportionately impacts some, and not others, and therefore how it is situated. In this way, queering shares with design its commitment to processes, to take the "where" and "how" seriously. Proposals might be good or well intentioned, but depending on where/how they are defined, put to work, shared, or discussed they might have un/desirable effects. Queering permits us, for example, to question established buzzwords in spatial design. Take for instance the "greening" of cities, buildings, sidewalks, roofs, interiors (and all its related terms like renaturalizing, etc.) that are often proposed as *the* way to deal with climate change. Greening cities is a "sustainable solution" that sustains the capitalist project. "Greening" is a new style—which can pollute the air too and, as political ecologies and environmental humanities scholar Malcom Ferdinand remarks, it also "preserves colonial inhabitation and the forms of human and non-human domination that come with it."[66] "Greening" is a real estate strategy that increases property value under the guise of sustainability. Sure, trees are attributed a

---

66   Malcom Ferdinand, *Decolonial Ecology: Thinking from the Caribbean World*, 115.
67   Cooking Sections, *Offsetted*.

productive role as large-scale atmosphere purifiers,[67] but what does greening all over actually do? Queering nature shows how notions of "green" are never neutral, they come with and reproduce all forms of exclusion and domination.[68]

But Aeropolis is also a queer(ing) territory. It is the space of bio- and necropolitics, life and death, at once. It is the city of ranges and spectrums, where materiality is fluid and mobile. As a queer urban political ecology—again, a wide umbrella that includes feminist political ecologies, decolonial, and queer ecologies—it brings together particles, bodies, the city, race, sexuality, gender, class... mediated by open air. And it pays special attention to all the different forms of environmental injustice—slow or fast, visible or not. This queer(ing) territory invites other bodies, other natures, other infrastructures, other forms of sensing—including the "othered" and those to whom the world has been denied.[69] Inhabiting them is an opportunity for critical and careful interventions as well as for thinking about other—queer—forms of living together.[70] Queering as a form of recognizing the potential to live differently. Vaporous and troubling spaces, physical and imaginary, where we breathe one another, where we let things grow, where we move slowly toward alternative presents and futures.

6.2

68 Natasha Myers, "From Edenic Apocalypse to Gardens against Eden."
69 What Ferdinand has callled the "(human and non human) off-worlders whose vital energy is forcibly dedicated to fuel lifestyles and ways of inhabiting the Earth of a minority whole being denied an existence of their own in the world." Ferdinand, *Decolonial Ecology*, 60.
70 I am referring to Ferdinand's definition of living together, as "the human political task of composing a world with other people." Ferdinand, *Decolonial Ecology*, 82.

6.3

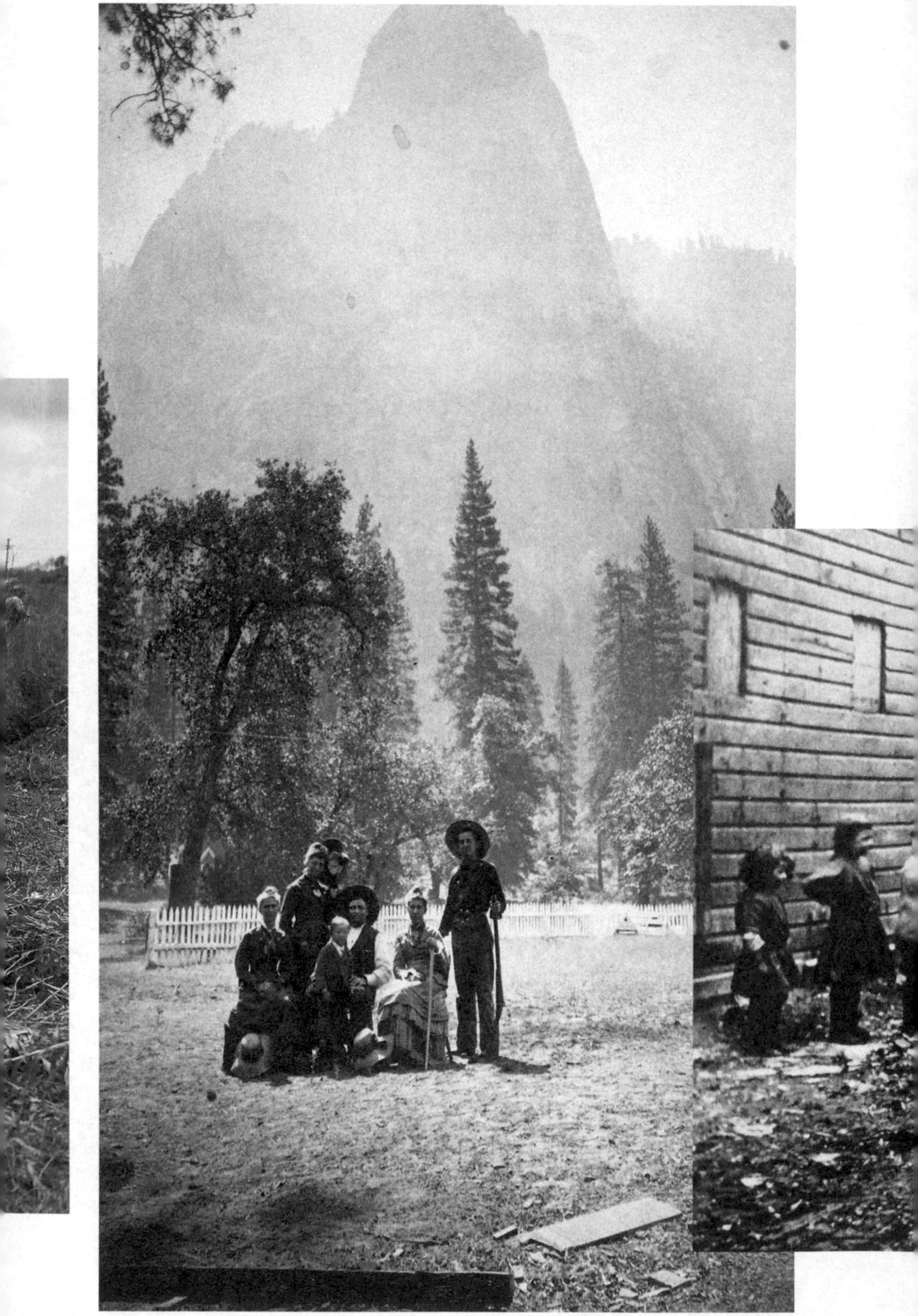

6.5

6.4

WORKS CITED

Allen, Irma. "Thinking with a Feminist Political Ecology of Air-and-Breathing-Bodies." *Body & Society* 26, no. 2 (June 2020): 79–105.

Borasi, Giovanna; Zardini, Mirko, ed. *Imperfect Health: The Medicalization of Architecture*. Lars Müller Publishers and CCA, Montreal, 2012.

Logan, William Bryant. *Air: The Restless Shaper of the World*. New York: W. W. Norton, 2012.

Child, Brenda J. "The Absence of Indigenous Histories in Ken Burns's *The National Parks: America's Best Idea*." *The Public Historian* 33, no. 2 (May 2011): 24–29.

Cooking Sections. *Offsetted*. Berlin: Hatje Cantz, 2022.

> *The Empire Remains Shop*. New York: Columbia Books on Architecture and the City, 2018.

DeLoughrey, Elizabeth, and George B. Handley, eds. *Postcolonial Ecologies: Literatures of the Environment*. Oxford: Oxford University Press, 2011.

Durham, Oren C. "Air-Borne Allergens in the National Parks." *Journal of Allergy* 20, no. 4 (July 1949): 255–268.

> *Your Hay Fever*. Indianapolis, IN: The Bobbs-Merrill Company, 1936.

Falck, Zachary. *Weeds: An Environmental History of Metropolitan America*. Pittsburgh: University of Pittsburgh Press, 2011.

> "Controlling the Weed Nuisance in Turn-of-the-Century American Cities." *Environmental History* 7, no. 4 (2002): 611–631.

Fanon, Frantz. *The Wretched of the Earth*. London: Penguin Books, 2014.

Ferdinand, Malcom. *Decolonial Ecology: Thinking from the Caribbean World*. Cambridge: Polity Press, 2022.

Fogué, Uriel. "Architectura Amandi: Hacia Una Cosmopolitical Del Deseo." In *Post Arcadia. Qué Arte Para Qué Naturaleza?*, edited by Miguel Mesa and Enrique Nieto, 185–218. Murcia: CENDEAC, 2020.

> *Las Arquitecturas Del Fin Del Mundo: Cosmotécnicas y Cosmopolíticas Para Un Futuro En Suspenso*. Barcelona: Puente Editores, 2022.

Gabriel, Nate. "Urban Political Ecology: Environmental Imaginary, Governance, and the Non-Human." *Geography Compass* 8, no. 1 (2014): 38–48.

Gandy, Matthew. "Queer Ecology: Nature, Sexuality, and Heterotopic Alliances." *Environment and Planning D: Society and Space* 20, no. 4 (August 2012): 727–747.

Gissen, David. *Subnature*. New York: Princeton Architectural Press, 2009.

Graham, Stephen. "Life Support: The Political Ecology of Urban Air." *City* 19, no. 2–3 (May 2015): 192–215.

Gray, Ros, and Shela Sheikh, eds. "The Wretched Earth: Botanical Conflicts and Artistic Interventions." *Third Text* 32 (2018): 163–175.

Halberstam, Jack. *Wild Things: The Disorder of Desire*. Durham, NC: Duke University Press, 2020.

> *In a Queer Time and Place: Transgender Bodies, Subcultural Lives*. New York: New York University Press, 2005.

Hampton, H. Duane. "Opposition to Natural Parks." *Journal of Forest History* 25, no. 1 (1981): 36–45.

Harcourt, Wendy, and Ingrid L. Nelson. *Practising Feminist Political Ecologies: Moving Beyond the "Green Economy."* London: Zed Books, 2015.

Heynen, Nik, Maria Kaika, and Erik Swyngedouw, eds. *In the Nature of Cities: Urban Political Ecology and the Politics of Urban Metabolism*. London: Routledge, 2006.

Hird, Myra J., and Noreen Giffney. *Queering the Non/Human*. London: Routledge, 2016.

Hoberman, Michael. *How Strange It Seems: The Cultural Life of Jews in Small-Town New England*. Amherst, MA: University of Massachusetts Press, 2008.

Hutton, Jane. "Inexhaustible Terrain." CCA, 2017.

Mah, Alice. *Industrial Ruination, Community, and Place: Landscapes and Legacies of Urban Decline*. Toronto: University of Toronto Press, 2012.

Martin, Emily. *Flexible Bodies. The Role of Immunity in American Culture from the Days of the Polio to the Age of AIDS*. Boston: Beacon Press, 1994.

Mbembe, Achille. *Necropolitics*. Durham, NC: Duke University Press, 2019.

McClellan, Guy. "Hippies in the Park: Yosemite and the Counterculture in the Sixties American West." *History ETDs*, July 12, 2014.

Meringolo, Denise D. *Museums, Monuments, and National Parks: Toward a New Genealogy of Public History*. Amherst, MA: University of Massachusetts Press, 2012.

Mitman, Gregg. *Breathing Space: How Allergies Shape Our Lives and Landscapes*. New Haven, CT: Yale University Press, 2007.

"Hay Fever Holiday: Health, Leisure, and Place in Gilded-Age America." *Bulletin of the History of Medicine* 77, no. 3 (2003): 600–635.

Mortimer-Sandilands, Catriona. "Unnatural Passions?: Notes Toward a Queer Ecology." *Invisible Culture* 9 (2005).

"Whose There Is There, There? Queer Directions and Ecocritical Orientations." *Ecozon@* 1, no. 1 (2010): 63–69.

Myers, Natasha. "From Edenic Apocalypse to Gardens against Eden." In *Infrastructure, Environment and Life in the Anthropocene*, 115–148. Durham, NC: Duke University Press, 2019.

Nash, Linda. *Inescapable Ecologies: A History of Environment, Disease, and Knowledge*. Berkeley, CA: University of California Press, 2006.

Ogren, Thomas Leo. "Botanical Sexism Cultivates Home-Grown Allergies." *Scientific American Blog Network*. https://blogs.scientificamerican.com/guest-blog/botanical-sexism-cultivates-home-grown-allergies.

Patrick, Darren J. "The Matter of Displacement: A Queer Urban Ecology of New York City's High Line." *Social & Cultural Geography* 15, no. 8 (2014): 920–941.

Papadopoulos, Dimitris. *Experimental Practice: Technoscience, Alterontologies, and More-Than Social Movements*. Durham, NC: Duke University Press, 2018.

Puig de la Bellacasa, María. *Matters of Care: Speculative Ethics in More Than Human Worlds*. Minneapolis, MN: University of Minnesota Press, 2017.

Rushkoff, Douglas. "The Super-Rich 'Preppers' Planning to Save Themselves from the Apocalypse." *The Observer*, September 4, 2022, sec. News. https://www.theguardian.com/news/2022/sep/04/super-rich-prepper-bunkers-apocalypse-survival-richest-rushkoff.

Scheppegrell, William. "Hay-Fever: Its Cause and Prevention." *The Journal of the American Medical Association* 66, no. 10 (1916): 707–712.

Seymour, Nicole. *Strange Natures: Futurity, Empathy, and the Queer Ecological Imagination*. Champaign, IL: University of Illinois Press, 2013.

Shiva, Vandana. *One Earth, One Humanity Vs. the 1%*. Oakland, CA: PM Press, 2019.

Snorton, C. Riley. *Black on Both Sides: A Racial History of Trans Identity*. Minneapolis, MN: University of Minnesota Press, 2017.

Taylor, Dorceta E. "Central Park as a Model for Social Control: Urban Parks, Social Class and Leisure Behavior in Nineteenth-Century America." *Journal of Leisure Research* 31, no. 4 (December 1999): 420–477.

Wodehouse, Roger P. "Hayfever, A Man-Made Disease." *Natural History, American Museum of Natural History* 43–44 (1939): 158–1963.

IMAGES

6.1, 6.6–6.9
Poplar fluff, London, 2020. Courtesy of the author and Ella Fathi.

6.2
Works Progress Administration workmen cutting ragweed in Lakeview, New Orleans, 1939. This crew launched the spring campaign against hay fever–causing weeds in New Orleans. Courtesy of WPA Photograph Collection 35.4004, City Archives & Special Collections, New Orleans Public Library.

6.3
A family poses in front of a mountain at Yosemite Park, 1880. Courtesy of US National Park Service.

6.4
Boys playing leapfrog in an alley, Chicago, c. 1900. JAMC_0000_0193_0296, Seven Settlement Houses-Database of Photos (University of Illinois at Chicago), University of Illinois at Chicago Library, Special Collections and University Archives.

6.5
A glimpse of the Mount Washington Hotel (a hay fever resort) in the White Mountains, New Hampshire, c. 1906. From the Detroit Publishing Company photograph collection. Courtesy of Library of Congress Prints and Photographs Division.

6.6

6.8

AFTER AEROPOLIS
BY TIMOTHY K. CHOY

1

Maybe begin by counting.

Testing a constraint used by others to study and characterize situational atmospheres seems fitting for thinking with *Aeropolis*, a textual concrescence of an ongoing air-bound sense-making that is at once analytic, aesthetic, and political. Nerea Calvillo—an architect of spaces, airs, concepts, gatherings, and machines—builds apparatuses for atmospheric attunement that surface both their surrounds and the specifications that ask for such attunement. Always situated and collaborative, her material and ideational arrangements yield techniques, sensations, and thoughts for breathing together—necessary lessons in compromised respiratory conditions—while eschewing aggrandizing Anthropocene airs.[+]

Counts are edges for cloud accounting.

Bodying air as toxicpolluting distribution, as sands from not-quite-elsewhere, as shared substrate, as remediating representational mist, or as a plenum of nonhuman neighbors, Aeropolis gathers its publics through "atmographies"—affective atmospheric techno-drawings. The atmographic pulls methods, materials, and metrics from air data politics, but it also willfully exceeds that arena's knowing gestures, arcing past aesthetics of evidence, endangerment, spectacle, and sublimity toward a hermeneutics of affection. No city of light, Aeropolis finds you already in the middle, suspended in an ambient medium of relations, touching and breathing air's residents and metabolizers, among other bodies and concerns that bring them to palpability.

In Aeropolis, data visualizations are vectors for "attentive speculation," specific queries of current and potential arrangements.

Where are the sensors registering this pollen? What if they were here instead? Why record this molecule, but not its cousins? Numbers open up, unfolding into materialist numeracies. The periodicity of readings. Abandoned equipment. The algorithm filling in the data's spatial and temporal gaps. How thresholds between colors are determined. "Every line or color," writes Calvillo, "requires taking a position toward the object of inquiry."

This, too, is atmospheric intimacy, feeling and stretching the edges of attention, infrastructure, and knowability. Other hues are possible.

4

The architect's atmographies elicit gasps
    —cognitive surprise!—
as they tangibilize   and problematize a given

substantiation of air,
    precluding its future relegation to background.
Stay longer,   though,
    and something else
        coalesces,
            possible
            shapes
                for atmospheric collectivity.

Part techne, part agora, part
celebration, Aeropolis's devices wear proud
    sociotechnical histories of small groups hashing
out   how to broach   intimate working

relations   with air   and
each other. Valuing   convivial
experimentation and sharing   over executive order,
Calvillo's gatherings draw out
    responsive forms of joined effort,
        responses in form
to problems of atmospheric co-subjection.

Invite.
Start small.
Test.
Ask
why. Listen.
Ask

how. Check.
Try together.

Material/Immaterial
The dualism can be tempting,
even if to critique, when trying to think
with air, but   *Aeropolis*
wonderfully makes such a gesture impossible—for across Calvillo's writing
and building,
air is always thick.

Thick and stuck in with bodies and things;
in re-mediations of pollution data, pollen
movements, swollen numbers, purity damage
contagion talk in environmental
politics, the unevenness of
toxic distribution in lands and lungs, or in feeling
for pressure and density in inflatable
architectures, airs come to matter and could be made
to matter differently through explicit practices
of fabrication. What makes it work

is that it is not (only) an argument; instead,
it's a sensibility
                    —a given—
                              permeating the practice and the writing.
Writing after testing after tweaking after talking after making after reading
and all of them all along.

This simple nugget reorganizes air's conceptualization for architecture,
the practical and political limits of environmental sense,
data and other epistemic embodiments.
With *Aeropolis*,   following it, concept work,
empirical study, and aesthetic production go
                                        hand in hand.

+ "... *constraint... situational atmospheres*..." Lauren Berlant and Kathleen Stewart are the inspirations here, particularly in their remarkable use of round word count as a formal structure within which to theorize and write the culturally generative work done in plays between structure, activity, form, language, and moment. See Berlant and Stewart, *The Hundreds* (Durham, NC: Duke University Press, 2019).

"... *textual concrescence*..." "Concrescence" signals for Alfred Whitehead a becoming whereby an event or object draws into unity. See Whitehead, *Process and Reality* (New York: Free Press, 1985). I call *Aeropolis* a textual concrescence because the book is one among other punctuating points in a current of both non-textual research creation and writing. A novel theorization of now-completed practices as well as a thinking practice in its own right, *Aeropolis* surfaces and works through problems specific to the academic monograph form, including how to enact a knowledge practice in which joined thinking replaces performances of individual mastery, as part of imagining and building conceptual and material responses to air-mediated problems when non-innocent legacies of dehumanization and harm are built into both distributions of breathability and the analytics (of, for instance, nature, environment, cleanliness, and safety) that demarcate airs as concerns in the first place.

"... *apparatuses of atmospheric attunement*..." This is another example of joined thinking. When I have used this series of words elsewhere to characterize assemblages of chemists, smells, gases, spores, laboratory equipment, mushroom hunters, dogs, and others as grounded thought and sense machines, Calvillo's projects have already shaped my attention. See Choy, "Tending to Suspension: Abstraction and Apparatuses of Atmospheric Attunement in Matsutake Worlds," in *Matsutake Worlds*, eds. Lieba Faier and Michael J. Hathaway (New York: Berghahn Books, 2021), 54–77; and Choy and Jerry Zee, "Condition—Suspension," *Cultural Anthropology* 30, no. 2 (2015): 210–223. Similarly, other writings, including those by Kathleen Stewart on atmospheric attunement and by Nicholas Shapiro on chemical sensoria, have by then already sensitized me to the ways tiny bits can charge a condition. See Stewart, "Atmospheric Attunements," *Environment and Planning D: Society and Space* 29, no. 3 (2011): 445–453; and Shapiro, "Attuning to the Chemosphere: Domestic Formaldehyde, Bodily Reasoning, and the Chemical Sublime," *Cultural Anthropology* 30, no. 3 (2015): 368–393. Meanwhile, Karen Barad and Hans-Jörg Rheinberger teach me to approach apparatuses and experimental systems as ontologically and epistemically generative. See Barad, *Meeting the Universe Halfway: Quantum Physics and the Entanglement of Matter and Meaning* (Durham, NC: Duke University Press, 2007); and Rheinberger, *Toward a History of Epistemic Things: Synthesizing Proteins in the Test Tube* (Stanford, CA: Stanford University Press, 1997).

6.9

ACKNOWLEDGMENTS

This book draws on work that has been in the making for more than fifteen years. This, together with my bad memory, makes proper acknowledgments an impossible task. I've also realized how limited the gratitude vocabulary is (at least in English and Spanish). So, since so much of this book is focused on *how* things are made, rather than quantify how grateful I am, I'd like to focus on what I am grateful *for*. As in film credits,[+] I'm using this space to identify the roles and people who have made this *book* possible. These roles are open and flexible, placeholders for the kinds of support I have received in and around these pages over time—in fact, most have played more than one role. Therefore, this list is just a snapshot, taken at the time of writing, of a network of connections, interactions, and affects. To avoid adding hierarchy where there is none, names have been listed in alphabetical order by first name.

THANK YOU, wholeheartedly, to my dear:

Aeropolians, aka all the inhabitants of *Aeropolis* (the book), who welcomed this project at various stages, who helped build it, who walked, wrote, and rewrote its lines with precision, who assembled and reassembled them with generosity, patience, care, and enthusiasm, who read and gave feedback on some or all of the manuscript: Alice Mah, Daniel López Pérez, Fernando Domínguez Rubio, Isabelle Kirkham-Lewitt, Jesse Connuck, Joanna Joseph, Uriel Fogué, my colleagues at the Centre for Interdisciplinary Methodologies (CIM), as well as James Graham, Jordi Ng, Marjeta Morinc. And my two amazing (and anonymous) reviewers, whoever and wherever you are.

Inspirers and conspirers, who continue to model the ideas, methods, ethics, ways of writing, and forms of living in this book

+   I borrow this idea from a tweet by Kareem Carr @kareem_carr, on August 25, 2022, who argued that "authorship of academic papers should be more like movie credits."

and beyond: Bent Bars, David Gissen, Lucas Platero, María Puig de la Bellacasa, Max Liboiron, Nicholas Shapiro, Timothy K. Choy, Tomás S. Criado.

Openers of knowledge, who introduced me to new forms of thinking concepts and making ideas, ways of being and doing in academia through references, patient feedback, role models, and forms of organizing: Celia Lury, Javier Lezaun, Nina Wakeford, Noortje Marres, and the Spanish STS Network. And, without knowing it: Bruno Latour, Donna Haraway, Natalie Jeremijenko, Paul Preciado, Toni Morrison, whose collective work was, literally, an entry point to the work of many others—especially during my independent research years.

Interlocutors, who enriched such treasured and in/productive conversations on air, ecology, pollution, the urban, feminisms, art, media, politics: Amparo Lassén, Cooking Sections, Daniel Barber, Desiree Foerster, Hannah le Roux, Ignacio Galán, Isabelle Doucet, Jesse LeCavalier, Jiat-Hwee Chang, Laura Forlano, Martin Savransky, Monika Krauss, Orit Halpern, Paulo Tavares, Sasha Engelmann. Also Michael Dieter, Nathaniel Tkacz, Scott Wark, and, again, the rest of my colleagues at CIM.

Enablers of experimentation, who commissioned the projects and texts this book draws on: Alejandro Zaera, Alex Wilkie, Benjamin Weill, Gonzalo Herrero, Iván López Munuera, Jose Luis de Vicente, Kitchen Budapest, Laura Fernandez, Marco Roso, Marcos Garcia, Michael Guggenheim, Nick Axel, Rafa Montilla, STS digital society, Valentina Montero.

Collaborators, who I've experimented and gotten my hands dirty with (stuff, words, ideas): Emma Garnett, Manuel Alba, Manuel Tironi, Marcos G. Mouronte, Marina Fernandez, Martin Nadal, Miguel Mesa del Castillo, Paula Vilaplana.

Nurturers, who provided all sorts of love, care, friendship, and ideas: Diego Viluendas, Elinor Carmi, Ella Fathi, Frank Mueller, Juana Canet, Mae Moll, Patricia Sacristán, and Rocio

Gracia. Also Daniel, Miguel, and Chan, Gon, Isa, Jorge, Mar, Nico, Ota.

Facilitators of presentations, workshops, travel, and exchanges (as well as the participants and audiences), who sharpened, clarified, rethought aspects of the book before it was even a book: Andrea Bagnato and Iván López Munuera (Vulnerable Beings: A Two-Part Public Assembly on the Space and Time of Epidemics, Museum of Art, Architecture and Technology); Andrés Jaque (On and Below the Planetary Garden, Manifesta 12); Catalina Mejía Moreno (Climate Care Symposium, University of Sheffield); David Gissen (Nature and Culture in Times of Climate Change, Academy of Fine Arts Vienna); Eduardo Castillo (LAB#01 Sentient Media, Medialab-Matadero); Emily Sargent (The Air We Breathe, Wellcome Collection); Eray Çaylı (Testimony as Environment: Violence, Aesthetics, Agency, London School of Economics); Ignacio Farías and Tomás S. Criado (The World/s at the Ends of the City: Explorations in Urban and Environmental Anthropology Seminar Series, Humboldt-Universität); Iñaki Abalos (ETSAM); Jaime Cantero; Jesse LeCavalier (Graphic Content: Drawing as Method Symposium, Daniels Faculty of Architecture, University of Toronto); João Ruivo (Research Architecture, Goldsmiths University of London); Julia Kaganskiy and José Luis de Vicente (Tentacular Festival about Critical Tech & Digital Adventures, Matadero Madrid); Jussi Parikka (Design and Aesthetics for Environmental Data, Aarhus University); Kim Förster (Contemporary Perspectives on Environmental Histories of Architecture, Manchester School of Architecture); Lydia Kallipoliti (Landing: Architecture in the Age of Extinction, Entanglements and Other Bodies, The Cooper Union); Marcos Garcia (URBANLAB-MAD: Air, Health and Wellbeing in Urban Environments, El Centro de Investigaciones Energéticas, Medioambientales y Tecnológicas, Instituto de Salud Carlos III, Medialab); Marisol de la Cadena, Fernando Domínguez

Rubio, Uriel Fogué, and Orkan Telhan (Encounters at the Edge seminar series); Multispecies Storytelling in Intermedial Practices Conference (Linnaeus University); Nick Ferguson (The Politics of Air symposium, Watermans Art Centre); Nicholas Shapiro (New Nature, Goethe-Institut Montreal); Tomás Saraceno Studio (Moving Atmospheres, Garage Museum of Contemporary Art).

Supporters, who made this possible financially, emotionally, logistically, and intellectually: Brené Brown, Canadian Center for Architecture (Mellon Multidisciplinary Research Program "Architecture and/for the Environment"), Columbia Books on Architecture and the City, Institute of Public Knowledge (Poiesis Fellowship, New York University), Maria Peters, Soledad Chamorro, UK Economic and Social Research Council. And in my early days: Amid/Cero 9, Ariadna Cantís, Jose María Torres Nadal, Medialab Madrid.

Companions in life and thought, who are colleagues, references, and allies—and most of the roles above: Andrés Jaque, Iván López Munuera, Uriel Fogué. As well as those who, behind the scenes, have opened, inspired, supported, and nurtured me to be curious, creative, and political: Germán Calvillo, Marisa Gonzalez.

In sum, my deepest gratitude to everyone who collaborated on each project included in this book. To everyone who has taught me how to think, how to write, and how to listen; how to be curious, how to navigate "interdisciplinarity," how to practice academia differently (and to take it less seriously). To everyone who has shared their life, their happiness and their sadness, with me; has stayed with the trouble; has showed their love for things and shared how to love (otherwise). To everyone who has encouraged me to enjoy life as much as possible; to be ethical. Who has supported a project around air and defended that Aeropolis *is* architecture (when it was most needed). To all the writers, activists, creatives whose work paved the way for *Aeropolis*.

This book was written across (and has survived) many trips, institutions, crises, and heartbreaks—a global health pandemic, two economic crises, Brexit, hormones gone wild. It was written amid thunderstorms and a too warm sea, in a weedy backyard and many, many cafés. It was written through several seasons, leaves, strikes, and TV series; through blood, laundry, rooftop drinks, outdoor swimming. It was written with colored pens, sticky notes, cinnamon buns, music, sweat, sweatpants, construction noise... by hunting for mental space, squeezing and stretching time. It was written under the blue, stormy, watercolor skies of London, New York, Madrid, and Montferri.

My entanglement with air began when air was mostly invisible (materially, socially, and politically), and this book is being wrapped up at a time when toxic, polluted air is at the center stage of politics (whether "action" is being taken, well, that's a different story). It's difficult to evaluate what is still relevant to be said or done. Dear reader, this is now on you.

Nerea Calvillo is an architect, lecturer, researcher, associate professor at the Centre for Interdisciplinary Methodologies, University of Warwick, and adjunct associate professor at Columbia University's Graduate School of Architecture, Planning, and Preservation. Calvillo founded the environmental mediations office C+ arquitectas and the collaborative project *In the Air*.

Columbia Books on Architecture and the City
An imprint of the Graduate School of Architecture,
Planning, and Preservation

Columbia University
1172 Amsterdam Ave
415 Avery Hall
New York, NY 10027

arch.columbia.edu/books
Distributed by Columbia University Press
cup.columbia.edu

Aeropolis: Queering Air in Toxicpolluted Worlds
By Nerea Calvillo
Preface by María Puig de la Bellacasa
Afterword by Timothy K. Choy

ISBN: 978-1-941332-78-8
Library of Congress Control Number: 2023932515

Graphic Design: Jordi Ng
Cover Pattern: John Provencher
Copyeditor: Rima Weinberg
Lithographer: Marjeta Morinc
Printer: Musumeci
Paper: Lessebo Natural Rough, Munken Print White
Typefaces: Immortel Infra, Tex Gyre Heros

This book has been produced through the Office
of the Dean, Andrés Jaque, and the Office of
Publications at Columbia University GSAPP.

Director of Publications: Isabelle Kirkham-Lewitt
Assistant Director: Joanna Joseph
Assistant Editor: Meriam Soltan